Beware the Masher

Beware the Masher

Sexual Harassment in American Public Places, 1880–1930

KERRY SEGRAVE

McFarland & Company, Inc., Publishers
Jefferson, North Carolina

Library of Congress Cataloguing-in-Publication Data

Segrave, Kerry, 1944–
    Beware the masher : sexual harassment in American public
places, 1880–1930 / Kerry Segrave.
        p.   cm.
    Includes bibliographical references and index.

    ISBN 978-0-7864-7927-6 (softcover : acid free paper) ∞
    ISBN 978-1-4766-1461-8 (ebook)

    1. Sexual harassment—United States—History.   2. Sexual
harassment of women—United States—History—19th century.
3. Sexual harassment of women—United States—History—20th
century.   I. Title.
HD6060.3.S4298 2014
364.15'3—dc23   2014002834

British Library cataloguing data are available

On the cover: A 1902 sketch showing mashers at work on L (elevated
transit) cars, *The Evening World*, October 28, 1902, Night Edition,
Page 12 (Library of Congress)

Printed in the United States of America

McFarland & Company, Inc., Publishers
  Box 611, Jefferson, North Carolina 28640
  www.mcfarlandpub.com

Contents

Preface

This book looks at the history of sexual harassers in the public spaces in the United States over the period 1880 to 1930. During this period the term "masher" was the word used to describe the behavior. The masher committed a mash, or attempted to commit a mash. I chose the period covered by this book because the term used to describe the behavior and the behavior itself seems to have emerged around that time, in the very late 1870s. The end date was chosen because it marked an end to the very large and aimless public gatherings of males from which so much sexual harassment was initiated. It was those gatherings that gave rise to so many communities passing vagrancy and loitering laws. It was the car culture, though, that did the most to eliminate such gatherings. As well, by 1930 or so, the strongly held social norm that men did not talk to strange women in public places had weakened considerably. While it had not disappeared entirely, it was well on its way to extinction.

For the purposes of this book, a sexual harasser (masher) is one who harasses a woman he does not know in the public places in America, such as on the streets of the nation's cities and on its transit vehicles.

Online databases were crucial in researching the subject of this book. Most useful were the Library of Congress, with its Chronicling America project, and newspaperarchive.com.

Introduction

Sexual harassment of women in the streets of America seems to have first become a problem around the very end of the 1870s. Prior to that time women had a more limited presence in the public spaces in the nation, at least on their own. The idea of the male "protector" who was always on hand to protect his woman was fading away. It had always been an upper-class phenomenon in any case, but the changing shape of the American landscape from rural to increasingly urban and industrial gave women more opportunity to be out and about on their own. The first feminist movement was well underway during the period covered by this book, and it demanded the right of free mobility, among other things. That increasing urbanization also meant an increasing anonymity for people in those ever-growing cities. It was harder to harass a woman in a small town, where everybody knew everyone else, than in a big city where anonymity was standard.

The first chapter of this book looks at the rules of conduct for people in social settings, specifically the rules for interacting with strangers in the public sphere. These were, of course, not laws but norms of social conduct. They exerted a strong control over people's behavior. Also discussed are the names used over time to describe sexual harassment. Chapter 2 discusses the description and extent of the problem as seen by a wide variety of observers over time. Chapter 3 features editorials from newspapers throughout this period, which alternately decried the situation and offered solutions. Also included here are comments from other public opinion shapers, such as religious leaders and columnists.

Chapter 4 focuses on the apparently timeless tactic of blaming the victim. What was that woman doing there in the first place? Why was she wearing that? Why did she have that manner about her? Reading today about some religious leader in 1912 urging women to wear their skirts a little longer, almost to the ground, to ensure their ankles were not visible only reinforces the ridiculousness of such notions. Men of 1912 were driven uncontrollably mad by such wantonness, don't you know.

Chapters 5 through nine cover responses made by individual women to their harassers. Specifically covered in those chapters are women responding through words, women responding with their fists, women responding with weapons, responses delivered by a "protector" (such as a husband or father), and women's responses delivered by one or more bystanders (that is, people who did not know the harassed woman but stepped in to deal physically with the harasser).

Chapter 10 looks at the various attempts at the state and local level to try and deal with the situation. Next follows a chapter focusing on the courts, their actions and reactions to the problem of sexual harassment on the streets throughout this period. Chapter 12 looks at the various remedies that have been proposed over time to help women deal with the problem, from the bizarre to the helpful. Women were often urged to take up one of the martial arts in order to be ready to deal with any harassers they might run into. Others urged women to take up sports, such as ice skating and fencing, in order to increase their general level of fitness so that they had a better chance of escaping from the harasser.

In Chapter 13 the various crusades that were undertaken are discussed. They varied from one-person wars on sexual harassers, to more formal organizations, with a number of members supposedly dedicated to eradicating the masher. These were all private individuals with no official capacity in their communities. Chapter 14 deals with the police, both their actions and reactions to the problem, with a subsection on how policewomen (who arrived on the scene in 1910) were used to deal with the harasser. Some of those police forces seemingly declared war on the mashers every other year or so. Finally, a conclusion provides an overview of the topic as discussed in the preceding chapters.

1

Rules of Conduct

An opinion piece that appeared in a newspaper in March 1875 dealt with the new style of promenading, with the gentleman hanging on the lady's arm. According to the piece, "This is a contemptible thing and should be cast out of all good society as evil." The author of the opinion asked rhetorically what difference it made who had hold of whose arm. The answer was: "A woman's safeguard is to keep a man's hands off her. If you need his assistance in walking, take his arm instead of his taking yours." She was advised to just tell him in plain English to keep "hands off." If you give a man your arm "he will take a great many privileges he would not take, if he was not permitted to do so." Other advice given was to "keep your girls off the [public] square except when they have business. Teach them that it is unnecessary to go to the post office every time they go out." And "if possible, instill into their very natures that they are safer in their own hands than they are in the hands of any man—preachers not excepted."[1]

Another opinion piece from 1875, originally published in the *New York Times*, declared, "The unwritten law of personal intercourse is constantly violated by the conductors of our street cars." He meant that "Many of them rarely allow a lady to enter or leave a car without taking her by the arm." They "pass her in" or they "pass her out," and they not infrequently put a hand on a woman's waist or shoulder. It was, of course, all well intentioned, "but it is none the less offensive to most of the women who are subjected to such handling on the part of a strange man." The only exception would be for illness or frailty.[2]

A piece from May 1876 that was originally published in the United Kingdom, then in a New York newspaper and reprinted in other American outlets, discussed the topic as to whether or not young women could walk about alone.

It was reported that it had become a lively theme of discussion at that time in the British press as to whether the young British lady of the period could or could not be trusted "to go about the public highway alone." The rule with young ladies of position in England heretofore had been to never venture into the streets without a governess, a maid, or a "protector" of some sort. According to this piece, that rule had lately been giving way a little under pressure from females who were not that favorably received (ladies of the "fast set"). That rule was in place to keep a young lady from meeting and falling in with "undesirable acquaintances." This stemmed partly from a fear of what men would do to young ladies, but mostly, perhaps, from the notion that women could not be trusted, being too naïve, childlike, and so on. That was much of the rationale to attempt to forestall female independence.

"Many a pale delicate girl, pining with dyspepsia and sedentary occupations, might become robust with joyous health, if she might go walking, rowing, riding, taking plenty of exercise, the sort of thing to make healthy, beautiful women, and strong brave children. But girls are so hedged round with proprieties that exercise becomes merely another form of restraint." The writer of this piece was clearly in favor of more freedom of mobility for women. Why should they not take walks and go to garden parties alone? This would spare their brothers the duty "of escorting their sisters, and men would learn not to annoy a girl merely because they see her alone, if it were considered ungentlemanly, and they knew that the Lady Mary This, or the Hon. Miss That, went about alone as much as Miss so-and-so, who is equally a gentlewoman, but has to go about getting her own living." This piece observed, "At present men, not a few wicked wretches, but great numbers of gentlemanly men, seem to think a young lady by herself is fair game, although, probably, one man in three has a sister who cannot always find a duenna [chaperon, older woman companion]." The way to remedy that, thought the author of the article, was not to place "more social trammels" upon women "but for men to feel how very mean and cowardly it is of them to try and mislead foolish girls. Yet I must say this for them, that if a girl goes out on her way without deigning to take the slightest notice of them they seldom persist farther than the length of one street, and surely it would be folly for a girl to neglect education and health rather than submit to that much annoyance." In conclusion, the writer declared, "Let it be the custom in Great Britain for women of all classes to be perfectly free, so that it is no matter of remark for any girl to be alone, and that custom in itself will be a vast protection to women, will raise their standard of health and intelligence, and we shall hear less of indelicate conversation."[3]

Harriet Hubbard Ayer (1849–1903) was an American cosmetic entrepreneur. She set up the first cosmetic company in America. During the last seven years of her life she reinvented herself as the highest paid newspaper woman in the United States. She was highly regarded as the author of articles about beauty, health and etiquette for Joseph Pulitzer's *New York World*. In a column that appeared in April 1903, some six months before her death, Ayer discussed the right and wrong ways of seeking an acquaintance:

> When a young man finds his ideal girl and wishes to win her for his wife the first thing in order is a proper introduction out of which an acquaintance can grow. He must gain this introduction in an honest, manly way. He must never degenerate from a man into a masher and attempt to make a girl's acquaintance by flirting with her on the street. No self-respecting girl will encourage such attentions. It is usually not difficult to find some obliging friend who knows the young lady and is willing to make the proper introduction.[4]

An unsigned advice piece that appeared in various newspapers in January 1904 dealt with a similar topic:

> Recognize no man to whom you have not been properly introduced by a mutual friend, who will give you some information about him. A casual acquaintance may prove a true gentleman, but the chances are he will not. You know nothing about him, and consequently the risk is very great. Many a girl has had cause to rue the day that she encouraged the advances of men she met by chance at the seaside, for instance, or at some place of amusement. When you have become acquainted with a man in the proper manner—which, although orthodox, is the only safe way in which to form an acquaintance—then a person could work on determining the man's character.

Continuing on, the piece declared the chief failing with many girls was "their lack of womanly dignity and self-respect, which enable them to be approached so easily by any member of the opposite sex…. It is the man who endeavors to scrape an acquaintance without the usual introduction who should be carefully guarded against." And, the piece declared, "the man who speaks to a girl in a public place, with the evident desire of forcing his companionship on her, is showing no respect for her, and consequently is not to be recommended for a place among her friends." In addition, "the man who tries to introduce himself by performing some unnecessary favor is to be included in the class of dangerous men whom it is well to avoid, or at any rate trust with caution."[5]

Nor was such advice limited to America. It was reported in the United States in November 1908 that American girls were bothered by mashers "whenever they attempt to go about unescorted in Paris. No French girl whose parents have a proper regard for her is ever allowed to do such a thing."[6]

In Wisconsin it was reported in December 1910 that the Milwaukee Socialist municipal dances were in reality nothing but schools of mashing, or at least that was the charge made by Catholic priests from three different churches in that city. Milwaukee Mayor Seidel refused to discuss the denunciations. The Reverend J. F. Ryan of St. Francis Seminary said, "The mashers who seek to know girls upon the streets without introductions are invited to the city's municipal dances. The admission of 15 cents is paid, and the announcement is that it is impossible to introduce people to each other, so the men are considered to be at liberty to invite any girl to dance, without formal presentation. If you love your children keep them away from the municipal dances."[7]

Betty Vincent was another bylined female advice columnist whose columns appeared in the *New York World*. In her column she answered letters from people seeking advice. Her column of June 19, 1914, started out with her offering her thoughts, without the spur of a letter from a reader, with a definition of masher:

> He's just a plain cad. The first article in a gentleman's code is to show all respect to ladies. The masher ignores this unwritten law. He forces his attentions on women to whom he is a stranger, thereby implying that they are the sort of persons who welcome informal acquaintances. This is of course a studied insult to a respectable girl. A masher is a coward too, for he knows that an unescorted girl can only express her resentment by ignoring him.[8]

An editor with a Tacoma, Washington, newspaper commented in June 1916:

> There's a lot of sanity in some rules of good form. There's "safety first" in the one which states that it is always a girl's privilege to speak to a man first whenever the two meet.... Every decent man observes it. Ask your brother. If you have none, ask you girl chum's brother. They will tell you that it's a common vulgar insult for a strange man to say to a good girl, "Beg pardon, where have we met before?" If there is any recognizing to be done, it's the girl's privilege to begin it. ... The cad with the movie hero bow who stops young girls on the street has no more soul than a shadow picture on a glass screen. By speaking to you, little girl, he had picked you as "easy." By replying to him, you accept his attention as flattery instead of as an insult. So don't appear interested, apologetic, supercilious or indignant.[9]

In November 1927, Sir Ernley Blackwell, legal assistant to the Under-Secretary of the Home Office in England, gave evidence at a public sitting of the government committee to investigate the profile of street offenses. He said, "In the West End of London a man merely takes off his hat to a girl and makes some passing remark. That is neither insulting nor threatening." He added, "But the law extends in villages in the London area where the conduct may be very different." Still, the times they were changing.[10]

However, throughout this period the idea that a man did not speak to a woman in open public spaces such as on city streets and on city transit vehicles was a very strong social norm, subscribed to by most people. It would have been common knowledge to virtually all citizens. The idea that a woman never went anywhere without a male protector was much less viable then, even in 1880s America. It remained in vogue to some degree among the upper classes but not so much in the other classes of society. Life in America was such that women of the lower classes often found themselves widowed or otherwise alone, with children and needing to support themselves as best they could. As a result, they often had to come and go on their own—for work reasons, to purchase food for themselves and their children, and so on. But the woman alone on the streets without a protector was often used as a justification by male harassers and their defenders to suggest that somehow the lone woman deserved the grief. That she was out and about by herself, using that type of rationale, was taken to mean she must be loose, a slut. A couple of judges received some publicity when they levied fines against harassers for the language they used while accosting women—for example, $5 for calling a woman "chicken," or $25 for calling her "cutie." In the vast majority of cases, though, it did not matter what the sexual harasser said to the woman he targeted. The violation lay in the fact that he had spoken to her at all, a woman he did not know and in the public streets. The content of the speech was irrelevant. It did not matter if a man accosted a woman to say "Ain't she a peach" or "Hello there." In both cases a violation had taken place, and the punishment was almost always the same. In this period an ordinary male citizen would never have gone up to a strange woman on the street with innocent intentions, such as to ask for directions to Main Street. It just was not done.

With respect to the origin of the word "masher," one suggestion, published in 1882, said it might have been a perversion of the French term "ma chere," or that, as the masher was apt to speak affectedly, he might originally have been a "macheur."[11]

A piece that originally appeared in the *San Francisco Examiner* (reprinted in a Los Angeles paper) in June 1883 declared that the term "masher" originated in the green room of the Union Square Theater in San Francisco in the autumn of 1878. Two comedians working there were McKee Rankin and Charles Thorne (both of whom had played in London). At a matinee where the audience consisted almost entirely of ladies, Thorne entered the green room after a strong scene and bragged about his performance to Rankin. The latter said, "I only touch their hearts, but by the gods you mash 'em." "Ha," laughed Thorne, "mash is a good word." Rankin replied, "Yes, my boy, you are the champion masher." At the end of the performance the two comics called in at the barroom of the Union Square Hotel and, over drinks, mentioned the phrase to a lot of journalists who were also drinking there. One of them, Chandos Fenton, made a note of it, and a week later, in the columns of a well known theatrical paper, the *Sunday Mercury*, he wrote an article titled "Heart Mashers at Matinees." The term amused the town, and, reportedly, it was instantly and widely adopted—"every well-dressed smart young man was individually called a masher (much as we call well got up men here swells), and the phrase was brought to England..."[12]

A piece published in November 1883 declared the term "masher" went over to England from the United States, into which it had been introduced by Irish emigrants. The word masher was said herein to be derived from the Gaelic "maise," pronounced masher and signifying fine or handsome, which was originally applied in derision to a dandy: "It is now in similar derision, appropriately applied to modern, underdeveloped men, whose sole aim is to dress well and ogle ladies."[13]

Later that same month in 1883 an even more specific derivation was given. Twenty years earlier, in New York City, it was customary in the slang of Broadway and Fifth Avenue to speak of a person hopelessly stricken with love as "mashed," an expression that succeeded the likes of "dead gone." The power of that infatuation reduced the victim of the passion to a "mash" or pulp, and to "mash" people of either sex was to bring them to a state of idiotic infatuation, softness, or pulpiness. Out of the verb "to mash" grew "masher," which became restricted to the male sex. That term, the piece argued, was a successor to other older terms used in reference to a man supposed to have exercised irresistible power over the opposite sex. In Elizabethan times it was a "gallant" in England and a "ruffian" in France. Then in France he became a "roué." In England successor terms included the "macaroni," the "buck," the "blood," the "dandy," the "fop," the "swell" (among others), and the "masher."[14]

A brief piece in September 1904 observed that Webster's dictionary defined a masher as "one who, or that which mashes; a charmer of women." Against that the article gave a definition from a "distinguished" judge [unnamed] in a Western state: "Any man who accosts on the street a woman whom he does not know and to whom he had no right to speak; any man who stands on the street corners and ogles women as they pass by; any man who makes grimaces at a woman."[15]

Overwhelmingly, the word masher was the descriptor of choice to apply to the harasser. Other words came and went as fads. During the early part of the 1880s the word "dude" became a fad for a time. It wasn't clear what the differences between the two words were except, perhaps, that dude referred specifically to a young masher. In the 1920s the word "sheik" became a craze for a period of time. And because it was the early 1920s the auto masher was getting a good deal of publicity. Therefore the fad required references to the "auto sheik." That fad, of course, sprang from the intense media attention given to legendary actor Rudolph Valentino after the 1921 release of his film *The Sheik*. Another term was "flirt," which saw use a little more often in the

1920s (that is, a masher was sometimes called a flirt in articles). No attempt was made to define the differences in those stories. Today we think of flirting as a rather innocuous behavior engaged in by members of either sex. It also takes place among people who know one another, as well as between strangers. If a Venn diagram were used, the smaller circle representing mashers would be fully contained in the much larger circle representing flirts.

Some time after the period covered by this book the term masher fell away into obscurity. It was largely replaced by the word "fresh," as in "My boss got fresh with me." Fresh, used in that way, appeared in newspaper articles as early as 1901, but its use was rare in this period. During the 1940s and 1950s, and into the start of the 1960s, it was fairly common for articles in women's magazines to deal with issues such as what to do about fresh co-workers, or fresh bosses, or fresh men they ran into on the streets. With the rise of feminism in the 1960s, the word "fresh" disappeared, with the result that the sexual harasser was described for what he was—a "sexual harasser."

2

Description and Extent

A reporter in Minnesota wrote a story in August 1880 wherein he told of a number of traveling salesmen who had met for dinner at the Merchants Hotel in St. Paul. Among those, he wrote, "was one of those disagreeable and disgusting fellows, aspiring to the role of masher—one of those fellows when in town who visits his barber two or three times a day, changes his clothes every time the sun passes under a cloud, and indulges in many other nonsensical practices only known to the fool masher."[1]

An American masher was "any foppish, overdressed fellow who parades more than he postures, and who may be a gambler who, in dull seasons, lives on the earnings of his mother's washings, or who may pick enough pockets to buy good clothes, while he resides at his mother's boarding-house," declared a journalist in the spring of 1883. And, he added, "the average American masher's points are a fine, noticeable overcoat and a waxed mustache."[2]

A month later in 1883, a masher, it was said, "may be described as a Moral Spittoon, and his mission on earth is to pester respectable girls with his nauseous attentions and to receive the scorn and contempt of all real men."[3]

Dud-de Dude.

An 1883 caricature of a masher. For a few years in the 1880s they were also called "dudes." This sketch shows one striking what was said to be a favorite pose of the breed—pausing to retie a shoe lace. Two women watch—admire?—the action.

In Brooklyn in October 1884 a journalist wondered, "Is there a being on earth who deserves such unmitigated contempt as the street masher? ... He is seldom or never a man of any pretensions to good looks, good manners or brains, and his alleged wide popularity with women is altogether inexplicable to the majority of men." What riled the average man, he thought, "is the pusillanimous fool who flirts in the cars, in the restaurants, the theater and on the streets ... they are men of all ages and conditions. A fat masher is no more of a novelty than a thin one, and mashers of forty years of age are quite as numerous as those of twenty."[4]

A masher was reportedly working the corner of Second and Fort Streets in Los Angeles in January 1889. On one night a woman went to the corner mailbox and was harassed by the masher both coming and going from the letter box. He followed her to the door of her

An 1885 caricature of an elderly, leering masher. Harassers were almost always depicted as well-dressed men.

house and frightened her. "Unfortunately," said a reporter, "there was no man at home to give the masher what he deserved." One or two nights later another woman was accosted on the same corner, and "a watch is now being kept on that locality by several gentlemen armed with clubs." That masher appeared at the same corner about a week later and harassed a woman visiting a drugstore. After she complained to the druggist, police kept a watch on the corner but nothing happened. Then he appeared again, after the police watch had ended, and harassed two women on their way home from a meeting. He even followed them for a block but turned away when a man approached from the opposite direction.[5]

According to a report from Minneapolis in January 1889, the shop girls of that city were all pretty because "a pretty girl can draw custom and make a sale where a homely girl cannot." And these girls were considered to be "legitimate prey" by the mashers. This account divided mashers into two or three classes. The first group contained the young clerk who spent all he earned in the purchase of loud and costly clothes. "He is not particularly dangerous, but is very tiresome.... He is what might be termed a 'milk-shake' masher, and

rarely gets any further than bowing to the object of his passion on the street."
That type had little or no money, and it was the young men with money who
were more dangerous. As a rule they were said to be more persistent in their
harassment. Those men did not confine themselves to shop girls alone, for
they also went after women at theaters and so forth. As far as this reporter was
concerned, the men old enough to know better, and who should have been at home with their wives and daughters, formed "the most reprehensible class of mashers in Minneapolis." The girl upon whom an old masher fixated was likely to get an unsigned note telling her if she wanted to have a good time she could have it simply by stepping into a carriage that would be waiting for her at a certain time and place. "The mashers haunt the street corners on every pleasant day, and the various places of amusement in the evening. They are ever on the alert for a pretty face, and when they see one their attacks begin," he summarized. "The masher generally knows enough to act decently at first, and not to seriously offend by making any public demonstration of his alleged affections. A rebuff seldom does any good, and as a rule it takes a sound thrashing to bring a masher to his senses, and cause him to cease annoying women."[6]

This 1889 sketch depicts a masher in a post office using a favorite ruse of the harasser. He would drop a letter he had with him and then approach a woman and suggest she had dropped her letter.

At the end of 1889 a reporter in Minneapolis declared his city was not as badly infested with mashers as some cities, but there were still a large number to be found. One of the favorite areas for them in Minneapolis was said to be the city's new post office. "He lingers in the broad corridors of the new public building, and subjects ladies to his insults." One of his methods in the post office was for him to drop a letter he had prepared and hidden on his person and then ask a woman if by chance she had dropped her letter.[7]

An article about the "masher hog" on public vehicles in New York City appeared in June 1890. "Every fair face is his victim, and no womanly modesty is too sacred for his assaults.... For him no punishment is too extreme.... A cowhide, club or the toe of a boot is the only adequate medicine." Why, the reporter wondered, should women silently submit to the insults of these creatures when there were decent men within call. "Often the grossest insults given by these sleek hogs are invisible or inaudible to other passengers. Is it unwomanly under such circumstances for an insulted woman to say to any gentleman present, 'May I appeal to you sir, to relieve me of this man's insults?'" And, thought the journalist, was there a decent man on Manhattan Island who would not respond to such an appeal? If he stepped forward and put the hog out of the car "with a few sound kicks and blows, he will have done a praiseworthy public service." He published part of a letter sent to his newspaper complaining about the harassers. "Hordes of women hunters parade the streets day and night, and no young or middle-aged woman, unless absolutely repulsive, is free from their attentions. The side streets as much as the prime thoroughfares are infested with these animals, and wives and daughters are persistently followed up and reach their homes on the verge of hysteria." The letter writer also worried that if a complaint was made to the police, and if the policeman asked the harassed woman if she wished to lodge a complaint, it would not happen because "the majority of women look with horror on such a thing as appearing in a police station or a courtroom."[8]

A reporter spoke of the masher scene in Pittsburgh in April 1891 by writing that his city, like many other large cities, "is infested with a class of idle young men who pass the earlier portions of the night lounging about the principal streets, leaning against anything that will afford support to an inert body and indulging in indecent comments on passersby." He continued, "Ladies without escorts are the particular targets for these beings and even when accompanied by a gentleman are often forced to overhear insulting remarks on their personal appearance which anyone, even of indifferent moral tone, would resent. Young girls even in daylight do not escape the remarks of these idlers intentionally uttered loud enough for them to hear." The police had reportedly tried to put a stop to the mashers and to some degree had been successful, but "nothing less than an army of officers could continually keep the downtown streets free from the human trash that frequents them."[9]

A piece in a Washington, D.C., newspaper in October 1891 took the form of a supposed letter from Alice to Louise. It said it had always been a Washington custom for young girls—and also older ones—to promenade on the sidewalks during the warm summer evenings, unattended by escorts, and seldom did anything disagreeable happen. Lately, though, girls had been complaining about a would-be masher who had appeared in different sections of the northwest of the city and "compelled the evening promenaders to beat a hasty retreat to the shelter of home." Policemen were not ubiquitous in those areas. Alice said that one woman had managed to ascertain his name and address, and it would have been a great service to her sex to make a formal complaint to the authorities, but, "as a rule, women shrink from appearing at a police court, and very natural is this feeling."[10]

The street corner mashers were out in force on a Saturday in January 1893 in Los Angeles, according to a report. Saturday was considered "the principal flirting day of the week." And, it was said, "These professional loafers stand upon the principal street corners, insulting by their leers and vulgar remarks every young lady who passes. Any stylish lady who passes is sure to attract their attention, and the fellows have the audacity to tip their hats, with the view of indulging in a flirtation." It was also stated that, "knowing that ladies do not like notoriety, and that complaints are not likely to be made to the police, these fellows feel secure.... The police should ferret them out and run them in."[11]

Lottie Collins (1865–1910) was an English singer and dancer, most famous for introducing the song "Ta-ra-ra Boom-de-ay" in England. She spoke to a New York City reporter in April 1893 during an extensive stage tour of America. She spoke on many topics, including mashers: "I don't think you have nearly as large a class of mashers here, anyhow, and they are not nearly so impertinent as they are in London. There they wait about the stage doors, these boys just up from school with more money than brains, to stare and ogle and follow you about." Collins added, "Perhaps it is because my husband has always been with me here, and I haven't had a fair chance at the American masher, save through letters, to see what kind of animal he is."[12]

Raids by the police upon the "cigar store statues" and mashers who infested Market and Kearney Streets in San Francisco early in 1893 were said to be successful in driving the "despicable class of human drones" from the street corners for a time, but a cessation of the arrests had resulted in the old haunts being again inhabited by these creatures by May of 1893. The great trouble, grumbled the reporter, was that women insulted by the mashers preferred to submit to the insult rather than the notoriety of the police court, and in nine cases out of 10, unless the police officer happened to overhear an insult, no conviction could be registered.[13]

An un-bylined female journalist writing in a Washington, D.C., newspaper in May 1893 remarked that the afternoon masher was somewhat on the increase, but "because he is more numerous it does not follow that he is any less disgusting than he was before." She had her own adventure in after-dark street manners one night that week; it was one she thought was "so frequent in occurrence" that nearly all the women would have experienced something similar. She was followed by a man for four or five blocks. She thought she had shaken him off in the better lit areas, but he soon reappeared. He finally disappeared when she entered a hotel. She wrote in her piece that the new style of masher had new methods. He walks up to a woman with her arms full of parcels and "hugs her. He generally succeeds in throwing her down, because he runs against her roughly, and then scampers away. By the time the lady regains her feet, if she is able to do so, he is out of the neighborhood."[14]

A letter to the editor of the *Washington Post* from H. Burke in January 1895 began by mentioning that now, while the police are so busy removing obstructions from the streets such as fruit stands, barber poles, signs, public clocks, and chicken coops, it would also be a good time to begin on "the worst obstruction of all—the street-corner masher." He thought most of the female citizens of Washington would much prefer stumbling over a fruit stand or running against a barber pole than "see-saw out of the way of one of these curbstone fiends." Burke thought the masher united all the objectionable points of all the other obstructions: "He is as gaudy as a barber pole; as pernicious as an Italian fruit vender; he stares like a big-lettered sign, cackles like a coop of chickens, and has wheels in his head like the public clock." And, unlike the other street nuisances, the masher was not stationary. Burke ended his letter with a plea: "Cannot the police spare a little time from their raid on the bootblack and the work of art and command this ubiquitous individual to 'Move on?'"[15]

A lengthy description of New York City's new tenderloin district was published in March 1896. One observer remarked to the reporter, "Now, you see the worst character of the new Tenderloin—the elderly masher. He is rich and adept in the art of staring a woman out of countenance, and he isn't to be abashed by any amount of snubbing." The elderly masher was said to be partial to harassing shop girls from the area in the street.[16]

There was a big craze for bicycling during the 1890s, and it soon spread among men and women. In a May 1896 article it was reported that "the pleasant freedom of comradeship which has arisen among cyclists has been seized upon by mounted mashers as an opportunity to approach women riders with masher impertinence. Look out for them." Those bicycle mashers had reportedly sprung up in number over the previous few weeks and were increasing rapidly. Central Park was a favorite haunt for them, but they could also be found on the boulevards and wherever cycling was most practiced. Like all mashers, these never hesitated to address women on the slightest pretext and to annoy them either with vulgarity or inanity. "Girls, decide the matter at once. Avoid this latest nuisance as you would a rattlesnake, or, better still, hand him over to the police while those of his kind are still few," urged the journalist.[17]

One year later a piece reported that the pleasures of cycling were being seriously impaired by a nuisance that the police and reputable wheelmen should combine to crush out—mashers. "They infest the path and make excuses to speak to the women and girls who sit for rest upon the benches provided." The reporter argued that the bicycle path should be as free and comfortable for the use of women as the streets, and there should be no more need of an escort in the daytime on the cycle paths than there was in a shopping excursion to the main downtown street.[18]

This 1896 drawing illustrates the idea that shop girls were in danger from mashers. They often hung around outside of the large retail outlets then employing many women, with a view to harassing them.

During the summer of 1899 the bicycle masher was still being reported as a problem, at least in New York City. A journalist worried that "unless summary measures are taken to discourage the tribe generally, the number of such persuasive criminals is likely to become large.... Already bicycle mashers of the impudent sort have multiplied with the increase of wheelwomen, and as no serious opposition to their effrontery has been made by the police authorities, they have taken it for granted that no one cares to disturb them and consequently have gone to extremes in their mashing arts." The account went into a fairly elaborate description of the bicycle masher:

He is always dressed in the pink of fashion, or what he regards as such. His eyes are roving, and the mobility of his face as a whole is striking. His head had a weathervane action, which is helpful to him in his maneuvers. He never keeps his back at more than thirty degrees. His wheel is never soiled, scarred or out of date. His handlebar is neither low nor high. He delights in riding "hands off" and with one foot on the pedal. He has a characteristic way of slowing down whenever he meets a comely wheelwoman, young or middle-aged, who he thinks might not be outraged by his attentions, and he is always able to dismount with grace and alacrity.[19]

A letter to the editor of a New York City newspaper in August 1899 described the situation, as seen by an anonymous female. She said it was then well nigh impossible for "a respectable young lady of facial attractiveness to travel through our great city without encountering these dregs of manhood. After nightfall she is liable to their grossest insults." She urged that something be done so that every woman "shall have protection on the streets.... To hear of a young lady's being accosted in the street during the hours she may with propriety venture out unaccompanied is not uncommon."[20]

Edna May Pettie (1878–1948, known onstage as Edna May) was a famous American actress and singer. Her autobiography was excerpted in newspapers in February 1900. One thing she spoke about was her time as a chorus girl and her experience with stage door Johnnies (as theater mashers were called). "No picture of stage depravity is complete without mention of the seductive 'Masher' or 'Johnnie' lying in wait outside the door." She called him "the silliest, most harmless thing that ever came down the pike. He doesn't know it. He thinks he is Don Juan, Mephistopheles and Cupid all rolled into one." She said that over the years she had received enough mash notes to paper St. Patrick's Cathedral. "I've laughed over some, yawned over others, and answered—none. Most other girls say the same thing."

Edna May said her "queerest" experience with a masher took place in Philadelphia. A youth called at the theater, said he was a reporter, and that his paper wanted Edna to take a tour of the city (with the masher as her escort) and then comment on the city. Edna checked with the newspaper to learn it had never heard of the youth or the suggested assignment. When the masher called at her hotel she told him she knew the truth. Still, he asked her to dine with him. She ordered him out.

In another town at another time she left the theater where she was working and noticed she was being followed all the way home. The next day a case of champagne was delivered to the house for her, signed XYZ. On the following Saturday night she received a note saying XYZ would meet her at the stage door after her performance. In separate deliveries from XYZ she also received a large box of candy and flowers. Each was accompanied by a mash note, signed XYZ. As she left the theater on that Saturday night the masher stepped up to her. Before he could speak to her, Edna's father ("who was my escort as usual") said, "So you are XYZ are you? My daughter and I have enjoyed your wine and candy very much. We want to thank you for them." Edna May never heard from XYZ again. She ended her section on mashers by saying, "So much for the silly stage-door masher, who thinks himself so irresistible and who is the laughing stock of the chorus."[21]

Clara Morris (1849–1925) was another American actress who had parts of her autobiography excerpted in the newspapers, in August 1901. She wrote that she was often asked what was the most unpleasant experience in the daily life of a young actress? She said, "Without pause for thought and most emphatically, too, I answer: Her passage unattended through city streets at night is made unalloyed misery through terror and humiliations ... the way through the city streets is mashed by blazing blushes." She called it an infamy that a girl's honesty should not protect her by night as well as by day. "But bring one of these men to brook, and he will declare that 'decent women have no right to be in the streets after nightfall.'" Clara said that some women never learned to face the homeward walk with steady nerves, while "others grow used to the swift approach, the rapidly spoken word, and receive them with set, stony face and deaf ears—but, oh, the terror and shame of it at first. And this horror of the night takes so many forms that it is hard to say which one is the most revolting—hard to choose between the vile innuendo whispered by a sober brute or the roared ribaldry of a drunken beast." She raised the question of why not appeal to a policeman but pointed out that of course a woman would—if one was about. "But believe me, they rarely appear together, your tormentor of women and your policeman.... And what good if he is arrested? Shame will prevent your appearing against him. Silence and speed are generally the best defensive weapons of the frightened, lonely girl."[22]

In a second installment of her autobiography, Clara Morris described the masher by declaring, "These creatures that, like poisonous toadstools, spring up at street corners to the torment of women should be taken in hand by the police, since they encumber the streets and are a menace and a mortification to female citizens. Let some brazen woman take the place of one of these street mashers and proceed to ogle the passerby, and see how quickly the police would gather her in."[23]

On the evening of August 28, 1901, shortly after 9 p.m. on a Capital Traction car in Washington, D.C., two men followed and made insulting remarks to two young women for several blocks as they rode along in the car. When arrested the men gave their names as James Green and Henry Wilson, and were charged with having assaulted one of the women and having acted in a disorderly manner on the streetcar. The men, "it is believed, gave fictitious names at the stationhouse," said the account. The men accosted 17-year-old Beatrice Hill and her companion, Miss Willie Walters. When approached by the men as they waited for a car, the women moved away. The men followed them and made several insulting remarks to them as they did so. When the car came they boarded it, but so did the two men, who continued to harass them. The men took seats near the women, and one kept nudging one of the women with his elbow. Both girls became increasingly frightened, and Hill finally jumped off the moving car. Alerted by the commotion, the conductor halted the car. Hill was assisted by other passengers and discovered to have suffered some injuries from her jump. Sergeant Kaucher was in the area, saw the commotion and arrived on the scene. When the men were pointed out to the officer by a passenger, Kaucher arrested the two men. At the station house it was said the police were trying to determine their real names. Several passengers expressed a willingness to appear in court to testify. According to the report, "No end of complaints have been received lately by the police officials regarding the rowdy actions of mashers aboard street cars, especially during the hot weather, when immense crowds journey to the nearby pleasure resorts."[24]

A brief characterization of the masher appeared in the newspaper in October 1901 as "this libel on the shape and morals of the monkey race."[25]

A description of the masher problem in Richmond, Virginia, was published in January 1902. One of the city's busiest streets was Broad Street, but the masher was also there. "His dress is flashy and his behavior impudent.... Richmond abound in this species and their presence on Broad Street in the afternoons has gotten to be so aggressive that it is regarded by many as a public nuisance." His chief characteristic was "self conceit," and "he is a wart on the fair face of creation for whose existence no reasonable excuse can be given; impediments only fit for handing raglans on and the consumption of cigarettes." His chief accomplishment was the art of "making goo-goo eyes. Nothing is sacred in his eyes and no woman is safe from his stare." On matinee days the mashers were out in full force on Broad Street. "That something should be done to abate the nuisance is admitted. There is a city ordinance against congregating on street corners and obstructing travel, but the masher appears to be superior to city and ordinances. The evil, instead of growing less, increases." In conclusion, the account said, "Richmond is sorely afflicted with this class who are old enough to know better. It's up to some one to find a remedy."[26]

A series of letters of complaint to a New York City newspaper in October 1902 led to a number of articles about the problem of mashers in that city. One woman wrote, "These hogs accomplish their insults in crowds that shield them from detection, and so they seem to have grown bold again." More letters poured in, and this article published excerpts from some of them. Wrote "Wage-earner":

I am glad to see that my fellow-workers have had the courage to complain at least of the way we've been treated for years. I could tell stories of the ways of brutes on L [elevated transit] and surface cars that would make every self-respecting man angry. They smile at us, speak to us and even squeeze our arms, knowing we can't protect ourselves in such a crowded and public place. Let it be stopped by law, say I.

Wrote "English Girl":

Last evening on the Sixth Avenue L a man pretended to miss his hold on the strap and caught my wrist. I thought it was an accident until next time the train twisted he swung across and actually kissed me. And this in the presence of over a hundred people. And no one noticed it. I could not help from crying I was so mortified. But what could I do? If I had screamed he would have lost himself quickly in the crowd.

"Saleslady" wrote:

This morning on the L I heard a voice in my ear say: "Good morning little girl." I looked around and it was a gray haired, gray side-whiskered man of probably sixty, who looked like a prosperous banker. I was surprised, but he went on paying me compliments. I tried to move away in the crowd but he linked his arm in mine and detained me. I could not escape without a struggle. When I reached the store I told about this, and two other young ladies had had just the same experience with the very same man. Can't you get him arrested?[27]

MASHERS WHO INSULT WOMEN IN CARS ARE BUSY

A day later there appeared an editorial in that newspaper about the situation. The editor said most of those letters "exhibit the innate and characteristic modesty which makes the victim of the insult shrink from the publicity of an open rebuke. A woman thus insulted is given the peculiarly distasteful alternative of putting up with the slight to her self-respect, mortifying as it is, or exposing herself to remark by taking notice of it. She should remember that if she 'calls down' the masher she will be commended, and if she takes pains to effect his arrest, as resolute women some-

A 1902 sketch showing mashers at work on L (elevated transit) cars. This was a particular problem in cities such as New York and Chicago.

times, though too rarely do, she will perform a public service." Concluded the editor, "A masher comes near being the ignoblest work of God. He counts on shielding himself behind the very modesty that he insults. It is a great gain for decency when he is exposed and punished."[28]

The series continued a day later when it was remarked, "It takes no clever detective work to discover the insults which are offered to girls and women. It is only necessary to be a woman to learn that the L masher's methods are as open as they are presumptuous ... the insidious tactics of the L masher makes the trip one of torture to a decent woman." The piece continued, "A woman's appearance nor her age do not save her from either the advances of these imitation men, for if the crowd of the car removes the youthful and pretty victim the next best will do." This is one of the only articles that ever made mention of this fact—all others always spoke of victims being young and pretty, and so on. That is, this was perhaps the only article in this period that said indirectly that what underlay the sexual harassment of women was not some nonsense about uncontrollable lust but the hatred for and toward women. Remarked in the piece was that if a female stood in a crowded car for a moment she would soon learn what it meant to be a woman in New York, for she would be pressed against, jostled, and hear a whisper in her ear. "You are helpless. The average woman detests a scene in public. It is woman's only salvation to ignore insults. But when they become so pronounced as to be unmistakable, the decent woman is up against a serious proposition." A female reporter for the newspaper, bent on investigation, was said to have been "so insulted" on the Third Avenue L "that the letters of the young women protesting to *The World* against the L mashers were only an intimation of what these cowardly oglers of women can do.... The L road tormentor is the agent of many a woman's nervous collapse." Mostly those women had no choice, for they had to rely on public transportation.[29]

A day later the series continued, featuring eight little sketches within one panel that illustrated the punishment that might be meted out on the L cars to mashers. In the text portion it was explained that on the previous evening a reporter for *The World* noticed two young women sitting opposite her suddenly become embarrassed and rise from their seats. After standing for a while, one of the young women began to cry. Investigation revealed that a masher "had made the most audacious advances to the women." He was promptly put off the train, but the distress of the women was not wholly eradicated. The reporter added, "Complaints from all conditions of respectable women are being continually made, and the L masher has assured a prominence in the social reform question which demands immediate attention." Something needed to be done to "the man who leers at women, who nudges them, who presses up against them, who take their arms ... [they are] a dangerous member of society and should be treated as all unruly citizens." Said a well-dressed

Some Things That Might Be Done to "L" Mashers.
Punishments Devised by Artist Powers.

The adoption of these and like masher-curbing devices would probably reduce the number of pinchers, nudgers and goo-gooers who infest the New York and Brooklyn cars during the rush hours.

So pervasive was the problem of mashers on New York City L cars in 1902 that a newspaper ran a series on the topic for several days in a row. This drawing depicts some humorous ideas on what to do with those mashers.

woman on the L that previous night, "It isn't safe for a decent woman to be out even at 6 o'clock, and at 7 her chances of being pursued by these mashers who made insinuating propositions on the L road are overwhelming." In conclusion, the piece declared, "The L masher is one of the greatest menaces to the woman of today, and the complaints asking the *Evening World* to suppress the evil show the long-endured suffering which the women of New York have long been subjected to."[30]

A week later a different newspaper in New York City discussed the masher problem. This reporter thought the hardest lesson for each woman to learn was that "the proper remedy is instant appeal to the biggest man in sight, preferably a policeman." Only then would the masher evil be reduced to a minimum. He observed that New York City had struggled with the masher evil for a good many years. The police had tried to curb it. Private citizens who had gone to the assistance of annoyed women without solicitation "have given some healthy illustrations of the way that mashers ought to be treated, in fact everything possible has been done to protect women in public places and yet the masher continued to flourish." Anyone could see that the species had flourished in recent years. Still, he thought that getting the harassed women to take prompt and vigorous action was the hardest thing to do. "The average woman will submit to almost limitless indignation before she will complain.... The truth is that most women suffer in silence because they are afraid of a scene and of the probable publicity that will follow a complaint."[31]

The Wadleigh High School for Girls, which opened in 1903, was the first public high school for girls in New York City. At the time, public secondary education for girls was considered highly novel and a bit scandalous. Newspapers devoted many stories to describing classroom scenes of girls receiving higher education. An article about the school that appeared on September 26, 1903, described the mashers, crowds of men age 23 to 34, who congregated on the corners near the Wadleigh institute in Harlem and accosted the females therein. They had become so numerous that area merchants were annoyed and had protested so much that there was talk of a vigilance committee being formed in the neighborhood to protect the high school girls. J. L. Brown, proprietor of a cigar store near the school, said, "These men hang around this corner and not only annoy the girls but make it extremely distasteful to the merchants in the neighborhood whose sense of decency is outraged by their behavior." The mashers always arrived just as school let out. Some of the female students were said to be so intimidated that they went home in groups. Several of the mashers held themselves out as Mormon elders and tried to start conversations with girls by pretending to try to proselytize them. There were several Mormon elders in Harlem, but these men mashing at the school were thought to be fakes.[32]

A wave of protest from women shoppers in New York City declared that 23rd Street was impossible for them to pass through without being "insulted by loafers." Those complaints surfaced in November 1904. A matron in Harlem told a reporter:

> Oh, it's outrageous. It's simply disgusting. Women can't come down here without being ogled. That isn't the worst of it. These fellows follow us and make remarks to us. They stand plastered up against the windows, and then as women look and say things.... When the women stop to look in the windows these mashers will step up also and that gives them a good excuse to talk.

Another New York woman stated:

> It's known as mashers' corner now. I was followed one night last week by a man who made such insulting remarks to me that I stepped up to a policeman to complain. The fellow disappeared. Three times in the past four days I have been followed, and I have been ogled and smiled at till my heart is sick at the thought that decent women have to endure such things on the streets here.

That corner was 23rd Street and Sixth Avenue.[33]

Without doubt the most famous masher to find his name in print over the offense was famed opera tenor Enrico Caruso. The star of the Metropolitan Opera House Company was arrested while he was a visitor at the menagerie in Central Park, New York City, on November 16, 1906, on a charge of disorderly conduct preferred by Mrs. Hannah Graham. The complainant, who said she did not know who the man was who had mashed her, alleged Caruso had repeatedly insulted her. After being locked up for an hour, Caruso was released on bail furnished by Heinrich Conried, director of the opera company. At the police station immediately after his arrest Caruso created a scene, and it was reported that it was only with great difficulty that he was induced to submit to the routine examination and search to which all those arrested were subjected. Throughout his stay at the station he insisted it was all a mistake. Conried had lodged a $500 cash bond.[34]

A report from a different newspaper gave a little more detail. Mrs. Graham and her small son were in the monkey house in Central Park leaning on the rail and watching the primates. A short, stout man arrived and stood beside her, ostensibly watching the monkeys; he was pressing himself against Graham's right side. Policeman James J. Kane was on duty; his beat included the monkey house and environs. One of his specific duties was to see that women in the park were not annoyed by mashers. Kane was walking by Graham and Caruso when he noticed the woman and child and a "foreign-looking man." He saw she appeared to be disturbed, and finally the woman wheeled around with a very red face and said to the man beside her, "See here, what are you doing?" At that point Kane ran over, grabbed the man by the arm, and said to the woman, "Do you want to make a complaint against this man?" She said, "I certainly do. He has insulted me." Throughout this part of the case Caruso reportedly spoke fairly good English—to Kane when he was arrested, to the police at the station house, and to Conried when he arrived to bail him out. Later that day the press agent for the Metropolitan Opera released the following:

> I have a statement to make for Mr. Caruso. He is utterly in the dark as to why he was arrested. He is enraged about it. Now he is sick in bed at the [Hotel] Savoy, but as soon as he is able he will sue the police department for false arrest. Mr. Caruso does not speak English, and does not understand a word of it, hence he didn't know what questions they put to him at the police station.[35]

A few days later Caruso was convicted and fined $10 for disturbing the peace of Graham. He vowed to fight on. But, said a reporter, "if he persists in appealing his case, it is intimated he may be accused of perjury over the evidence he gave at his trial." In the wake of that case, the article went on to say that "sensational prosecutions," beside which the fining of Caruso will appear insignificant, were promised against mashers in Central Park. "Men who are reputed to be worth millions are expected to be dragged into police court and forced to stand trial on charges similar to that which brought woe to Caruso. The names of prospective defendants are carefully suppressed by the authorities, but it is announced the publicity given the Caruso case brought forth complaints that had been undreamed of." Said Deputy Police Commissioner Mathot, "I have spent much time in Central Park trying to get some of these fellows. We have other complaints against men like Caruso. Some of them are a great deal more important that Caruso." The hint that the rich and the famous were among the (hidden) mashers was no doubt accurate. But the notion that mashers from that class would be arrested and prosecuted was, of course, completely inaccurate. Caruso would always remain the only famous and/or rich masher.[36]

The first appeal launched by Caruso was rejected by the courts at the very end of 1906. He vowed to fight on and appeal to the next level. However, in New York City on May 14, 1907, Frederick W. Spelling, counsel for Caruso, came forward to pay the $10 fine originally imposed on the singer and to announce the appeal to the appellate division of the state supreme court had been withdrawn. That ended the Caruso case.[37]

The Caruso case produced an article that discussed the difference with respect to mashers in the United States and those in Europe. In America, it was said, "women are followed and annoyed during shopping hours. Women who work are subjected to worse persecutions on their way home after the day's work in the streets and public conveyances. The police could find work to do in many of the busy thoroughfares during shopping hours and after. The well dressed loafer is found there smirking, ogling, trailing, insulting." The American masher knew that public indignation could at any moment punish him. That was not so for his European counterpart. Over there it was the opinion of the majority that women who objected to insults "should not go forth unless properly chaperoned. The principal thoroughfares of the capitals of Europe are thus to a certain extent unsafe for women who visit them unprotected." In the United States a word of appeal spoken by a woman would make the mashing offence the concern of every man within hearing, a matter of immediate danger to the offender. On the other hand, "In Europe woman does not dream of appealing to the chivalry of one man against the offense of another.... It is the business of nobody but the offender, the victim and her own men folk, who should be there to defend her, and are not." Annoying women was said to be one of the established diversions of the street life of the great cities of Europe. And there was no public opinion there to be crossed. As well, there was no punishment of the masher in Europe, except through private vengeance.[38]

A report from March 1908 declared that mashers "infested" State Street in Salt Lake City, and the police had been unable to drive them from the street because the insulted women were unwilling to appear in court. Some mashers, it was said, even insult "women who are accompanied by escorts." According to the story, State Street, from First South to Fourth South, "is infested with gangs of young rowdies, who are out for the purpose of insulting every woman, old and young, who happens to pass." Those mashers were said to walk the streets in pairs or in small groups, being too cowardly to annoy passers when alone.[39]

In reply to a complaint by a New York newspaper woman in March 1908 that she was "insulted almost every time she appeared here [in Washington, D.C.] at night, and that bad manners and the absence of chivalry are the rule here rather than the exception," Major Richard Sylvester of the police declared Washington was not overrun with the masher and that women were as safe from the insults of ogling men on the streets in his city as they were in any other large city in the nation. The female reporter added that even in the most prominent residential and business sections she was approached by strangers, spoken to, and otherwise annoyed. She declared that Pennsylvania Avenue was more lawless than the Bowery. She gave numerous examples of having been personally harassed.[40]

A letter to the editor of the *New York Times* in November 1909 from an 18-year-old girl who had just arrived in New York City after having spent all of her life in New Orleans complained of the situation. In her letter she wondered why she "should be grossly insulted at least a dozen times a day by that despicable creature, the New York masher?" She went on to say, "Unless escorted by a man there is no place day or night, that I feel safe from the specimens that pass as men who prowl your streets and fill your restaurants, your elevators, your theatres, and your shops—men that I don't even see until they come smirking up beside me and, without encouragement or provocation, insult me." She declared that in all her 18 years in New Orleans she had never been insulted even once. A follow-up to that letter came from a woman from Detroit. She, too, complained about the number of mashers. She said, "Like the girl from New Orleans, I ask, 'Is there no safety or comfort for an unescorted woman in the streets of New York City?'"[41]

Convinced that a great deal of mashing was being done by men who owned canoes, motorboats, and other kinds of small pleasure craft on the Tidal Basin and Potomac River, the police in Washington, D.C., in the summer of 1912 had determined to break up the practice so far as it lay in their power and to deal heavily with perpetrators. Recently several canoeists had been seen paddling slowly around the Tidal Basin near the walks and driveways of Potomac Park, smiling at the women on shore. The park police, under the direction of Colonel Spencer Cosby, superintendent of public buildings and grounds, had instructions to put a stop to such practices. The police had also noticed a number of canoeists at different times lingering in the vicinity of the Aqueduct bridge, and whistling to girls and women walking across the bridge. Complaints had also been heard from Alexandria, Virginia, where it was claimed men in motorboats from Washington hung around the wharves and waterfront, and invited women to go for rides with them. So far, it was said, the Alexandria police had been "powerless" to break up that practice. Commissioner Rudolph said that he wished there was some way of breaking up the mashing, but it was hard for the police to do anything: "We want to stop all mashing and are doing all that we can."[42]

According to a news story published in August 1912, within the previous several weeks reports of mashing cases in which automobiles were used had come in from Washington, D.C., Detroit, and Richmond, Virginia. The auto masher was a comparatively recent addition to the "preying fraternity." His kind had been made possible by the lowering in price of the automobile—it was then more affordable to many more people.[43]

A report that same month declared, "It seems that the days when women and girls could walk the streets of Honolulu any time of day or night, unmolested, are past. There have been many instances lately where girls have been accosted in town, in broad daylight, too, where the cases have not been reported to the authorities." It was also said that "many young women hesitate long before telling of these things because of the notoriety it gives them.... The saying in Honolulu used to be that women were as safe on the streets as they were at home."[44]

One month later, in September 1912, a report noted that the rowboat masher was the latest pest of young girls without escorts in Chicago spending the cool of the evening on the lagoons in the parks. A forerunner of his class was said to be Louis Revnor. He was arrested while plying his pastime in Douglas Park. A policeman testified Revnor rowed his boat beside a boat occupied by several girls and tried to get their names and telephone numbers. The girls screamed, and a police officer made an arrest. The masher was fined $5 and costs.[45]

A first-person account of a working girl's experiences with mashers in Philadelphia appeared in print in April 1915. The woman involved had just moved to Philadelphia from New York City. Before she moved she regarded Philadelphia as safe and New York as dangerous and full of mashers. But her personal experiences in Philadelphia "led me to the conclusion that the obnoxious breed of humanity known as the masher is particularly indigenous to these parts." She, like so many others, subscribed to the idea that few girls liked notoriety, and therefore "the masher abounds as a result." On one of her first walks in her new city a man in a car completely blocked her way, saying, "Come, sweet little one, come have a ride with me." Another man lurched out of the shadows and accosted her. "The friends whom I have made since that night are conservative girls. They dress as inconspicuously as it is possible to dress in 1915 attire, and yet they tell me that mine was no unusual experience." Even the beautiful driveway in Fairmount Park along the Schuylkill was not immune from mashers: "Let a girl walk out there alone in the afternoon and the majority of the men who pass her in motors consider her to be open to their advances. One rebuff does not discourage them. Sometimes, like persistent flies, they circle round and round, and only when their victim threatens them with arrest do they desist." She went on to say, "Usually there is at least one on every corner of the business district." Sometimes they stood around in groups, thus making it impossible for a female to stop for a bit to look in a store window without being mashed. She concluded by declaring, "I know that I would rather be ogled at 50 times a day than have to go to court and testify," thus making the police job much more difficult, as she admitted.[46]

Philadelphia's director of public safety, Porter, was asked to comment on the above article. He said, "The chief cause for the existence of the masher in Philadelphia is the leniency with which he is treated by the corrupt Magistrates in this city." He was not asking that mashers be jailed, only that magistrates would fine them "severely." He felt that if every man brought before a magistrate on the charge of mashing was fined $7.50 consistently and regularly, that annoyance of women would soon cease. He went on to argue that women with the courage to prosecute could not be assured of justice because of politics. When the masher was brought before the magistrate the ward boss came along and said, "He's my man," to the magistrate, and that ended it. Either there was no fine levied or a very tiny one was exacted, which had no effect. The Director of Public Safety concluded, "Every woman should report every man who so insults her, and then, in time, the streets of this city would be absolutely safe for women to appear on unaccompanied."[47]

Mrs. Libby Bresley of New York City engaged Samuel Danneberg in "interesting conversation on the telephone," in 1916, while police rushed to arrest him, and, said the report, the first telephone masher—ever—was caught. He received a sentence of six months.[48]

A complaint in a Burlington, Iowa, newspaper in 1925 reported the city's "sheiks" did not live up to the qualifications of skillful mashers, as the "book of etiquette" said that they should not accost girls on the street [but should be out doing that in autos], and that was the fault of the local talent. In any case, it was reported the streets of Burlington "seem to be the 'hunting ground' for the mashers," those "glucose haired slickers" whose opening lines included "let's eat," "what do you say we see a show," and "let's take a spin in my buzz-wagon."[49]

In 1928 a reporter for the *Decatur Herald* described his town's streets as "fertile hunting rounds" for mashers after nightfall. That reporter followed four women through the business district of Decatur as they walked along the streets. An average of two offers from cars were shouted to them as they walked the streets. The circuit the women traveled was never completed by any of the four without at least one offer. The women made no attempt to invite attention as they walked. A car would drive up to a woman (supposedly waiting for a streetcar), the door would swing open and a hand was held up in invitation. The reporter found that women walking in pairs received more invitations than when they were either alone or in threes or fours. In only a few cases, he found, were the men persistent enough to try more than twice with the same girl. The reporter made no mention of mashers on the sidewalks approaching any of these women on foot. Apparently all of the mashers were in automobiles.[50]

3

Editorials and Opinions

Perhaps the earliest editorial on the subject of mashers was one that appeared in the *Brooklyn Eagle* on March 11, 1881. On the preceding day a "flashily dressed man" entered a Broadway stage [streetcar] and began trying to attract the attention of two ladies. "He was a type of a certain class of well to do American blackguards known by the generic title of 'mashers.'" His attentions became so offensive that the women felt compelled to appeal to the other passengers. That enraged the masher to the point that he grabbed one of the women and started to shake her with some violence. Other passengers quickly intervened at that point, beat up the masher, kicked him off the stage and had him arrested. When arraigned in court the masher "attempted to blacken the character of the lady he had assaulted." He was fined, put under a bond to behave himself in the future, and returned to the lock-up pending the appearance of a bondsman. The editor commented, "Too much severity can hardly be shown in such a case. He worried that justice could not always be relied upon (as in this case), "for good clothes and influence too often go together to protect the masher." He felt it would be far more effective if some of the gentlemen of the town were to organize a little society for the protection of women and children, and take an occasional cruise of the streets, two or three men together, looking for just such fellows as that masher. And those men in such a society "could have plenty of fun in the performance of a public service, and would be likely to avenge many an insulting demonstration directed by the masher to their own wives, sisters, sweethearts and lady acquaintances." Concluded the editor, "A street car or stage ought to be as safe a place for a lady as her own parlor, and the conceited jackass who affronts her self respect after the fashion of the masher ought to understand that the community purposes to make it so."[1]

A year and a half later an editor in Colorado asked himself what was a masher. He answered by writing: "a creation indigenous to American soil, and which grows profusely on the steps of hotels, at the intersection of streets and around theater entrances, or at such parts of the promenade as are most frequented by young ladies without escorts." As well, he was always airing his accomplishments, and when an object of prey appeared, "the masher writhes and twists like a subtle anaconda, whom he resembles, indeed, and is at once afflicted with a facial difficulty; his features work convulsively, one eye is partially closed; a smile intended to be an inspiration of love, but which in its idiotic vacancy more nearly resembles a suggestion of colic, wreathes his bland features...." In conclusion, he said, "There are great differences in mashers, but the line begins with a fool and ends with a villain."[2]

An editorial that made the rounds of newspapers in September 1882 but originated in Evansville, Indiana, was written by an editor who said he had made a close observation of the masher as he existed in Evansville. It convinced the newsman that "he is a cross between an incurable idiot and a bilious ape. He is made up of a cheap suit of clothes, a ten-cent cane, a flashy necktie, a variegated hat, an oroide [an alloy used in imitation gold jewelry] watch chain minus a watch, a 99 cent diamond pin, low cost shoes, red stockings that cost 8 cents a pair, an idiotic grin, an empty skull and barren purse. He possesses lots of cheek and no education." Continuing on, the editor remarked that the masher's actions when he was pursuing prey "would draw forth from an orangoutang expressions of contempt, and yet his microscopic brain tells him that he is pretty and positively irresistible." This editor assessed the masher to be "a foul blot upon society, a disgrace to his sex and an insult to the human race.... He has no laudable ambition, no worthy traits of character, no commendable aim in life and no sense, but staggers along basking in the sun of his own admiration."[3]

A Texas editor declared in August 1883 that to people of good sense and intelligence "there is nothing so despicable as the sneer and petty insults to which needy women, who work for a living, are subjected by a large number of street loafers, rowdies and roughs." He believed that women with "spirit enough" to work for their own support should be protected to the full extent of the law. He decried the usually token punishment mashers received when convicted. He suggested the only way to protect women from mashers was to have them imprisoned for 30 or 60 days, "and while the guilty ones suffer from disgrace and humiliation, an admiring world and thousands of misused women will stand back and applaud."[4]

An editor with the *New York Times*, in July 1884, mentioned the case of a woman who caused the arrest of a party of street-corner mashers who made insulting remarks and gestures to her as she passed by. He thought she was deserving of special credit for her actions because those Broadway mashers "got off too lightly with a night in the station house and a fine in the police court, but even if that penalty were uniformly the result of such behavior the streets would be made more agreeable for unprotected ladies."[5]

An editor with a New York City newspaper in January 1888 commended a woman who had slapped the face of a masher on the Brooklyn Bridge the night before and held him by the collar until a policeman came. The writer declared that she "showed unusual pluck," and that she showed still more courage in going to the police station and filing a complaint against the masher. He concluded, "If every muscular man who sees a masher plying his avocation would apply his toe rigorously to the despicable creature, unescorted girls and women would be subject to fewer annoyances. This pest is getting to be a nuisance. Mash the masher."[6]

On a Sunday in July 1889 a Catholic clergyman in San Francisco preached what was described as a "red hot" sermon against the class of mashers who congregated around church doors at the close of services. Father Fassnot's sermon was such, thought an editor, that "the indignation of the priest should be shared by all other men who despise the masher." According to the editor, there was a sort of fraternity among "those fellows who are known as street statues, since they gather in groups on the walk-ways in the evenings, and make every sensitive woman who passes the object of staring and low-voiced exclamations that mortify, if they do not positively insult her." It was time, the newspaper man thought, to enter into a crusade against the masher, "who, if anything, is the most offensive of all the nuisances of the street."[7]

"The vanity of the masher is insufferable. Nothing can be more revolting than the galvanized smirk with which his simian countenance is perpetually wreathed. As a spectacle which passersby must witness many times in a day going to and fro in the performance of customary duties, the masher becomes unendurable." So thought a Colorado newspaper editor in October 1898. He added that "a stunted mind and a well developed body are the principal ingredients in the composition of the masher. His manner and conduct proclaim his degraded instincts.... He is given to libelous comments about girls and women who are compelled to undergo his impertinent scrutiny on the streets."[8]

An editor from a Newark, New Jersey, paper described the masher, in July 1900, by writing:

> He is a coward of the first water, with such idea of the dignity and honor of
> womanhood as would disgrace a brute. He has neither brains or conscience or
> sense of propriety. He is a foe to society, a conceited, insufferable little pest....
> Nothing short of the fist of a manly man or a horsewhip applied is really adequate to his case. Unhappily these are forbidden by law.[9]

In November 1901 an editor in Washington, D.C., delivered a rant against the masher, declaring:

> They are the evilest things that walk the streets. Their number has multiplied enormously of late years. They have become so bold that no woman walking alone is sure of escaping their insults.... Arrest and a fine is too feeble a punishment. They should be clubbed into behaving themselves.... It is time for drastic measures.

Five days later he returned to add to his rant. After noting that "we" had something to say about the mashing evil in Washington a few days earlier, he stated, "These poor, pitiful pinhead creatures, with their feeble brains and immeasurable audacity, continue to molest and insult unescorted women who have the temerity to stroll about the parks in broad daylight." There were not enough police, he said, to guard the city, and he again urged that an example by made of some of the mashers. And these were the times when policemen, like ex–Inspector Williams of the NYPD, were desirable. He was known as "clubber" Williams because he proved that the policeman's favorite weapon was more effective in breaking up rowdyism than police courts.[10]

In St. Louis in the spring of 1903, an editor was happy to report, in brief, that a large number of mashers were "getting theirs" from an army of hatpins, parasols, fans, umbrellas, gloved fists, and so on.[11]

A New York City editor in July 1903 mentioned three cases of mashing in the previous week when the offenders had been physically dealt with. Then he wondered, "Is there not a duty devolving on every husband and brother to frown upon a masher's advances wherever seen? When the frown proves ineffective, let him interpose with his good right arm and visit physical chastisement upon the offender, if a man of action, or if a man of peace, secure the masher's arrest and expedite his punishment by appearing as a witness against him."[12]

In September 1903 an editor with a newspaper in Ocala, Florida, described a situation in which a woman had arrived in Ocala just one day earlier, knowing no one in the community. She had been in the city for only about six hours when she received a mash note at her landlady's home. The editor grumbled, "Both the young lady and her landlady were very indignant at the affront.... Any man who will take advantage of an unprotected girl in such a manner deserves a horse whipping and the contempt of all decent people."[13]

When a correspondent from San Jose wrote a letter to the editor of a San Francisco paper in December 1903, he complained that it was time for a crusade against mashers. Ladies from the country who went to San Francisco to look around were "insulted all along Market Street." The letter writer wondered what the remedy was, and worried that "no woman is going to make a complaint to police." The editor said that San Franciscans were well aware of the problem: "The nuisance is great, but it lies with the ladies themselves to cure the evil. A mere scornful glance at one of these insulters profits nothing." A remedy for the nuisance, he went on, was provided by the court: "If ladies who are insulted by these sidewalk gallants would resolutely put their pride in their pockets and secure the cooperation of the police, the nuisance would be rapidly abated."[14]

A Salt Lake City editor came out in February 1904 in favor of dealing out justice to the mashers when and where the offense took place. With respect to male citizens "helping out," he said, "We do not believe there is a court in Utah that would inflict any penalty whatsoever on a man who whips a masher within an inch of his life. On the contrary, we believe any court into which such a matter might be taken would dismiss the defendant with words of commendation." He wanted the time to come when women could walk along the streets at any hour of the day and be perfectly free from unwelcome attentions from "bums and loafers and rowdies." That was not then the case, because "on street corners, in front of hotels and saloons, gangs of these beasts stand and ogle passing women, making remarks to and at them, and causing them the greatest suffering and embarrassment. It is a pity there is not always some strong man to resent such proceedings with a prompt blow."[15]

An editor with a paper in Washington state mused in April 1904 that one of the most difficult things to understand was the mind of the masher: "What possible pleasure there can be in insulting women, following girls, ogling, smiling and acting the malicious fool generally is a mystery to the decent man." He then observed that it was "natural" for a modest woman to stand much insult in order to avoid publicity, and that the average woman did not want to appeal to the law. Therefore, "it is a good plan to make an example of these human pests every time an opportunity comes. Here is one instance where there can be no objection to a man taking the law in his own hands. The average masher is a coward. He deserves to be thrashed."[16]

In Pittsburgh in September 1904 an editor said his city had found a new source of revenue for the municipal treasury. And, by extension, he thought other cities might want to use it. One evening the Pittsburgh police force arrested 30 mashers for ogling women on the street, and they deposited in collateral some $1,600, "most of which was forfeited." Said the editor, "A man who makes a business of standing on street corners and annoying decent women deserves to be mulcted [fined] of his cash. There is no room for him on the street, and until he reforms there should be no room for him on the earth." The money referred to was the money extracted from each alleged offender as bail to allow him to be released until his case came up, usually the next morning. If the man did not show up, he forfeited that money. Typically, then, the judge would issue a bench warrant for the arrest of the no-show.

However, there was a high proportion of no-shows because most of those men used fictitious names. Hence the warrant was largely useless, and the bail posted amounted to, in reality, a small fine.[17]

An irate editor on a Salt Lake City newspaper fumed in October 1904 that "no young girl is free to walk down Main Street or the side business streets after 6 o'clock in the afternoon without being spoken to." He declared that Salt Lake was said to have a worse problem with mashers than many, if not most, American cities. "They not only speak, but as a woman waits for a street-car, these mashers edge near her in the most disgusting fashion, staring into her face with the foolish smile customary to such men." Unless something was done to call the public's attention to this problem, he worried that "the women of Salt Lake will either have to remain indoors, be escorted or suffer the insults of the streets. And yet this is an American city."[18]

"A human cur, without manners, morals or decency; an insulter of women; the lowest type of humanity," was how a Seattle newspaperman described the masher in December 1904. And "the man takes his place in front of a theater or store, and as women pass along he makes remarks, generally about their personal appearance—his own disgusting passion. Perhaps he selects a victim and follows her to a car, pouring remarks that should land him in the penitentiary into her unwilling ear."[19]

When he gave a sermon at the YMCA in Salt Lake City in April 1906, the Reverend P. A. Simpkin scored mashers as "things who gather on the street corners and scan every face of passing women and make remarks." He said it was a great pleasure to everyone to see those "things" squelched "by the searching look of purity and innocence bestowed on them by some, and then the look of shame and disgrace that flushes the faces of the mashers."[20]

Illustrating how pervasive was the concept of the masher and how familiar it was to the average American was an editorial cartoon that appeared in newspapers in August 1906. It featured three politicians after the GOP presidential nomination. The GOP nomination was depicted as a large elephant decked out in a dress and with a parasol, walking along. The politicians—Cannon, Fairbanks, and Taft—were depicted separately, with each making a mash comment to the GOP nomination. The cartoon was titled simply "The Mashers."[21]

An editor for a Portland, Oregon, newspaper said in December 1906:

The man with the goo-goo eyes is rather an ubiquitous person. You may find him on the street corner or in all public places, especially the post-office and on the street car. He exists in a large variety of forms, for the victims of the ailment are young and old, rich and poor—but all of them lacking in self-respect or respect for womankind. This is the fundamental requisite, for teach a man the meaning of the word decency and he uses his eyes for observations purposes and not as the complement of a gross and debased nature.[22]

The Mashers.

This political cartoon shows three politicians in 1906 seeking the GOP nomination for the next presidential election. The GOP elephant is dressed as a woman and the politicians are issuing "mash" comments. The cartoon was titled "The Mashers" and illustrated how common the term was and how familiar the public must have been with mashing.

When W. Lester Bodine, superintendent of compulsory education in Chicago, delivered a lecture before a group at the First Congregational Church of Evanston, Illinois, at the beginning of 1907, he said he had given instruction to patrolmen on duty at schools to call an ambulance instead of a patrol wagon when they saw a masher approaching a girl. Then instead of leading the fellow to the patrol box, the cop was to "take him around the corner and put him in such shape that he will be received without question when he arrives at the Cook County Hospital." As the chief of truancy officers in Chicago, Bodine said his method would eradicate mashing in Chicago in six months.[23]

An editor in Newport News, Virginia, grumbled in April 1907 over the lack of a city ordinance that would "absolutely prohibit" street lounging. The lack of such an ordinance meant the police were powerless to prevent men from congregating. Such crowds, of course, were full of mashers. "If there is a more contemptible and despicable specimen than the street masher we do not know where he can be found. He is of the class that should not be given the least bit of liberty," said the editor. "Surely it would be a wise act for the common council to pass an ordinance that would not only protect the ladies of Newport News, but the strangers that we expect to have as our guests during the next six months as well…. It is an easily remedied evil and should be taken care of immediately."[24]

On the evening of November 9, 1913, in a sermon on "Love" delivered by the Reverend Dr. James Shera Montgomery of Washington, D.C., he suggested the whipping post as the proper punishment for the masher. He said, "The masher—how despicable the word. How it has come to us in the atmosphere of much that is low and degrading and abominable. The whipping post should be his portion, as the lash of the public gaze and sentiment cuts him. The word stands for all the impoverishment of mind, soul, and body."[25]

A newspaper editor in Cape Girardeau, Missouri, declared in March 1917 that

> mashers, and men who make offensive remarks as women pass certain corners in this city, have become a menace to society, and it is a matter that is neglected by the police. Every city has a clique of moral delinquents who feel themselves privileged to annoy women, whether in street cars or as they pass by on the public streets. Cape Girardeau has its quota, and they are becoming particularly bold in recent months.

He went on to say that such men belonged in jail, and it was the duty of the police force to see that women could enjoy the right to move about the streets without molestation. But he added that the police of his city had never attempted to enforce any laws against mashers. "When a city reaches the stage when women cannot board a street car or stop to observe the bargains in a store window without being annoyed by men who have lost respect for humanity, then the city deserves condemnation," he declared. He demanded the police begin to take action. If not, he promised that his newspaper would start to publish the names of the victims and the accosters in its pages, because "we can think of no criminal more to be despised than the degenerate who stands on a street corner and preys on the defenseless woman."[26]

Sophie Irene Loeb (1876–1929) was a U.S. journalist and social-welfare advocate. She wrote a column on the subject of mashers that appearing in papers in April 1917. In it she told the story of a woman being accosted and finally having the courage to call a policeman and prosecute the case. "I gloried in the courage of this girl. Of course she had to 'make a scene,' and I could see she disliked doing it very much, but, as she explained, 'I am strong enough to go and tell the policeman, where another girl might hesitate and put up with the nuisance and thus let the dastardly cur go free.'" Loeb urged women to do the same as that girl. "She should realize that she is doing it not only to rectify the wrong that has been done to her but for the weak sister as well, who has not enough nerve to fight the issue at the time, and as a consequence suffers because of her timidity."[27]

When a Missouri newsman remarked in April 1917 that with the coming of spring the mashers were back in his city of St. Joseph, he declared, "And of all the unholy two-legged polecats who are permitted for some reason beyond the understanding of mere humans, to remain upon the face of the earth, the mashers smell the worse." The editor added that if no policeman was around when a woman was harassed, "the fact that you take the law into your own hands and inflict swift and deserved punishment will not cause you any trouble with the law. Swat the masher."[28]

In Bemidji, Minnesota, in June 1918 an editor complained about the problem by writing:

> It seems to be growing in popularity, the disgusting actions of certain individuals who should be stood upon their head to allow their brains to get into the proper place, provided, of course, they are supplied with any gray matter at all. When the women, girls and children of Bemidji cannot take strolls along the lake shore, the most beautiful, healthful and invigorating spot in Minnesota, without becoming a target for some poor non-discriminating fool, it is time the matter was taken in hand and drastically remedied.[29]

An editor in Washington, D.C., discussed the problem of mashers in August 1921. He noted the problem existed in cities around the nation and then went on to say the phenomenon was in some sense a corollary of "feminine emancipation. The growing independence of the fair sex is leading it to regard a night-time escort more as a pleasurable adjunct than a sine qua non for trips abroad after the lamps are lighted, as was the case not many years ago." He thought that was even truer in Washington because of the imbalance of females to males—more work opportunities there for women. The editor went on, "It is a common sight to see girls awaiting trains or buses approached not once but several times during a few minutes, and not by one but by several mashers."[30]

Sophie Irene Loeb returned with another column on the subject, this one in August 1922. It was similar to the first column in that it praised women who took action against their harassers:

> Somehow I cannot help feel that woman owes it to herself and every woman has a civic duty to do her part in bringing to justice such men who try to molest women. And the girl who does take the initiative to go through with it until he is punished is indeed to be appreciated and applauded. The way to manage is to have them punished and not to let them go scot free after they have been offensive.[31]

An editor with an Iowa newspaper launched into a tirade against auto mashers in June 1925, deriding "several half-witted idiots in Carroll [Iowa] who own automobiles and who are simple-minded enough to think that every girl they meet on the streets is crazy enough to take a ride with them." Their method, he explained, was to drive up to the curb near a woman walking on the sidewalk and invite her to take a ride with him, "but to heap insult upon injury, some of these would-be sheiks follow the girls for blocks, insisting on them riding with them." The editor urged those harassed women to get the license number of the car and to phone the police, "or better still, call some relative or friend who may be near. If two or three of these street comedians would get their faces punched good and proper about this time, the practice would be discontinued—and that is what is going to happen."[32]

In the city of Owosso, Michigan, Reverend Lawrence, pastor of the First Baptist Church there, was advocating in the fall of 1926 the addition of "pretty girls" to the city's police department to "act as policewomen" to catch mashers. He said there was a great need for protection of girls accosted by men inviting them to go riding.[33]

After an inspection of New York City's subways during the rush hour periods in early 1927, famed Los Angeles revivalist Aimee Semple McPherson wondered what chance the poor working girl had against the hordes of subway mashers. Said McPherson, "Subways are the mashers' playgrounds. Girls must go through hell to get to work and home. There should be separate cars for men and women."[34]

Another editorial against auto mashers surfaced in June 1927, in a Wisconsin newspaper:

Of all the annoyers of women, the auto masher is the worst. The old-time sidewalk masher was bad enough. But when he made a mistake he had to take the consequences at close range or take to his heels. The cowardly automobile masher is not so easily dealt with. If he finds his advances repulsed and trouble in sight, he promptly steps on the accelerator and speeds away.

The author thought the auto masher was a bigger problem for the police to deal with because of their mobility. "Courts view mashing as disorderly conduct, but usually women shrink from court ordeals. They seldom take the offender's auto license number and have him arrested." The editor had no solution to offer for the problem, despite the title of the piece being "Let's Mash the Curbing Mashers."[35]

4

Blame the Victim

While many identified and described the problem of sexual harassment in America's streets and public places, there were some that did not. For them there was no problem except perhaps with the female victims—as in "What was she doing there?" or "Why was she wearing that?" Then, as now, there was no shortage of people ready to blame the victim.

One of the earliest of the blame-the-victim accounts appeared originally in a Philadelphia newspaper in the spring of 1883, and was reprinted in other papers. It began by arguing that as brazen as the street flirt appeared, "he will not often speak to a woman who offers him no encouragement." Continuing on, the piece declared, "It is manifest that the girls are to blame for his presence upon the streets. Let them lay aside their dashing boldness of manner, which they often foolishly imagine denotes independence, but which is as dangerous as it is unseemly.... Many girls are lacking in that modesty which would entitle them to consideration." Very few girls wished to be considered "fast," the account argued, yet there could be a certain recklessness of conduct while in public places that could easily earn that appellation. "In no other country are unmarried women allowed so much freedom as in our own. In view of the disastrous results of this custom, it would seem to be the part of wisdom to adopt the Old World fashion of chaperones."[1]

An editor with a St. Paul, Minnesota, newspaper mentioned in an editorial on September 6, 1887, the case in his city a day or two earlier of a masher who had harassed a young woman only to be himself "mashed" by the girl's big brother. The editor observed, "The law unfortunately can not take cognizance of the masher if he stops short of actual insult, but the big brother can. And he shouldn't hesitate to do it. In no other way can the evil be stamped out." Then the editor abruptly changed course. He declared that it had to be confessed that the masher was not always without excuse for his advances, saying there were many "silly girls" who would do anything to attract attention, or what passed for it. It was with girls of that type that the masher found his opportunity, for, "as a general proposition, a modest, self-respecting girl, armed with the dignity of her innocence, is in no danger of molestation."[2]

Clara Belle was the bylined author of a piece appearing in a Texas newspaper in March 1890. Perhaps she was a syndicated columnist, perhaps not. The piece was set in New York City. In her column she claimed a number of women told her that it was more dangerous for a pretty woman to go on the streets alone during the daytime than at night. One matron told Clara that the time would come before long when New York parents would adopt the rule of the French and never permit a young woman to go on the street alone without an attendant. Clara remarked that ladies while walking were then exposed to more rudeness than ever before. Supposedly another woman said to Clara, "I know that there are thousands of women who influence badly the habits of the street, as our careless men go about they find at every turn some woman who encourages them to be insulting." (The women Belle quotes were never named nor even vaguely described.) And, Belle continued, that encouragement caused some men to be "impudent" to any woman that caught their fancy. "And that is why you see men sidle up alongside of a pretty girl when she stops to look in at a shop window, or crowd unnecessarily close to her in a street car. She may despise their advances, but she is compelled to suffer an infliction reared by her own sex. Those insulting men have on more than one occasion been met with encouragement." Belle added, "I certainly do blame my own sex for the increase of masculine brutality." (Note that all the above quotes were supposedly from an unnamed woman.) Then, speaking for herself, Belle declared she found considerable truth in those words (from the supposed woman cited above); and if women offered no encouragement, "street mashing would be a starvation employment in very short order." (The first third of this article declared and described the high incidence of mashing; the rest of the article went on the blame the victim.)[3]

Six weeks later the entire Clara Belle article cited above was reprinted in a Kansas newspaper under the title "Street Mashing in Gotham." It included a couple of extra paragraphs added at the end of the piece, but there was no mention anywhere of the name of "Clara Belle." The author byline went to Jennie Dean.[4]

Florence Thorp, 15, was arraigned before Justice Goetting in the Lee Avenue Police Court in Brooklyn on January 25, 1892, charged with being wayward and disobedient. The specific act of disobedience was visiting a merry-go-round in opposition to her mother's wishes. She promised the judge to refrain from going there hereafter, and the sentence (unspecified) was suspended. She was the fifth girl who had been before Goetting on a similar charge. Mashers were said to infest the vicinity of the merry-go-round.[5]

A piece that appeared in a Los Angeles newspaper in November 1892 said that the girl or woman who paraded the streets of Los Angeles looking for a flirtation generally found one, but she who "looks neither to the right nor to the left" is never accosted. "It is only those who trip along in a semi-inviting manner and look as if they had lost somebody, that are accosted by the bipeds who stand at street corners." To make matters worse, "troops of young girls are seen on the streets at all hours of the day and late at night, laughing, talking loudly, and even acting in a boisterous manner, inviting the attention of just such men who stand at the prominent street corners. These girls are not attended by their parents or guardians," and thus tended to fall into bad company. As well, the piece added, there was another class of older girls and even mature women "who parade the streets in costumes purposely to attract. Their eyes are 'here, there and everywhere,' and they glow upon a masher as they pass, half inviting him to venture a remark."[6]

A letter to the editor of a Washington, D.C., newspaper in September 1899 from a Thomas W. Gilmer discussed a recently published article that interviewed some of the officials of the city's police department who complained about a number of "insolent mashers" said to infest a certain area of town. Gilmer thought the trouble was exaggerated because "it takes two to make a flirtation. In almost every case the woman who is addressed by a stranger can silence him with a look or a word without calling a policeman or raising an alarm and therefore attract unpleasant attention."[7]

A story in a Salt Lake City newspaper in January 1904 declared that the masher should be treated with the contempt he deserved, but "it must be said that the blame does not always rest upon him alone. One often hears of girls complaining that men go so far as to speak to them on the streets, stare them out of countenance, etc. In the majority of cases, if they themselves do not look at the men, they will not be troubled with the objectionable glances and remarks. The girl who goes modestly about her own business will rarely be subjected to insults." And, it was added, "as a rule, the well behaved girl is free to come and go as she pleases, secure from obnoxious looks or remarks."[8]

An editorial in a Salt Lake City newspaper in September 1904 called attention to a recent sermon delivered in that city that denounced "that class of ogling and worthless humanity known as the masher." After saying he was in agreement with such sentiments, the editor then devoted the rest of his lengthy piece to something else. He wanted to state that his newspaper wished to call attention to the fact that "the mothers of these silly giggling daughters who become the victims of the mashers, are almost as much to blame as the mashers." He wanted the women of Salt Lake to open their eyes and look around them and "observe the girls that throng the walks and flock to the soda water counters, and who promenade with swagger strides, winking and smiling at the men they meet. Who is to blame if these giggling misses become the victims of the masher? There is only one answer. The mother who permits her daughter to parade the streets instead of keeping her at home, where she belongs." When innocent girls wandered the streets alone or in company with others of their own age, "they encourage and invite disaster, and the parents are to blame." Uttering a dire warning, the editor exclaimed, "Disgrace is the inevitable end of the girl who frequents the public streets alone or with chums of her own sex." Furthermore, "no girl or woman need have fear of the masher if she be attending to her own business." The police, he argued, could not protect the girl who smiled upon the masher and invited his attentions. "There is a limit to the guardianship of the law. Something must be done at home. Mash the masher but—mothers, keep your daughters at home."[9]

In an editorial that appeared in a Washington, D.C., newspaper in January 1905, the editor declared that the modern young woman, even while she protested against being ogled, usually considered it a tribute to her beauty "instead of counting it merely as curiosity excited by something wrong or eccentric in her appearance." As far as this newsman was concerned, nine out of every ten men who stared at a woman did so "wondering why you look as you do—some type of silliness or fashion error." In other words, almost every time a man stared at a woman it was because he thought she looked like a goof. With respect to the masher, this editor viewed him as being in the trying position of a "naughty child" in a big family who was indulged and encouraged by half of the family's members, and punished for his misdemeanors by the other half—"For many young women do encourage him." It was the woman "who wears her hats just a trifle larger than necessary for beauty or comfort, her heels just a trifle higher than they need be, a little more fur, a bigger bunch of violets, and a huger muff than is actually in keeping with her face and figure. It is she who enters the street car with swish and a dash, who hold her skirts just a trifle high, and also talks across the aisle at her chums in an unnecessarily vibrating key." She did all these things because it made people look at her, and she liked that. "The masher eyes her and unconsciously he knows she likes his stare.... He is encouraged."[10]

A strange article appeared in *The Sun* in New York City in November 1905 in which three female night workers were interviewed, and in which all three declared they found the streets of New York safe and completely free of mashers. It was a fairly long piece and featured a physician in New York City who was out on the streets at all hours and had been for 20 years. She had never been mashed a single time and had never even seen a masher in all those years. Second was a female journalist who had been out on the streets of New York at all hours for five years and had never been mashed a single time and had never even seen a masher in all those years. Third was a night school teacher in New York City who had been out on the streets at all hours for eight years and had never been mashed a single time and had never even seen a masher in all those years. The teacher went on to mention her home in Chicago and said it was worse there for an unescorted woman than it was in New York City. In New York a woman had to worry about the likes of holdup men, burglars, highwaymen, and so forth, but there were no mashers. This article used a different method of blaming the victim, eschewing the usual editorial rant about why the women were at fault. This account pretended to talk to three women in the street who should know the score. The problem is that none of these women were identified in any way. There seemed to be no reason to withhold their names, and there was no explanation given in the article as to why they were not named.[11]

Later that same month an editor with the *Washington Times* started off by mentioning the type of cases usually published in the papers where the man "is dragged into court to answer the charge of forcing his attentions on women on the street and is usually reprimanded. The woman who boldly defends herself is praised." However, he continued, getting to the real point of his rant, "but the fact remains that in ninety-nine cases out of a hundred the woman, either ignorantly, unconsciously, or intentionally, encouraged the attentions to which she afterward objected. Charitably he said that some young girls did this innocently. For example, they became frightened when they thought a man was following them and kept looking over their shoulders to see if he was still there. As well, there were various ways in which girls could attract these attentions "but always it is the woman's fault. She cannot sometimes prevent a man's speaking to her, but no man continues to talk to, or follow, a woman who ignores him utterly." He concluded by observing:

> The woman that attends to her own business looks where she is going, and neither sees nor hears any attempts at flirtation, is subjected to very little if any annoyance. Men may speak to her, but they don't carry on any extensive conversation. They may follow her, but not for any distance. And certainly she comes out of any chance encounter of the kind with more credit to herself than the woman who airs the affair in police court.[12]

Also published in November 1905 was an article that featured a collection of letters to the editor and bits and pieces that blamed women's clothing for the "epidemic" of mashing. Wrote one man who saw a girl walking "whose costume was such that it made certain portions of her figure very much in evidence, and, old sinner that I am, I found myself making goo-goo eyes at her. How could I help it." Fashions such as peek-a-boo waists and tight skirts were held up for special blame. Also coming in for negative mentions were the low corset and the "princess one-piece gown." Apparently the piece originated in a New York City newspaper but was reprinted in various other papers. This article concluded by saying, "So girls, you'll have to confine your décolleté wear to evening affairs indoors with the shades down. At any rate, wear more clothing on the street, or the goo-goo man will get you if you don't."[13]

Reporter Winifred Black mocked the idea that mashers were all over the place in a January 1906 piece that appeared originally in a New York newspaper but was also reprinted. "No man is too old and doddering, no boy is too young and inoffensive to pursue her with his unwelcome attentions," Black sneered. "They spring up on street cars, bound out from behind ribbon counters, leap into terrifying activity in church aisles, these pursuing monsters of her imagination." She mentioned an unnamed friend of hers who was fat, forty, and not in the least fair, who could never step outside her home without having those kinds of adventures. Black's conclusion? "If you don't want to see mashers, ladies, don't look for them." Winifred Black (1864–1936) worked for a time as an actor in Chicago before being recruited by William Randolph Hearst to work for his newspaper the *San Francisco Examiner*.

These two sketches were used to illustrate the idea that women were to blame for being harassed. It was their fashions, the clothes they wore they caused all the problems. Blaming the victim is a very old strategy indeed.

Hearst wanted Black to fill a similar role to that of Nellie Bly for Joseph Pulitzer's *New York World*. Over the years Black also used the pseudonym Annie Laurie.[14]

Los Angeles police commissioner John Topham was peeved, in May 1911, about the many complaints received against Broadway oglers, and on May 31 he advised the women's club to begin a campaign against the fashions of the day—the hobble, the harem and the peek-a-boo—which, he said, invite attention and insult. Said Topham:

> Any woman regaling herself in such apparel should expect to be greeted with "whoops my dear" or similar salutations. Such apparel has a tendency to make a man "feel frolicsome" for he looks upon the wearer in the nature of a freak. The way some women appear on the street is degrading, and if they would give a little more attention to such matters there would be fewer complaints against mashers. I am heartily in favor of a city ordinance making it a misdemeanor for a woman to appear on the streets garbed in either a hobble or a harem skirt.[15]

Clarence Cullen wrote a piece in July 1911 in which he said, with respect to the great deal of media publicity about mashers, "Most of them, it is fair to say, are males of foreign birth. The native-born very rarely is a masher." This article appeared originally in a New York City newspaper and was reprinted in other outlets. His idea was incorrect, or at least was not testable, for the simple reason that the vast majority of men charged with mashing gave fictitious names. It was very easy to do that and to get away with it. And so they did. Cullen noted that New York City magistrate McAdoo voiced the other side of the argument recently when he said, "I am going to send every justly convicted masher to jail," but "to convict every man arrested on this charge on the complaint of a woman would put too dangerous a weapon of revenge into the hands of unscrupulous and vindictive women, of whom, unfortunately, there are too many in all communities like New York." He meant that he was going to be careful to see that these men were properly tried and heard when they came before him. He continued, "I have seen thoroughly respectable men haled before magistrates on the charge of mashing—men wholly incapable of engaging in that sort of thing—and investigation of these cases has always shown that the charges were preferred by women who sought only to get even with these men for slights or fancied slights." McAdoo said no such case would get by him, and while the real masher would get no mercy from him, so the man arrested and brought before him on a trumped up charge would get every protection from him. Reporter Cullen, stating first that he too hated real mashers, went on to declare he agreed with McAdoo. Then he went on to explain that some years ago there were a number of girls and women in New York City "who derived a highly plethoric income from threatening to have perfectly on-the-level men pinched for alleged mashing." It was said that Police Chief Bill Devery ran them out of town by the Blackwell's Island prison route.

(William Stephen Devery was superintendent of the New York police from 1898 to 1901, at which time the title of the post was changed to Chief of Police, in 1898. Thus Devery was the last superintendent and first chief of the NYPD.) The supposed method of the offenders was to pick out a likely target and approach him with some ruse—asking directions, for the time, and so on. Having got him stopped, the female would then say to him, "You have stopped me and insulted me. You are a masher. If you don't give me twenty-five dollars I shall have you arrested. If you are arrested on the charge of mashing you will be disgraced. I have nothing to lose. You have. It makes no difference whether you are guilty or not, your disgrace will be the same. If you don't give me the twenty-five dollars instantly I shall scream and faint and you will be arrested." Invariably, said Cullen, they paid up. There were a number of problems involved if one wished to believe that story. For one thing, there was no disgrace involved in being charged with mashing since most of those charged apparently used a fictitious name successfully. They were still fined and/or jailed, but their real name never emerged for any disgrace to attach. Cullen gave no details or names about this supposed scam run by women. Devery had not been police chief since 1901, ten years before Cullen's story appeared. The perpetrators were jailed, according to Cullen, so the whole incident was a matter of public record. Why then no names?[16]

The Reverend Walter T. Sumner, chairman of the Chicago vice commission and member of the board of education in that city, entered the campaign against mashers on August 4, 1912, with a warning to Chicago women to revise their dress as the first step in that movement. He described the present-day female fashions as "indecent and built along the lines which contribute to sensuality." He declared the nation was passing through the "era of suggestive dressing," and that this was the main reason Chicago's streets "swarm with insulting and obnoxious mashers." Added Sumner:

> My opinion is that men generally persist in accosting women only as they receive the impression that they are being given some sort of encouragement to do so.... If there be an increase in this annoyance to women I am inclined to think it can be traced largely to the dress of women of today. We are going through a period when women are making many efforts to accentuate those lines which contribute to sensuality.

He further argued that the average working girl of the time was taking, in ignorance, as her standard of dress that of the demimonde (prostitutes, more or less). It was thus no wonder that she consciously or unconsciously invited men's attention. "The pity of it is that many of the women who should have the instincts of modesty and refinement — the effect of good breeding — to whom we should look to set the right standards for society are no freer from criticism. They are quite as flagrant in suggestiveness of dress as the working girl." Sumner went on to urge dress reform. "If girls do not want to be accosted by men, then let them select such clothes as have less the appearance of those worn by women of the underworld, whose lives, alas, are spent inviting such attentions from men." He waxed eloquently about no influence being more inspiring that that of a "good and beautiful woman," whether wealthy or poor.[17]

Sumner's comments caused the clergy of Washington, D.C., to come forward, ready to reinforce his statements. Said the Reverend Earle Wilfley, pastor of the Vermont Avenue Christian Church, "One must agree very largely with Dean Sumner. Present feminine fashions with respect to tight-fitting skirts are so immodest that they make men wonder if the wearer is not purposely trying to attract attention. Young women clad in more decorous garb than the so-called tube skirt rarely if ever are troubled by the masher." He added that the custom of "penciling the eyebrows and carmining the lips" seemed to accompany the wearing of such skirts. "It is to be deplored that such underworld marks as those are assumed by good women. In some cases it is true that women or girls who are not of actually evil life wear the tightest skirts or the most rouge, and this with the intent of attracting the greatest amount of attention and gazing by men." While this article spoke of clergymen [plural] ready to join in and reinforce Sumner's position, none were mentioned or alluded to except Wilfley.[18]

The Reverend Norman B. Barr, pastor of the Olivet Memorial Church in Chicago, added to the dress debate in September 1912 when he declared, "No woman who dresses modestly and carries herself in a modest manner need fear being annoyed by mashers in the streets." He continued, "If women could be induced to abandon the present day fashions I believe the masher would become a thing of the past. Twenty-five years ago a woman being accosted on the streets was an unheard of occurrence. Nowadays women are becoming active in every line of endeavor and are becoming less modest than formerly."[19]

The issue continued to draw media attention for a little bit longer. Later in September 1912 an article declared, "There seems to be widespread revolt against the present mode of women's dress. From all over the United States, and from many classes of people, came harsh criticisms of the short, clinging skirt, the low-necked waist, short sleeve and other alleged 'abominations.'" The Atlanta vice commission, then investigating the Georgia capital, had given official attention to the matter and declared that much of the "freshness of men" was caused by women's clothes rather than the men's "cussedness." The Reverend O. N. Jackson of Atlanta issued this edict to the women attending his church: "There must be no nudeness of the arms, no nudeness of the neck, shoulders and adjacent territory; no nudeness of any part except the face. Everything must be eliminated in the attire of women that is calculated to distract the minds of men from bold things." Jackson added, "Some dresses of the latest fashion bring ideas of lax morale to the young men who view them." Bishop Austin Dowling of Des Moines Iowa said, "It is because women's gowns are designed in a country which is frankly immoral." The Civic League of Chicago declared in their statement about mashing, "Clean men constantly condemn men who speak to girls and women, or treat them in such manner as they would not tolerate from any man toward their own sister, sweetheart, wife or mother. But the big cry of annoyance on the street and in public places from men which girls are now making is largely due to their foolish mode of dress and manner." Mary F. Balcombe, president of the league, added, "Women should wear longer and wider skirts not long enough to touch the ground, but sufficient to conceal the ankles, and that the waists should not be cut so low." Joseph A. McCord, chairman of the Atlanta vice commission, fumed, "Present feminine fashions are so suggestive and immodest that they make mashers out of the most timid of men." The Reverend Frederick W. Fraser of the Presbyterian Church of Massillon, Ohio, also decried current fashions: "There never was a time when it is so difficult to distinguish the good women from the other kind. Highly respectable women are actually being accosted by strange men who, misled by their immodest fashionable attire, take them for other than they really are. Christian women must desist from wearing in public costumes which provoke men into infractions of the seventh commandment [adultery]." In St. Martin's Catholic Church in Baltimore, the Reverend Thomas Broylick declared that some of the current fashions worn in the churches "are profane to the temple of God." In a lecture delivered at Columbus, Indiana, Mrs. Leonora M. Lake of St. Louis stated that women were suffering from "fashionitis," and that ballet dancers and acrobats were more becomingly attired; it is the present tight skirts give men reason to make the vulgar remarks. Said the Reverend Finis Idleman, "Suggestive attire is a hint for mashing in men, and this evil has multiplied five-fold in the last few years."[20]

Dorothy Dix was the pseudonym of Elizabeth Meriweather Gilmer (1861–1951), a forerunner of the popular advice columnists of today. She was a hugely popular journalist in her time. In one of her columns in May 1913 (likely nationally syndicated) she gave some homilies about the evil mashers but went on to mostly blame the victim. All of it came in a supposed response to a letter written to Dix by a young woman complaining about the pervasiveness of mashers both in public places and in places of employment. Dix said, "Generally speaking, the girl whose employer makes love to her, and the young woman who is followed on the streets, have only themselves to blame. They have at least looked willing." And, she declared, "the girl who dresses quietly and who conducts herself with dignity, who keeps her eyes steadily before her and goes sedately about her own affairs, can go unmolested from one end of the country to another." Dix mentioned that the peril was often imaginary because "there is nothing more common than for a woman's vanity to make her think that men are in love with her when they are not, and she is pursued by those who, in reality, have never given her a second thought." Of the supposed letter writer, Dix concluded, "I will warrant that if she will dress sensibly and act sensibly men will not further molest her." Dressing conspicuously and "flashily" on the street was, after all, "asking for trouble."[21]

A decade later Dix wrote a column on flirts. She saw a variety of the species—one of which was the masher—but she did not define the differences. She asserted, "The most common of these [flirts] is the masher—the varnished-hair, pinched-in waisted, overdressed Lotharios that you may see lounging against store windows and hanging around the lobbies of theatres, ogling everything in skirts that passes." Dix added, "The masher's methods are simple to the verge of childishness. He does not exert himself to charm the fair sex. He does not have to. He had merely to 'give them the eye,' and the treat of looking at him, and the trick is done."[22]

In October 1915 a reporter in New York City submitted several questions to Magistrate Samuel D. Levy in connection with the frequent cases of mashing in that city. Those questions were: (1) "Are men solely to blame for the conditions that might be termed an epidemic of mashing?" (2) "Do women court such insults by their present mode of dress?" (3) "Have you found any women who are prompted in making outcries against alleged mashers by a craving for the attendant notoriety?" Levy held that men were not always alone in the responsibility, that women by their dress invited insults, and that many complaints were "wholly insincere," seeking merely the publicity that accompanied their thrashing a masher. Said Levy, "There are many girls looking for publicity—they ache for it.... They want to be written up.... It is the zenith of their attainment." Thus, all manner of false charges came before him, some of those from females "with tainted or questionable records." Magistrates, as a matter of routine, Levy said, asked for and obtained the probation officer's record of the defendant. (Actually, they almost never did. That was one of the reasons it was so easy to use fictitious identities in court. In misdemeanor cases, as all harassment cases were, background checks were almost never ordered.) He also argued that "I think the time has now come to also obtain the probation officer's record of the complainant." He observed that several cases had come to his attention wherein "I have felt that if the complainant was a really modest, good girl she would simply have walked away and paid no attention to any remark made to her. But in all these cases the complainant, in her anxiety to rush into public print, proceeds to have the defendant arrested, brought into court and tried." Levy said there was much to be said against the current fashion styles "as an incitement to impressionable men," and he welcomed the day when females "will wear high-necked dresses and proper length of skirt. I believe such apparel is decent and invites respect from the male sex. These low-cut shoes and fancy silk stockings effect in a great measure sensitive or supersensitive men. I consider the present styles of women the cause of many of these peculiar happenings."[23]

Four months later, in February 1916, Magistrate Levy returned with comments on female fashions: "A decent woman never has anything to dread when it comes to annoying attentions from the other sex. But the clothes worn by women today tend, in my opinion, to lessen that delicate sense of the conventions and the proprieties that we expect of our women folk, our wives and our daughters." He reiterated that he had no use for the masher, but "if women wore a little more material and were not so desirous of unenviable attention, they would not be subjected to the annoyance of which they complain."[24]

5

Women Respond with Words and Guile

Victims responded directly against their harassers in a variety of ways throughout this period. One way was by using words and/or guile. A young girl riding in a horse-drawn streetcar on a November day in 1882 in Hartford, Connecticut, found herself greatly annoyed by a well-dressed young man who was determined to make her acquaintance. According to the news account, "The young man was of the masher class and only had his good clothes and his impudence to recommend him—two qualities which often go together." The masher had taken a seat close to the woman, although there was room enough for him to have maintained "a respectful distance." He tried to engage the woman in conversation, without success. Finally the car passed a stately mansion and the man asked if she happened to know who owned it. She blushed and said, "Husband owns it." (It was owned by a man named W. P. Husband.) Thinking she meant her husband, the masher stammered something and hurriedly left the car. The few passengers who had witnessed the scene were said to have enjoyed his confusion and laughed outright as he left the car.[1]

She was a woman caught in the rain in Detroit in late 1886, spoiling a $14 hat in the shower. He was a masher who thought a perfect opportunity had presented itself. Raising his umbrella, he hurried along, overtook the woman, and said, "Madam, permit me to offer you the use...." "Oh, thank you," she interrupted as she took it from his hand and walked away quickly, leaving him to take shelter in a doorway.[2]

On a spring evening in 1889 in Minnesota a woman was walking along on the street when she was accosted by a masher, or, as a reporter put it, "one of these animated store dummies." Smiling broadly, he said, "Ah, good evening, miss" to his prey. Stopping short, the woman gave him an icy stare for a moment or two and then exclaimed, "You miserable dirty little cur. Don't you know any better than to speak to a woman you do not know on the street. If I were a man I would feel tempted to thrash you, but as you are such a dirty little puppy and so far beneath any decent woman's notice that I will let you go this time. If you ever speak to me again I'll spank you." Taking the tongue-lashing meekly, the masher turned on his heel and walked away without a word.[3]

A Frenchman named L. R. de Sante Foy announced in November 1889 that he was suing the *Chicago Tribune* newspaper for $20,000 because it had called him a masher in print. In its pages the paper had printed an account of Mr. Sante Foy having sent a note to a respectable young lady asking her for a meeting. She took that note to the newspaper's editor, and a reply penned by the newspaper staff was dispatched to the Frenchman. That letter and Sante Foy's reply were subsequently published in the newspaper with some comments attached that alluded to the idea that the professor (as Sante Foy was said to be) was a masher. The writer of the article also ridiculed the Frenchman's blonde mustache and hair, and "crushed the Gaul" by calling him "an albino."[4]

Eleanor Stackhouse (1863–1942) was an American author, journalist and teacher. She wrote for the *Chicago Tribune* under the pseudonym "Nora Marks" in the 1890s. Early in the year 1890 she visited Omaha and in an interview with a reporter from one of that city's newspapers was asked if she had much trouble in traveling alone. She said she was so used to taking care of herself that she was seldom annoyed, although she did admit that occasionally a would-be masher tried to get up a flirtation. Stackhouse told the reporter that not that long ago a Chicago drummer [traveling salesman] occupied a seat just back of her reclining train car seat. He went through the usual mash attempts—shall I open the window for you, allow me to lower your chair for you, and so on. Finally, after several banal remarks about the weather and other topics of equally absorbing interest, he said to her, "Aren't you frequently annoyed by the attentions of men when traveling?" Replied Stackhouse, "Very seldom, except by Chicago drummers." In a very few moments the drummer found something interesting in another train car, or so she supposed he did, because he went out, luggage and all, and did not return to her car.[5]

A masher boarded a train in Batavia, New York, in May 1892. "He had all the appearance of a professional lady-killer, including a red necktie and an India-rubber smile," wrote a journalist. He stared at all the ladies as he walked down the aisle of the car. Apparently he was picking out a victim. Finally he sat down near a married woman whose child was playing in the aisle. Writing something on a card, the masher gave it to the little girl to take to her mother.

He had written, "I should be delighted to make your acquaintance." The mother turned red as she read the note, but she wrote a reply and gave it to the child to deliver. She wrote, "Perhaps you can get my husband, who is sitting directly behind you, to introduce us." Looking around, the masher found a man staring hard at him. "Suddenly the India-rubber smile lost its elasticity," remarked the account, and the masher fled the car.[6]

A woman was riding on the Sixth Avenue L (elevated transit line) in New York City on a January day in 1893 when she was accosted by a masher. She "encouraged" him as the car traveled along. At the 23rd Street station she got up and made her way to the front of the car, joining a crowd preparing to get off. He was sitting farther back and made his way to a different door and jumped off the train quickly, positioning himself to await his designated target alighting. However, at the last moment she held back and did not get off the train, and as it pulled away she left the would-be masher with a "now-I'd-like-to-see-you-catch-me smile."[7]

A woman entered a stage (transit vehicle) on Fifth Avenue in New York City in March 1895. A masher got aboard the vehicle and sat beside her, noted a report, "accosting her exactly as if he were an acquaintance." To his surprise she answered politely, and after a few more blocks she got off, followed by the harasser. After a few paces she turned and said to him, "I have stopped on the beat of the largest policeman on the avenue, and if you are not a block away within five minutes I will have you arrested. I spoke to you because I knew three women on the opposite side of that stage, and I wasn't going to have it get around that I had been spoken to by a man I didn't know." Apparently the masher believed her—there was a large cop in the vicinity—for he stammered an apology and left in a hurry.[8]

A sexual harasser, described as not youthful, was staying at a downtown Los Angeles hotel in the spring of 1895. One day he went out and walked along Spring Street. Soon he picked a victim and began to follow her, close enough to try and attract her attention by a series of delicate coughs. She stopped and went into a store, came out and continued on her way. He had lingered outside and recommenced following her. Finally, she dropped a small packet and her handkerchief, both retrieved by the would-be masher. She took only her handkerchief before boarding a car. The harasser stayed behind and opened the packet, which contained only a note and a few confections. Said the note: "Cough drops for grandpa."[9]

The omnibus was about half full in March 1896 in New York City when the masher got on and took a seat next to the pretty young woman. He placed himself close to her, and she edged away, but little by little he crowded up to her until she was jammed into the corner. Other women on the bus glared at the masher. The girl in question turned to her harasser and exclaimed, "If you want my place, sir, I shall be happy to rise and give it to you, but please don't try to occupy it while I am in it." The masher pulled the stop cord and got out.[10]

During the summer of 1896 a woman in Paris, France, was out shopping at a local flower market. Soon a masher appeared and began to follow her. She paid no attention to his harassing. Finally she purchased two big geraniums. He quickly stepped up and offered to carry them home for her. She agreed, making him carry both big plants. At her building she stopped and thanked him for his help, but he insisted on carrying them right to her apartment door. When she told him she lived on the top floor of the building and that there was no elevator, he still insisted. She agreed. When the pair arrived at her door she rang the bell and a man opened it. The woman said to the masher, let me introduce you to my husband. Addressing her husband, she told him the masher had been kind enough to carry her geraniums home for her. The husband thanked him for aiding his wife and began to reach for 20 cents to give him as a tip. However, the masher did not wait around and was already on his way down the stairs.[11]

A masher was walking along State Street in Chicago one evening in February 1900 when the theaters were letting out. He noticed a woman and stepped into her path. When she tried to step around him he gave a cough and muttered an unintelligible remark. The woman paid him no attention and walked on. He followed, coughing and issuing a variety of other sounds to attract her attention. She stopped in front of the Palmer House hotel where a group of well-dressed people were talking. She said to the masher, in a voice loud enough to be heard by the others, "You have been at considerable pains to attract my attention. Evidently you imagine I might encourage your advances ... what indicates I would tolerate you for a second." Then she added, "One glance at your face reveals your dwarfed mind. You are dressed in atrocious taste, and your tailor had better be carrying the hod instead of making clothes, as yours fit you shockingly." By this time more passersby had joined the group, and all awaited his answer. He tried to move away, but a bystander grabbed him and said he could not go until he had answered the lady's question. "I can't. Let me go. I don't know," he wailed. They let him go and he swiftly departed.[12]

A New York City nurse had gone out for a little shopping in the summer of 1900 and was walking back towards the nurses' residence where she had a room when it started to rain a bit. She was caught in the shower without an umbrella. Then a stranger walked up to her with his umbrella open and tried to make her acquaintance and act as her escort, "without any encouragement from her," noted the story. He persisted in walking with her even though she gave him the cold shoulder. Finally she stopped, opened her purse, pulled out a penny and held it out to him. Caught off guard, the masher exclaimed, "What do you take me for?" To which she promptly replied, "A beggar!" Without delay he disappeared.[13]

Miss Alfa Hudspeth, 17, of St. Louis, pretended to fall victim to a masher's charms until she reached the city's Carr Street police station. She was walking home from Union Station on a Sunday night in October 1904. Hudspeth noticed that she was being followed by a man. She was frightened and tried to avoid the stranger, who winked, spoke, and raised his hat to her. Although nervous, she continued to walk along, looking for a policeman. None could be found, so she pretended to be interested in the man who had accosted her. She became friendly, and the masher appeared to be delighted. On they walked. Soon they came to the police station. Hudspeth told him to wait while she went inside for a moment. Suddenly he realized where he was and took off. However, she had told the duty officer inside what had happened, and he chased the masher down and arrested him. He told the police his name was Diogenes Sulerneo and that he was 30 years old. No more was reported on this case.[14]

PRETTY GIRL HAS A NEW CURE FOR MASHERS

Josie Davis of Los Angeles discouraged mashers with words. Whatever they said to her she embarrassed them by pretending they were beggars.

In Indianapolis, on September 22, 1906, Miss Lenore Cross, 17, and a girl friend were walking along the street when they were accosted by two men. Cross said she was frightened, as the men followed them, but the thought then struck her that she should lead the men to the police station. She and her friend smiled at the men and led them to the nearest police station. Once outside that building the women ran inside and told the desk sergeant that two men had insulted them and would he please arrest them. He did so and jailed Harry Smith and John Lyons, who were both later fined.[15]

The experience of Miss Josie Davis of Los Angeles in dealing with her harasser was present in the newspapers as something to be thought of not as an isolated case but as a remedy for all such women who were set upon by harassers. Davis, it was reported, placed no faith in the revolver, the hatpin or the punch as a way of dealing with the masher, but relied on her tongue. When a masher approached her and said something to her, she gave him the same reply, no matter what he had uttered. "What, neither dinner nor supper? You poor fellow. You must be starved. Here's two bits for you. Now run along and get a good meal." It was a method that worked every time, insisted Davis.[16]

Someone described as a "well known" American society woman was out walking in Paris, France, in June 1907, leading her three dogs on a leash. As she turned into a secluded pathway in the park a Frenchman passed and said, "Good morning, mademoiselle." She stared at him icily, but he followed and repeated his greeting. Determined to end such annoyances, she faced him, glared, and said, "Monsieur sees that I am accompanied by three dogs. They are English. When I need a French dog for an escort I'll send monsieur my card."[17]

When the steamship Carmania arrived in New York City in August 1907 from Liverpool, it was revealed that a masher had been at work aboard the liner. One of the passengers was Mrs. Henry O. Jackson of Norfolk, Virginia, who was accompanied on the trip by her husband. The masher, whose name was withheld by the ship's officers, had ogled the woman for several days. According to the account, several of the other passengers on the liner had threatened to whip him, but then a better plan was decided on. Mrs. Jackson got a lemon and walked to the promenade deck. Some of the 400 first class passengers were in the big saloon at the time. When the masher accosted her there, she handed him the yellow fruit, whereupon, it was reported, the other passengers jeered loudly and to such an extent that the masher took to his stateroom where he remained for the rest of the voyage.[18]

In November 1930 in Philadelphia, Goldie Laskowicz and her sister [unnamed] were walking along a street one evening when they found themselves being harassed by two men who were following them in their car. They were Cornelius Bowman and LaMarr Moberly. They persistently drove up near them and accosted them. Under the pretext that they were interested in the men, the two women guided them for a bit until they were at a Philadelphia police department station house. The women went in and lodged a complaint; the men were arrested.[19]

6

Women Respond Physically

Social conventions of this era, along with ideas of how a respectable woman behaved and a woman's "proper place" in the universe, all militated strongly against any sort of physical response by a woman to a sexual harasser. Yet so frustrated and angry did some women become in the face of egregious and persistent harassment that they sometimes did respond physically. One of the earliest such reported incidents took place in Berks County, Pennsylvania, in August 1877. An extremely brief report noted only that a girl in that region had "thrashed" two young men who had insulted her at a dance.[1]

In a September 1892 report from St. Louis a man related the story of his friend's wife. He observed, "Like most handsome women, especially those who lived in the smaller cities, she had been much annoyed by the rude staring and smirking of street-corner loungers," and she determined to respond. Her husband was an "expert boxer," and without telling him why, she induced him to give her daily lessons. Six months later she was ready. Soon she came across a masher who gave her a prolonged and insolent stare. She gave him a lecture and then pummeled him with her fists.[2]

Late in 1895 an exposition of some type was underway in St. Louis. Miss Mabel Puthoff was working at that exposition as part of the Quaker Oats display. Mabel and her sister were down in the basement one day having lunch when a young man happened by. He was, by appearance, said a report, "a swell of the first order." Seeing the women, he went and spoke to them but was unrecognized by the women, who were confident they had never met the man before. As was to be expected, they ignored him. After finishing lunch, the pair returned to their exhibit work and were "much surprised when the man put in an appearance and at once began to make overtures as though an acquaintance." The climax to the story came when the "swell" asked Mabel for a hairpin, or "just anything to remember you by." At that point Mabel hauled off and punched him in the face. A crowd began to gather, but before a security guard arrived the man had disappeared into the crowd. An exposition detective was detailed to find the man, but he could not locate the masher.[3]

Eugene Flash, 18, described as a "prominent" young man of Mount Vernon, New York, was assaulted on a night in October 1896 by six females employed in Police Commissioner Taylor's Lenox Laundry in that town. When the girls passed his place of business as they went to and from work, Flash would cry out at them, "There go the Lenox girls," and other such words. Having had enough of such insults from Flash, one day at noon the women agreed among themselves to take matters into their own hands and punish the masher. That night, as the women passed on their way home, Flash spoke to them in the usual way. Three of the females had lunch baskets with them, which they let fly at their harasser, one of which hit him in the face. Two other women jumped on him and threw him to the ground. While he was down they all joined in and kicked him around a bit. Flash had to promise to never again cry out at them such expressions as "There go the Lenox girls." Then he was allowed to get up; immediately he ran off home.[4]

Soon after a woman entered a Broadway cable car in New York in December 1897, an elderly masher took a seat not far from her. After ogling her for a time, he began to edge nearer and nearer to her. He finally got so close she was squeezed against the passenger on the other side. She got up and stood by the door. However, he followed and stood so close to her that they touched. The other passengers had noticed what was going on and watched to see what would happen next. Suddenly and swiftly she slapped her harasser soundly in the face. He doubled up his fists as if to strike her. At that point two of the other men on the car rose from their seats. Said one of them to the masher, "You hound, if you lay your hand on the lady I'll throw you from the car." Said the other man, "You got what you deserved." The masher then got off the car at the first opportunity.[5]

H. C. Moseley made "goo-goo eyes" at Ida and Madeline Shaw, sisters, on an electric car in Norfolk, Virginia, and afterward approached them as they sat in their seats. In response, the sisters jumped up from their seats and gave masher Moseley what was described in a news account as "a severe punching with their fists."[6]

Blanche Bates (1873–1941) was an American actress, well known in this period of time. She was on her way home from the matinee performance at the Garden Theater on April 22, 1901. She was then appearing in the role of "Cigarette" in the Broadway play *Under Two Flags*. Produced by Charles Frohman and directed by David Belasco, that play ran at the Garden Theater for 135 performances. Bates was the star of the piece. Walking home with her that day was her maid. A man stepped between the two women and thrust his head beneath the actor's umbrella. He pushed the maid away, taking her place. Reported Bates, "I was dumbfounded at the man's impertinence, especially when he leered at me and asked permission to walk with me." Bates said to the harasser, "What do you mean by speaking to an unprotected woman?" He made no reply. Then she gave him a "good, sturdy push" away from her. He lost his balance, fell against a railing, and then slipped to the ground. "That's what you get for insulting a defenseless woman," she said to him as she moved away. And, as she reported, "I left him scrambling to his feet."[7]

J. M. Rousseau, who said he was an electrical engineer, was arraigned in the Harlem Police Court in New York City on October 12, 1901, charged with disorderly conduct and assault. Miss Bertha Streit said he accosted her on the street, and that when she caught the tail of his dress suit to prevent his boarding a cross-town car after she had called for the police, he turned and struck her in the mouth with his clenched fist, cutting her lips. Streit and her friend Miss Alice Horner were walking along 125th Street near Madison Avenue when Rousseau stopped them with his hat in his hand, claimed acquaintance and asked them to go to a drugstore with him for a soda. He persisted in harassing the pair even after repeated refusals. Streit struck his hat, knocking it to the ground. He picked it up and ran to a car at the corner. Streit followed and grabbed him by the coat, calling for the police. After he struck her, he was "roughly handled" by several men in the vicinity. Rousseau explained to Magistrate Mayo that he "had been dining too well" and made abject apologies to Streit. He was held on a bond of $1,000 to be on good behavior for six months. He furnished the bond.[8]

Miss Georgie Coker of St. Louis used her fist on the face of a would-be masher who accosted her on the evening of April 1, 1902, as she entered a streetcar. Several times within the previous two weeks Coker had been annoyed by the same man. Once, also on a car, Coker had felt compelled to ask the conductor to come to her aid. On April 1 the man grasped at her arm and whispered something in her ear. She turned quickly and gave him a punch in the face. Then Coker asked the men on the rear platform for help. Several had witnessed the incident and started running after the masher, who by this time had jumped from the car. The masher managed to escape.[9]

Mrs. Margaret Sidney, from Minneapolis, was sitting alone in Paris, France, at a table at an open-air restaurant on August 16, 1902, awaiting her husband, who had been delayed. Seeing the lady alone, a man who was dining at the next table "smirked" and, gradually growing bolder, finally raised his glass as if drinking to her health. Sidney called a waiter and asked him to tell the masher to cease his annoyances. The masher resented the waiter's intervention rather loudly and approached the woman, smiling, and said, "Now, dear girl, don't be foolish." Before he could say any more, Sidney sprang up and punched him in the face, sending him sprawling. Once the uproar in the restaurant had died down, the masher was given his hat and ordered to leave the establishment.[10]

After the matinee performance at the Madison Square Theatre in New York City on May 14, 1903, Anita Bridger, the leading lady of *A Fool and His Money*, had, she said, an encounter with a masher. She was on her way home when the masher appeared, just after she had left the theater. When he approached her and asked to take her to dinner, she slapped his face. That sent him scurrying away. When Bridger returned to the theater later that day for the evening performance, said the article, "she told the press agent of her experience and he hastened to make it public."[11]

A masher was standing on Washington Avenue in Minneapolis on September 7, 1903, when Miss Helen Lewis of Red Wing, Minnesota, passed by. He spoke to her, and she stopped and looked him squarely in the face. Thinking he had made a "mash," the harasser attempted to grab her arm, at which point Lewis punched him a stinging blow between the eyes. The force of the blow staggered him, and before he could regain his equilibrium she struck him again and knocked him down into the gutter. As he tried to regain his feet a third blow from Lewis brought him down again. Taking offense at this treatment, the masher reported the matter to Patrolman William McLeod. The officer told the sexual harasser that it "served him right."[12]

Mrs. Mary Collins took her two children to Huber's Museum, one of New York's oldest and best known dime museums, on a day late in 1903. Dime museums were very popular in this era and offered a combination of education displays, entertainment displays, and freaks. Aimed at the lower classes, a dime museum was where you went if you wanted to see the six-legged dog or the two-headed baby. Collins and her children sat down inside the museum to watch a film, part of the show. Suddenly she heard a man's voice in her ear whispering, "Hello, dear." Then the voice suggested they sneak out and go next door for a drink. Then the film ended and the lights came up, and for the first time she saw the masher—one Isaac Moses. Collins let fly with a punch that landed on his chin. He struggled to get up and she hit him again. Once again he struggled upward only to be punched again. By this time Policeman Abrams arrived and took charge of the situation. Mrs. Collins filed a complaint, and Moses was in court on that charge on December 3. When the facts were told, Magistrate Poole expressed a desire to shake the hand of Collins for the way she had dealt with the masher. "If our men and policemen are not able to protect us," said Mrs. Collins, "we will have to protect ourselves. I have been an advocate of physical training for women all my life and have cultivated my

HOW PRETTY MRS. MARY COLLINS THRASHED A MASHER WHO
ANNOYED HER WHILE SHE WAS IN A MUSEUM WITH HER CHILDREN.

SHE PUNISHES
THE MAN WHO
INSULTED
HER
IN THE
MUSEUM.

SHE ASKS
THE CAPTAIN
TO FEEL
HER MUSCLE.

"I HAD NO ONE TO PROTECT ME
BUT MY GOOD RIGHT
ARM."

MAGISTRATE
POOL
CONGRATULATES HER
IN COURT.

Artist's rendition of Mary Collins subduing her harasser with her fists. These exaggerated drawings show Collins flexing her muscles for a policeman. That did not happen.

muscles until I feel that I can take care of myself." Moses was held over for trial on $1,000 bond. At home later that day Collins told a reporter, "While I deeply regret the notoriety that this had brought upon me and my husband, I must say that I do not regret what I did to this offensive person."[13]

The Collins case caused the editor of a New York City newspaper to weigh in on the matter. He noted that cases of personal chastisement of a masher by the object of his unwelcome attentions occurred periodically. Referring specifically to Collins, the editor observed, "It is a painful thing to see a woman figure in such a role. More painful, however, is the low standard of masculine chivalry which in the circumstances justifies the deed." If men were honorable and considerate there would be no need for that sort of thing, and no court cases would arise out of ogling on the L cars, he thought. But men's honor was not so high, and so such cases would continue. He argued that the remedy was internal with men, "and an occasional rebuke by the woman insulted affects little to suppress the nuisance." However, he believed physical chastisement might serve the good by punishing the individual offense and exposing the offender "to the detestation which he so richly deserves," and that "an example made of one may discourage the practice in others."[14]

On December 11, 1903, Isaac Moses was convicted and sentenced in the Court of Special Sessions. Judge McKean fixed his sentence at two months in jail.[15]

William Nichols, an engineer, was arrested on the night of May 7, 1904, at Twelfth and Olive Streets in St. Louis, charged with disturbing the peace of Mrs. Emma Scoville. She was on her way home from the Post Office when she was approached by a man unknown to her who, nevertheless, insisted on making her acquaintance. Scoville paid no attention to his remarks until she saw he was following her. At that point she turned and struck him in the face. Nichols started to run off, but she grabbed him by the coat and shouted for a police officer. When Patrolman Byrnes arrived, she was still holding Nichols, despite his efforts to tear away from her grasp.[16]

Miss Maud White, an actor, claimed she was not treated fairly in the published account of her encounter with a masher on Broadway in New York City one week earlier. Speaking in the middle of July 1904, she said, "I regret very much that my name got into print in a matter of this kind. The man whose face I slapped had grossly insulted me on two occasions. I told him if he ever spoke to me again I should have him arrested. When he had the effrontery to come up to me in the street and speak to me a third time, I slapped his face."[17]

On August 18, 1904, Mrs. Anna Brammer passed through Harlem on foot. Specifically, she went along 125th Street where it crossed Lexington Avenue, an area said to be known as "Mashers' Corner." One of the oglers lounging on that corner followed her and addressed her. She paid no attention at first, but he continued to follow and harass her, so she turned and slapped his face. He only laughed and persisted in trying to force his attentions on her. Then she used her fists on him. Men passing by joined in the fray, and by the time a policeman arrived the masher was getting the worst of it. All were taken to Harlem Court that same day. Arraigned therein, the masher said there must have been some mistake, that he was William Snow, 26, and "a member of a good family." Magistrate Crane found him guilty and imposed a fine of $10, which, said a reporter, "he paid from a fat roll of bills." Snow was then released.[18]

A scene took place in front of the courthouse at Logansport, Indiana, in August 1904 when Miss Myrtle Robertson, daughter of Sheriff S. C. Robertson of South Bend, Indiana, dealt with a masher. Sheriff Robertson had arrived in Logansport to pick up a detainee. He was accompanied by his daughter. The masher walked up to Myrtle outside the courthouse while she was by herself. He spoke to her, saying, "It's a lovely day." According to the article, "Miss

WOULD-BE MASHER REBUKED

An unidentified woman on board the Pennsylvania ferry boats out of Philadelphia was said to have dealt with a masher in August 1904 by suddenly hiking her skirts and letting fly with a kick that caught the man on the point of the chin. As he lay stunned on the deck she delivered several slaps to his face.

Robertson drew back in astonishment. Her big eyes blazed and her face flushed. Her pretty fingers clenched themselves into a firm, symmetrical knot, and her little arm unfolded itself in a hook that would do credit to [boxing champion Bob] Fitzsimmons." The masher went down, attempted to rise, tripped and fell back down. Then he ran.[19]

Miss Anna Schine, a waitress in Minneapolis, was accosted by a masher on her way home from work on a night in October 1904. As she walked along, a man approached her. She made no reply to his remarks, and when he started to follow her she turned and hit him squarely in the eye. She then reported the matter to the police, who were looking for a well-dressed man with a black eye.[20]

Miss Estelle Wyman of San Francisco arrived in New York City in the middle of December 1904. At 8 p.m. on December 29 she was waiting at a car stop at Madison Avenue and 59th Street. A young man came by and walked back and forth several times, ogling her. She ignored him. Finally he approached near her, raised his hat and spoke to her. Suddenly she turned on him, grabbed him and flipped him over her own body. The dazed masher picked himself up and tried to brush some of the mud off his clothing before hurrying off down Madison Avenue. Men waiting at the stop told Wyman they would have the man arrested if she wanted to. "Oh, no thanks," she replied. "I guess he has been punished enough. I learned some tricks of wrestling in the San Francisco High School." Whether she flipped the masher with a wrestling move was not clear, but the media all decided she had bested the harasser with jiu jitsu moves, one of the Asian martial arts.[21]

The Wyman incident caused well-known columnist Nixola Greeley-Smith to give her opinion. She started off by asking what the solution to the masher problem was—and then promptly answered her own question by declaring, "It is contained in those words of hyphenated magic: Jiu-Jitsu." She then mentioned the Wyman incident and said there was the odd woman who punched a masher "But the feminine right arm strong enough to administer fistic punishment is the exception, and only the Japanese art of jiu-jitsu seems to meet the requirements of strong and weak alike." She wondered rhetorically if women would then organize them- selves into one gigantic jiu-jitsu club to exterminate the offender. But she an- swered this query by declaring they would do nothing of the kind. For if young women really resented the mash- ers' attentions with half the seriousness they would have us believe, the number of that despised class would be radically diminished. "Of course, it is foolish to contend, as some women and men do, that a girl who attends strictly to her own business and does nothing to chal- lenge attention will always escape the masher. For she will not." While Nixola did not fall for the easy—and false— idea of blaming the victims by declaring they must have been doing something wrong or inappropriate, she went on to argue that the main thing in dealing

This is a sketch of Myrtle Robertson dealing with a masher with her fists in Logansport, Indiana, in the summer of 1904.

with the masher "is not to seem afraid of him. For if you do he is very apt to continue his persecution just to frighten when he sees that he cannot impress." Then she declared there was a "jiu-jitsu manner that any young woman accus- tomed to going about alone will often unconsciously find herself acquiring and that is usually entirely adequate to managing any little mashing incident that may arise without obliging her to have recourse to actual physical vio- lence." Nixola did not explain just what that jiu-jitsu manner was or how women in the Anglo-Saxon culture of North America could unconsciously adopt a manner that was part of a Japanese martial art that was very much unknown in North America at that time.[22]

One day later Nixola devoted another column to the subject. She observed that the average woman knows nothing of the art of self-defense, "yet the feminine invasion of the commercial world has made it necessary and customary for young women to go unattended, frequently at a late hour." She again mentioned the Wyman case. This column featured a series of photos and text designed to teach a woman how to defend against a masher who came up to her on a deserted street at night. The man who posed in the series of four photos for Nixola's column was the famous boxer Tom Sharkey, then retired from the ring for about a year.[23]

After she had hurled the masher through the store window in August 1905, Miss Josie Sanchez was arrested and booked for malicious mischief on a complaint from the person who owned the store and whose window had been shattered. She quickly gave bail for her appearance in court and then handed $8.50 to the complainant as compensation for her destruction of his property. "I don't begrudge the money," she told Judge Conlan in San Francisco, "for the satisfaction I derived from chucking that impudent cur through the window was worth twice eight and a half." She and a girlfriend were walking to the theater, she told the judge. They came upon a masher who was standing in front of an office at 404 O'Farrell Street, and as the women passed he uttered an offensive remark. "He had done the same thing several times before, so I thought it was time to stop him," she added. "I just turned around, picked him up and threw him into the window." Said Conlan to Sanchez, "You did what was perfectly right, and if you could have chucked him through a skyscraper skylight instead of a first-floor window he

A sketch of Josie Sanchez throwing her harasser through a retail store's window. She was charged with mischief for breaking the window.

would have been properly served." A reporter described Josie as "Amazonian in stature and breadth of shoulder." The case against Sanchez was dismissed.[24]

On the evening of August 24, 1905, in Cleveland, Ohio, Mrs. Frank Gilbert, described as "prominent in society and noted for her beauty," rained blow after blow upon a masher on a crowded Euclid Avenue car, rendering the man unconscious. Annoyed for some time by his attentions, she rose from her seat and dealt the harasser several blows to the face. Friends picked him up and took him away while, a reporter wrote, "the passengers applauded." Said Gilbert, "I learned to box when I was young. Perhaps I was too hasty."[25]

Miss Margaret Jordan of Brooklyn was accosted on a streetcar in the spring of 1906 by Joseph Sowalsky. She turned on him and delivered a hard blow to the jaw. Jordan then had him arrested. When the case came to court, the prisoner claimed Jordan and her female companion had been flirting with him. Not believing that story for a minute, the judge commented favorably upon the method of defense adopted by Jordan, remarking that she was a brave girl to hit the masher the way she did. Jordan was the niece of American vaude-

SHE SMASHED MASHER WITH HER WHITE FISTS

Left: On an August evening in 1905 Mrs. Frank Gilbert of Cleveland was harassed by a masher. According to press reports she beat the crap out of him. *Right:* Margaret Jordan was another woman who repulsed her harasser with a punch to his face. In court the judge had words of praise for Jordan and her method.

ville star Maggie Cline (1857–1934), an immensely popular vaudeville singer who was most famous for her song "Throw Him Down, McCloskey."[26]

Later that same year Mrs. William Wagar, "a society woman" in Cleveland, Ohio, slugged a masher while wheeling her baby along the street. The masher, Frank Tyndall, tried to flirt with her and then tried to throw his arms around her. "I gave him uppercuts and tripped him," Wagar told the police officer who arrested Tyndall. When the officer arrived on the scene, the man was lying in the gutter, with Wagar kneeling on his body and punching him in the face. Tyndall was fined and sent to the workhouse for an unstated period.[27]

On a summer day in 1906 Miss Viola Keech was sitting in Central Park in New York City, busy with her crocheting. Along came a masher. Undismayed by the first rebuff from his prey, he advanced again. At that point Keech decided to put an end to the harassment. Keech jumped to her feet and punched him in the face. The masher picked himself up and ran a little way off. A policeman was called, and he managed to find and arrest the man, who said in court that his name was Raymond Meyer and that he was employed as a clerk. Observed Keech, "I hope other girls will do as I did. It's outrageous the insults the girls are forced to take if they are out alone." An editor for a New York City newspaper added his opinion that "it is a pleasure to wish for mashers in general the exemplary fortune of Mr. Meyer in selecting the wrong girl for a subject of approach."[28]

"How are you, darling? Let's take a walk." In that manner James Hall, bartender, accosted Miss Genevieve Hayes on a night in August 1906 in Sacramento, California, taking hold of her arm in a familiar way as he spoke to her. Instantly she slapped his face. Then Hall punched her in the face with his fist. But she got up and began to scratch and slap the face of Hall with such persistency that he took to his heels and ran. Hayes reported the matter to a deputy sheriff, and Hall was arrested and jailed within 30 minutes after the offense had occurred. However, within another few hours Hall was a fugitive from justice. After being bailed out by the amount of $200 posted by friends, he fled the city, reportedly to Portland, Oregon. Most likely he had adopted the practice of so many men brought up on such charges and gave a fictitious name to the police and the courts. Which meant, of course, that he would almost certainly never be found. A reporter ended his account by remarking, "Miss Hayes is the heroine of the hour and has earned the respect of all classes by her earnest endeavor to suppress the most detestable type of masher that prowls the streets."[29]

On a day in January 1908 a man followed a woman along Upper Broadway in New York City. As it was the middle of winter her hands were contained in a huge muff. The masher had been harassing her for some time. Suddenly, at 45th Street, she stopped and turned on the man. One of her hands, clad in a two-ounce boxing glove, lashed out, landed on his jaw, and sent him sprawling into the gutter. The masher picked himself up and dashed off. Detective Leigh of the NYPD came along and said, "Young lady, you mustn't come around here knocking people down." She told the officer she was a stranger, and alone, in New York City, just having arrived from Alabama. "I put this boxing glove on and hid it in my muff because every time I walk down Broadway to get the fresh air some hoodlum accosts me, and as the police can't be everywhere at once, I decided to take care of myself," she explained. "I've knocked about four of them this evening— and there'll be more." She added, "But I'll tell you, officer, there's no man in this city that can insult me with impunity. I taught women boxing in the south—and I'll teach New York mashers boxing in the north." After bystanders told the officer she had acted in self-defense, Leigh changed his tone and said to her, "I admire you." He asked her name, but she would not say.[30]

Mrs. Louise Rice, 24, of Chicago was accosted in that city by a masher in May 1908. He stopped her on the street, smiled and said something she didn't understand. Rice told him to let her alone and continued on her way. He kept following her and talking. Then she struck him in the

On a winter evening in 1908 a woman out walking in New York was stopped by a masher. Since it was cold weather she had both hands encased in a large muff. To the surprise of the masher she dropped the muff to reveal a boxing glove on one of her hands. She hammered him and he fled. She refused to give her name to the authorities.

face three times, cutting him with her rings. She said, "I took him by the collar and beat him until a policeman came up." The masher identified himself as Joseph Rusicle. Rice added that Rusicle was not the first masher that she had chastised. About a year earlier she had been accosted by a harasser, but she did not have that one arrested. Rather, she said, "I just beat him with an umbrella until he ran for all he was worth."[31]

During the morning rush hour on March 30, 1909, Miss Isabelle Graham, 20, was on a packed car of a Third Avenue L line in New York City on her way to her job. She suddenly cried out and gave a man a shove that sent him sprawling into the aisle. Then she worked through the crowded car to appeal to a platform guard for protection. A group of male passengers volunteered to watch the masher and see that he stayed on the train until a police officer could be summoned. When the officer arrived, Graham told him the masher had offended her with "flagrant indignities" and that she was willing to prosecute him in court. "I'm perfectly willing to lose a day's pay and even to risk my place if I can put this creature where he will not be able to annoy respectable girls on their way to work," she exclaimed. Graham's last statement concisely summarized the very real difficulties that were sometimes involved in prosecuting a masher in court. Her masher was named as Frank Feloneno, 35. He told the court his wages in a jewelry shop were $4.50 a week, and out of that he had to care for a wife and five children. He denied doing anything improper. Magistrate Hermann believed Graham's story, and he intended at first to send Feloneno to the Workhouse for a long term. However, because that would have left his family as charges upon the county, the Court let the man off with a fine of $1. But Feloneno had no money at all and could not pay the $1, so he was locked up.[32]

In Oakland, California, in September 1909 Mrs. Josie Woods was walking along the street on her way home when masher Peter Bogas approached her and made what was described as "an impertinent remark." Then Woods slapped him hard on the cheek and delivered a series of slaps to the man which left him in a daze. Soon the police arrived and took Bogas into custody on a charge of disturbing the peace. Bogas then made things worse for himself by offering the two arresting officers $10 to split between them if they would let him go. They reported the attempted bribery to Police Chief Lynch, who then ordered detectives to investigate the man thoroughly. Nothing else was reported on this case.[33]

Margaret Illington (1879–1934) was an American stage actress popular in the first decade of the 1900s. In January 1911 she was playing at the Lyric Theater in Cincinnati, starring in *The Encounter*. She was on her way home from the theater one day, accompanied by her husband Edward Bowes, when a young man jostled her and winked at her. Margaret's husband landed on him, surprising the masher. Then Illington went for him. She slapped him around and punched him until he went down. Said Bowes, "Why, Margaret, can't you let me handle these fellows?" Replied Margaret, "Well, I guess I have a right to hit him if I want to, I'm not going to let anybody harm you." She added, "A fight's a fight, and I expect I can hold my own with any of them." Then Bowes got in another punch. By this time the masher's companions had all scattered, and the actor and her husband proceeded on their way. The couple married in 1910, and at the time of her death in 1934 he was just starting his run as a radio superstar, host of the amateur talent show that bore his name, *Major Bowes' Amateur Hour*.[34]

Mrs. Nina Hatcher rebuked a stranger in Seattle in August 1911 who, she said, had accosted her three times in a span of 10 minutes. She rebuked him by delivering a severe blow to his jaw. Before he could recover from the blow, Hatcher grabbed him by the lapels of his coat and shook him vigorously and then led him to a policeman and caused his arrest. At the police station the man told Hatcher that she had made a grievous mistake, to which she replied, "If I made a mistake it was in not hitting harder." The masher gave his name at the station as John Brown but was later identified as A. Z. Washburn. He was released on his own recognizance.[35]

On the evening of December 12, 1911, in New York City, Mrs. Mary O'Donnell, 27, went outside to mail a letter. At Seventh Avenue and 125th Street there was a crowd of young men lounging about, Harry Barnett among them. Barnett followed O'Donnell, who turned down Seventh Avenue. A short distance from the corner he caught up with her and tried to converse with her. O'Donnell pulled his tie and pulled it so sharply that it acted as a noose around his neck. She held him like that until Policeman Davis arrived and arrested the 200-pound masher. Magistrate Corrigan fined Barnett $10. He paid his fine and hurried from the courtroom.[36]

On a June evening in 1912 in Los Angeles, Miss Dorothy Watson had just come off her shift at the telephone company and was going along the street, walking home. E. W. Simpson approached her and insulted her. He then attacked her, blackening her eye, and hit her on the side of the head. As she said later, "I didn't see any one to protect me, so I protected myself. My handbag broke at the first whack and I started in with my fists. A taxicab chauffeur seized me and Simpson got away. I chased him and found out where he went. Then I called an officer and had him arrested." Simpson denied that he insulted or attacked the girl. He said that he thought he knew her and for that reason greeted her. Nothing more was reported on this case.[37]

A masher nudged Miss Nellie Hight, 17, on an elevated car on a May morning in 1913 in Chicago and then smiled at her. During the next second the masher received three swift blows in the face, a blow on the head with an umbrella and an uppercut on the chin, all from Nellie. Not a word was spoken by either party until the man disappeared down the steps at the next station. Then she turned to the conductor and said, "There, I guess that will hold the old fool for a while." The first time he nudged her Hight thought it was an accident and ignored it. Then he did it again. Then out of the corner of her eye she saw him grin. Then she hit him with her umbrella, three times in the face with her left hand and then one on the chin with her right hand. She explained, "After he ran I was so mad that I smashed his hat. I never saw him before. I do not know whether I should have acted that way or not but he made me so angry that I could have done anything." Hight added that she thought the masher was the same man who had bothered several of her friends on the L during the last month. And, "if every girl would start in and give every masher a few punches they would not worry us any more. I do not care whether it is ladylike or not. I felt like hitting him and I did. He was a silly old goose, and next time he will know better than to try and flirt with the first girl he meets."[38]

Miss Esther Grossman, stenographer, collared a man who she said had been annoying her on the way uptown on the subway in New York City on the evening of March 23, 1914. She then pulled him off the train at 135th Street and dragged him five blocks to the nearest police station, where she accused him before the desk sergeant. While she was on the subway, she told the sergeant, Alfred Orlando persistently tried to embrace her. Grossman ignored him for a time, but eventually her patience ran out. The pair went off to court, where he was held without bail for sentencing on the following day.[39]

In court the next day before Magistrate Marsh, Orlando's wife appeared and declared she did not believe her husband could do such a thing. Apparently it worked, as Marsh suspended the sentence.[40]

Esther's case caused the editor of a New York City newspaper, *The Evening World*, to weigh in with an editorial on the incident. After summarizing how Grossman had grabbed the masher and dragged him by herself, alone, all the way to the police station, the editor noted she "has the sympathy and approval of the public. Apparently that is all she got from the passengers on the train. Although the man is said to have made repeated attempts to hug and embrace her, no one interfered." Then he commented on New Yorkers priding themselves on their ability to mind their own business. He went on to decry that lack of involvement when he concluded, "In many ways it is wise policy for the man in the street not to be officious or interfering. Serious trouble often descends upon the citizen who tries to set things straight without a policeman. But maybe if bystanders were a little less cautious in showing what they think of the ordinary masher who annoys a woman in a public place, he would be fewer."[41]

Virginia Mercereau was window shopping in Chicago in July 1929 when George Duffy came along and tried to strike up a conversation with her. She ignored him, but he kept harassing her. Then she punched him in the eye, got him in a headlock and flattened him with another blow. At the police station where Duffy was booked for disorderly conduct, Mercereau told officers she was a claimant to the title of "world's middleweight woman champion wrestler." And she was indeed a female wrestler of note.[42]

7

Women Respond with Weapons

Some women, when annoyed beyond endurance by a sexual harasser, responded with weapons. For the most part those weapons were not the ones we think of today, as items with no other purpose than to be weapons. Women most often responded by turning something they carried with them, or wore, into weapons. Most popular by far were the umbrella, the ubiquitous (in the era) hatpin, and the whip (the equivalent to today's car key).

In the summer of 1894, reported a Minnesota newspaper, a young lady entered a streetcar and sat down opposite a man who, on first appearance, seemed to be alright. However, he soon showed himself to be "that contemptible creature, a masher," said the account. Almost at once he "proceeded to mash; he stared, ogled, smiled insinuatingly, and made a second-class fool of himself." The woman was annoyed, and she seized her parasol—but not to wield as a weapon. She simply opened the parasol inside the car and spread it in his face. Thus she was invisible to him under her protective screen. The chagrined masher got out at the next corner and disappeared. When he had gone, the woman closed her parasol and said, "I have heard of fighting wild beasts with such a weapon opened suddenly in their faces and I find it serves a good turn with tame ones."[1]

Very early in the morning of January 13, 1886, in Palestine, Texas, a cowhiding scene took place at the Watson Hotel. One John Gray, a masher who worked in Charley Finger's paint shop, had been trying to force his attentions on a "respectable" young servant who worked at the Watson Hotel. When she rebuffed him he began circulating false rumors about her character, claiming, among other things, that he had seduced her. On the night in question several men boarding at the hotel assured the woman they would stand by her if she wanted to redress the wrongs done to her. A heavy cowhide whip was produced, and Gray was invited into the parlor. No sooner had he entered than the woman whipped him. Gray took his castigation, it was reported, "without a word or movement."[2]

An editorial in a St. Paul, Minnesota, newspaper in February 1886 observed that mashers have "a habit of attempting to form the acquaintance of ladies without the formality of an introduction. One of these miserable excuses for a man attempted the arts of the professional masher with a St. Louis lady yesterday and as a result received a well laid on horsewhipping from the young woman he had insulted." Then the editor offered the thought that "it would be a most excellent plan for the young ladies in all our Western cities to form cowhiding societies for the purpose of dealing out punishment to the street masher."[3]

Two Boston women were sightseeing in New York City in May 1890. They were sitting in a car, while opposite them sat, said a reporter, "one of the most offensive of the masher tribe." He stared impudently and then tried to place a foot between the feet, accidentally, of one of the two women, the one carrying a parasol. Apparently by accident she brought the parasol (it was long and ended in a point) down smartly on the man's foot. He gave a cry of pain and withdrew to a seat closer to the second woman. A few minutes later he insulted her. The woman with the parasol saw that and, leaning over to supposedly look out the window, jammed the point of the parasol into the man's instep and gave it a quick twist. The masher cried out in pain, limped away from the women and left the car at the next stop. The passengers, reportedly, did not know what had happened, and the woman with the parasol was said to look as surprised as everybody else at the cries of pain and the limping man.[4]

A masher boarded a Cottage Grove Avenue car in Chicago in October 1890 and took a seat beside a woman. He crowded close to the lady, who didn't seem to notice him, and persisted in crowding. She said nothing, and he got so bold, said a news story, "that he became offensive in his actions, although he never said a word to her." The lady was wearing a silk belt that was fastened to her skirt by a long, stout steel pin with a silver head. Once more the masher pressed his knee against her. She quickly pulled out the stiletto-like pin and, with a strong thrust, jabbed it into the masher's leg. He yelled out in pain, got up, and rushed off the car. The passengers, reportedly, laughed with delight; the woman wiped off the pin with her handkerchief and replaced it in her belt. Said the journalist, "This is the proper way to serve all men of this stamp. A few lessons like this and the disreputable practice would be materially lessened; at least the masher would show more respect for his intended victim."[5]

As a young woman was walking alone on a downtown Pittsburgh street in April 1891, a masher fell in step behind her and finally accosted her by saying, "Taking a walk, I presume?" She took no notice, but he continued to follow her. When he repeated his question she came to an abrupt halt. Raising her hand, in which she carried a heavy pocketbook, she hit the masher twice in the face, saying, with the second blow, "When I want you I shall send for you. Goodbye."[6]

Would-be masher Gil Monroe received what was described by a journalist as "a severe, but deserved horse-whipping" at the hands of Miss Nellie Bourn-gresser. It took place on Vernon Street in Lawrence, Kansas, on January 29, 1892. Monroe sent a "very insulting" note to Nellie requesting her to meet him at a certain place. The young woman, "whose character is above reproach," laid the matter before the city marshal, who advised her to go to the place designated by the masher and deal with him as she thought best. Nellie did so, and when she met him at the appointed time she immediately proceeded to give him a severe whipping. He attempted to flee, but at that point the marshal and the county attorney came out from where they had been hiding and caught Monroe and held him while the woman finished whipping him. After she was finished, Monroe was taken to jail but released the next morning by the authorities, who thought he had received sufficient punishment.[7]

On the morning of June 20, 1894, James Reilly, 18, was sent to Blackwell's Island from the Jefferson Market Court for six months for having insulted Mrs. Alice Young. On the evening before, she had been walking along Greenwich Street when Reilly, who was "flashily dressed," stepped up to her and tried to engage her in conversation. She paid him no attention at first, but when he renewed his harassments a second time and a third time, she raised her umbrella and belabored the would-be masher over the head. Policeman Patrick Harley started to arrest her but changed his mind and took Reilly into custody instead when bystanders explained the situation.[8]

Three women with rawhide whips took vengeance on an alleged masher at Wilkes-Barre, Pennsylvania, on the night of September 22, 1895. Theodore Hirner was severely lashed, and when he tried to fight back he was floored by one of the women. The masher was well-known for what he was, and the police had received many complaints about him. He had a favorite street corner where, it was reported, he would ogle girls that came along. "Whenever the opportunity appeared he would address them." Hirner always carried a dozen or more ladies' handkerchiefs with him, and when he wanted to strike up a conversation with a woman he would drop a handkerchief on the pavement and then exclaim, "Oh, here, Miss, you have dropped your handkerchief." Several of the harassed girls complained to their mothers, and a plan was designed to take care of the masher. On the Saturday night in question the three women lay in wait for Hirner. A fourth woman was also involved in the plot. She was used to lure Hirner into a trap. At the appointed hour she passed Hirner's usual spot and was accosted by him. A brief conversation followed, and then the pair walked down the street a short distance. At that spot the girl gave a signal and the three women, armed with cowhide whips, sprang out and surrounded the masher. They began to whip him without mercy. Initially the man showed fight and struck at one of the women. As he did so he received a blow from behind that sent him sprawling. Picking himself up, blood running from several cuts, Hirner ran off down the street, crying with pain.[9]

Shortly after 12 noon on January 11, 1896, in Baltimore, Mrs. Mattie V. Anglier, wife of Frank, a cigar dealer and poolroom proprietor, shot Charles H. Parker, 33, an agent for the Leavitt Machine Company of Athol, Massachusetts. The shooting took place in her husband's store at 1431 North Charles Street. Parker was taken to City Hospital where he died at 2 p.m. He had two bullet wounds in the back of his head and another in his left breast. Mrs. Anglier, 30 years old and described as "a frail little woman," was then locked up. She told the arresting officer that Parker came into the store several days earlier and tried to take liberties with her (her husband was not well, and thus Mattie was usually alone in the store). He grabbed her about the waist. She freed herself and told him if he tried anything like that again she would murder him. Fearful that he might indeed come back to the store and of what he might do, Mattie put a revolver in her pocket. He did come back, and once again he tried to grab her. She pulled out the gun and shot him. "I do not regret it, because I did it in self-defense. He should have let me alone, and I would not have shot him," she explained. The couple had several small children and were described as "respectable and thrifty people."[10]

Frank and Mattie Anglier both stood trial for murder in April. However, on April 3 the jury reported itself hung and was dismissed by the judge. The final vote by the jury was 11 to 1 in favor of acquittal. The lone holdout wanted a verdict of guilty of murder in the second degree. Having been held in custody since that fateful January 11 day, the couple were then released on $10,000 bail. Nothing more was reported about the couple.[11]

Late in the evening of June 18, 1896, Maggie West and Gracie Lynch boarded a ferry in New York City. The women were song and dance artists finishing a night's engagement and on their way home. A man got on the ferry after them and followed the pair into the women's cabin. The women had first noticed him when they left the music hall. Apparently he had been outside and then followed them to the ferry. In the cabin, said a report, "he winked and smiled at the two girls, took off his hat to them, and finally took a flower from his buttonhole and tossed it across the cabin into the lap of Lynch." All he got in return were cold stares. When the boat was in mid-stream, one of the other male passengers offered to go to the assistance of the women. Said Lynch, "We won't trouble you. We have met mashers before, and I guess we can handle them." Then the women moved to a different part of the ship.

Again the masher followed them, and he became bolder, reaching for Lynch's hand. Lynch battered him with her umbrella, and West joined in by using her fists. Then a passenger joined in and decked the masher with a punch. When the boat docked the police came and arrested the masher, who said his name was Walter Linden. When he was arraigned before Magistrate Wentworth the next morning he was held for trial on $500 bail. Nothing more was reported about this case.[12]

On one of the main streets of Milwaukee one evening in December 1897 was seen a woman roundly chastising a man with her umbrella. After severely belaboring him about the head with it for several seconds she went on her way, not stopping, said the reporter, "to enjoy the cheers of the spectators." The story, as told by a friend of the woman, was that while walking along the street on her way to an art exhibit a man approached her and said, "Good evening." She ignored him, thinking he had made a mistake. But he followed her. He approached her again with the same remark. By then she was frightened as she continued on, but he still followed. Finally the man placed himself directly in front of her on the street just opposite Gimbels department store. Lots of people were on that part of the street coming and going. For an instant the two faced each other—then she attacked him with her umbrella.[13]

Pedestrians who happened to be out for a stroll on Washington Street in Hoboken, New Jersey, on the evening of July 20, 1900, saw a horsewhipping scene. Mr. and Mrs. Allen H. Webb were in front of their home on that street when William Blackmore passed by and tried to force his attentions upon Mrs. Webb. The woman ran into the house, grabbed a "stout" rawhide whip, chased Blackmore up the street, whipping him as she went and cutting him "viciously about the head and shoulders," according to the account. Blackmore finally managed to run away from his pursuer. For some time past, said Mrs. Webb, Blackmore had annoyed her, so much so that a few weeks earlier she had him arrested. Mr. Webb watched his wife chastise Blackmore but took no part in it, believing his wife would prefer to do the punishing herself.[14]

The masher stood for two hours one afternoon in May 1901 ogling the women who passed the corner of State Street and Jackson Boulevard in Chicago. The area was thronged with shoppers. One woman passed him a few times as she went back and forth between several stores. One of the times she passed him "the cad raised his hat," observed a reporter. On her way past him again (she had by this time raised her umbrella in the slight rain) he harassed her yet again. She charged at him with her umbrella lowered and speared him in the stomach with the steel point of the umbrella. That sent him running off, "and as he fled the laughs and jeers of the crowd followed him."[15]

A party of six to eight young women who went down to Coney Island in New York for the day on August 4, 1901, created some excitement in the

Sea Beach line depot at the island that night when they punished a young man who, according to the girls, was "entirely too fresh." Principal complainant was Annie McIntyre, 19. The masher said his name was George Carr. None of the women knew Carr. According to the females, Carr pushed into the same seat with several of the women as they boarded a car to go home. Then he put a hand on McIntyre and made some remark. McIntyre got up and smashed him on the top of his head with her umbrella, driving his straw fedora hat down over his ears with her umbrella. Several of the other women grabbed him and held him, while the others beat him with their umbrellas and the straps in which they carried their lunch boxes. James W. Pierce, a railroad official, ran for Policeman Snyder who "rescued" Carr and took him to the Coney Island police station where he was locked up on McIntyre's complaint.[16]

Mrs. Adelaide Bitman (perhaps Bittman) of New York City thought she slashed a masher with a bread knife on Tuesday night, December 30, 1903. She also thought he could have been missing part of his left ear, although, because she fainted, she was not sure. Bitman's story was that a masher, whom she had never seen before, annoyed her in a crowded Columbus Avenue car on that evening as she was on her way home. He got off at the same stop as she did and followed her. When they neared her home he brushed up against her and asked if he might see her home. She ignored him but ran off to the door and upstairs to her flat. Shortly after that the bell rang, and Bitman, thinking it was her husband (who was expected home around that time), pressed the button to open the hall door. However, it was the masher. Bitman had been cutting bread and was holding the knife in her hand when the masher tried to enter the flat. Bitman blocked the door. "I just thought I'd drop in for a few minutes," he said. "Don't make any fuss. It's all right." She tried to close the door, while he tried to grab her. The bread knife was brought into play. What she did

A woman fending off a masher with her umbrella on State Street in Chicago in May 1901.

with it she did not know for sure because around that time she fainted. Her husband, who arrived home soon after, found her unconscious on the floor.[17]

When the New York City newspaper *The Evening World* reported the Bitman incident it made a humorous story out of Bitman's knife defense. It started with a poem: "He tried to mash Mr. Bitman's wife / But she cut off his ear with a carving knife / Did you ever see such stars in your life / You bold, bad man?" As well, the article came up with a sketch illustrating a woman with a proposed defensive weapon—an ear-punch (something like the modern day hole punch for paper) to be used on mashers. This article took more than a few liberties with the story, as Bitman recalled little of the events and may not even have used the knife on the masher at all. Said the article, "Seeing the

After a celebrated incident in 1903 during which a woman had, perhaps, cut off a masher's ear a number of articles appeared on the topic. One of them, in a humorous vein, suggested that what was needed for women to use on mashers was an ear punch. This would also help judges determine how often a man appearing before him had harassed women—one hole punch in the ear for each mash. At the time the use of fictitious identities made it difficult for judges to know if the accused man had harassed in the past or not.

masher who had persistently annoyed her an hour before determined her at once upon summary action. Swiftly she raised the bread knife and without a world of warning cut off a tiny piece of the masher's ear. With a yell he vanished into the darkness...." While that may have happened, it was pure invention herein. The story went on to say that after she dispatched the masher, and pending the return of her husband, she, "like a well-conducted person, went on cutting bread and butter." Getting back to its hypothetical ear-punch, the newspaper thought it would be a great aid to judges, who could then determine, by looking at the prisoner's ears, how many times he had been dealt with as a masher. Because of the pervasive problem in this time period with fictitious identities, judges almost never had any idea if an accused masher stood before the bench for the first time for that offense or the thirty-first. "By all means, let us have the ear punch," concluded the piece. "And may the stupidity which prompts the masher in the first place preserve him from wearing ear-protectors."[18]

Miss Mayme Andrews of East St. Louis used a hatpin effectively on a would-be masher near the corner of Thirteenth Street and Broadway, East St. Louis, on a Saturday evening in April 1903. The masher insisted on walking alongside her. When he continued to harass her, Andrews reached up into her hat, withdrew her hatpin and pricked him on the shoulder. She was employed in a St. Louis department store and was on her way home when the man accosted her. She did not reply to him and walked faster. However, he kept pace and walked close enough to almost touch her arm. It was at that point, as a last resort, that she used her hatpin. After being pricked, the masher ran off down the street. When Andrews got home and told her family what had happened, some of them set off to hunt for him but could not find him.[19]

Miss Maybelle Courtney was one of the Sadie girls in the Anna Held company. Held was a Polish-born American stage performer who was a superstar in this period; she was also the common-law wife of Broadway legend Flo Ziegfeld. One of the numbers she was famous for was the 1903 "Sadie" production, which included a number of lavishly-costumed chorus girls who surrounded Held. Maybelle Courtney was one of these women in the Chicago show in May 1903. After one of the shows, Maybelle left the theater and was heading for her hotel when a man accosted her on Clark Street. She paid no attention to him but did quicken her pace. He followed, all the while keeping up a series of "insulting questions. Finally, he tried to take her arm. In response she swung her umbrella at him and hit him a hard blow in the face. As the man staggered back she renewed the attack, hitting him again and again over the head. His hat was knocked off and his face considerably cut. The masher then ran off."[20]

The subhead for a New York City newspaper article read: "Kansas girl

Leoti Blaker jabs her harasser with a hatpin in 1903. The hatpin was ubiquitous in this era and women often used it to fend off harassers. Hatpins tended to be relatively long and sturdy.

gave an elderly exponent of the 'Goo-goo Eye' a hard jab in a Fifth Avenue coach." The age of the "elderly" masher was estimated at 50. According to the piece, Miss Leoti Blaker ran a hatpin into the masher's arm with such violence that the occupants of the coach were thrown into confusion by the "screams of the elderly stickee." Blaker came from Kansas and had only been in New York for a few days when the incident occurred, in May 1903. She told the reporter, after the event, "If New York women will tolerate mashing, Kansas girls will not." Leoti got on the Fifth Avenue coach and sat down near an elderly looking man in the corner. She said, "I didn't pay any attention to him, but finally his actions became so annoying that I could scarcely stand it." She kept edging away from him, but he kept pushing closer; finally he put his arm in back of her. "I became so enraged that I didn't know what to do. At last I reached up and took a hatpin from my hat. I slid it around so that I could give him a good dig, and ran that hatpin into him with all the force I possessed," she explained to the journalist. "Of course, all the time I was looking calmly in front of me, so that when he let out a terrible scream of pain no one in the coach had any idea what had happened. They all looked at him inquiringly, but he didn't have a word to say. He got up and left the coach at the next corner." Blaker added that she thought of the hatpin as a weapon of self-defense that was without equal. As a final comment, she said that out in Oskaloosa, Iowa (where she had spent her earliest years), "a man would be tarred and feathered for daring to insult a woman by such persistent actions."[21]

A masher in a Wells Street car in Chicago in December 1903 tried to become familiar with what turned out to be the wrong female when he forced his attentions on Miss Mabel Roberts, a stenographer in the Marquette building. She drew a toy revolver and drove him from the car. Roberts was on her way home when the man got on the car, stood opposite her, stared at her, and then harassed her. She then reached into her purse, drew the revolver, pointed it at him and ordered him from the car. He left.[22]

Cecile Vogel was a stenographer who said she was accosted on the evening of August 14, 1905, near her home in Marinette, Wisconsin, by a young man named Bert Williams. She rebuked her harasser by picking up a slab (unspecified) and trouncing the fellow with it. Vogel knocked him down and pounded him until he cried for mercy. During this event a crowd had gathered and, said a reporter, "cheered the young lady on in her work." Williams eventually slipped free and ran off. She told a reporter that this was the third time Williams had annoyed her.[23]

During November 1905, Mrs. Amy Congelton, a "wealthy society widow," was troubled by a masher for more than a week. At last she armed herself with a small revolver and a cowhide whip. As she was out walking on a Thursday night, the masher came out from a side street and rushed after her. When he pulled level with her, his "insulting 'good evening'" was cut short by a blow from the whip. Amy lashed him a few more times before he recovered from the shock and ran off. She felt he was the same man of whom so many neighborhood women had complained about for mashing them. His usual method of operation was to accost strange women on the street, tip his hat to them and, if possible, strike up a conversation with them.[24]

Mrs. Waller of Fremont, Nebraska, gave a masher a blow one night in September 1906. She was walking on East Ninth Street when she found herself followed by a stranger who overtook her and made an insulting remark. Waller picked up a bottle which lay near the sidewalk and smacked him over the head with it. She was not further molested.[25]

After finishing her late shift as a cashier in Martin's Restaurant at the corner of 40th Street and Broadway in New York City at 2 a.m. on September 14, 1906, Miss Ellen Pierson, 28, set off to walk home. Two men approached her as she walked. The first one asked that they be allowed to carry her umbrella. She paid no attention to them but they continued to follow her, and then one started to make "insulting" remarks. Instantly she attacked him, striking a blow to his head with her umbrella. He fell, and she stood over him, raining blows down on him. His companion tried to come to his aid, but Ellen felled him with a blow from her umbrella. Policeman McDonough heard the cries of the men and rushed to the scene. "They insulted me," said Pierson to the officer. At the station house the two bleeding men gave their names as Conrad Kimball, advertising man, and David Peters, diamond broker. When the pair were arraigned later that morning in the Jefferson Market Court, both wore bandages and pleaded a lapse of memory. Said Pierson to Magistrate Baker, "I leave the restaurant at 2 o'clock every morning and am very often spoken to and insulted by men who hang about the Metropolitan Opera House entrance. I was not afraid, and I am glad I did this one up." The two men were fined $10 each, which they promptly paid. Pierson was congratulated by the magistrate for her spirit.[26]

The daughter of a prominent Sparks, Nevada, family, 18-year-old Myrtle Thacker, routed two mashers on January 23, 1908, in that city with a gun. The pair of mashers were following her and addressed her. When they did that she turned on them and said, "Stand back." They ignored that and continued to follow her and to address her. Then Thacker drew a revolver and fired three shots—seemingly at them, but she deliberately fired high. The mashers turned and ran. According to a reporter, "Women residents of Reno and Sparks have been greatly annoyed by mashers lately, and Miss Thacker had armed herself in anticipation of just such an occurrence as that of tonight." Said Thacker, "I had no intention of shooting them for I could not kill a human being. I knew they were cowards or they would not force their attentions upon any woman, so I just fired to scare them and hope I have taught them a lesson they will remember."[27]

As she was walking home alone in New York City on the evening of October 17, 1908, Miss Marguerite Le Blanc was accosted by a man. He approached her and put his arm around her. She grabbed one of her hatpins and stabbed the man twice, one in the arm and once in the face. A number of bystanders who were on the street at the time ran after him, but he managed to escape from his pursuers.[28]

Early on the morning of November 9, 1909, Miss Hope Whitacre was walking homeward in Los Angeles when she was accosted by Erich Eich. She pulled out a small police whistle and used it to good effect; it drew a policeman, who arrested the masher. In police court later that same day Eich pled guilty to a charge of disturbing the peace and was fined $30 by Judge Rose. Hope worked at a café on South Main Street and got off work at 1 a.m. When Eich harassed her he approached her and bowed to her, and then spoke. She ignored him, but he continued to harass her and finally grabbed her by the arm. She broke free from his grasp and then used her whistle. On the way to the station in the custody of Patrolman Blaisdell, the prisoner begged to be released, and as they neared the station he drew some money from his pocket and offered it to the officer.[29]

E. L. Dickson was arrested in January 1910 for annoying women in film theaters on South Main Street in Los Angeles. Later in court he pled guilty to a charge of disturbing the peace, preferred by a Miss Marcia Taylor. According to the police, a number of complaints were made by proprietors of the theaters that women in the darkened places were molested by a man who would sit near them and grasp them by the arms, and otherwise annoy them. Two plainclothes officers were detailed to investigate and traced the masher to the Olympic Theater, where they saw him take a seat next to Taylor. They saw him grab the woman's arm. Then they watched as Taylor moved to another seat, only to observe Dickson follow her to the new seat. Then Taylor pulled a long hatpin from her head and told Dickson to move away or she would jab him with the hatpin. At that point Dickson was arrested. After he pled guilty, Judge Frederickson sentenced him to a fine of $50 or serve the alternative of 50 days in the city jail.[30]

When Mrs. Julia Della Vivini and her friend Mrs. Antoinette St. Marie were out walking on East 149th Street in New York City on August 8, 1916, they discovered a man was following them. After their patience had worn thin, they both turned on him and belabored him with their parasols. Despite that treatment, the next time they turned around they discovered that he was still following them. They had him arrested. In night court he gave his name as Harry Monganeni. He told Magistrate Simms that the arrest was a shock to him, as he had been so persistently followed by the two women that he had fled into the cigar store, where he was arrested. He was found guilty of disorderly conduct. No sentence was reported.[31]

One of the more unusual weapons used was wielded by Miss May Ebert in November 1916 in Orange County, New York. She and her friend, Miss Esther Van Auken, were accosted on the street by a masher. They rebuked him, but he grabbed Ebert and continued to harass her. She pulled a loaded powder puff from her purse and smashed him in the face with it. It was full of powder, and, half blinded, he staggered away. Half an hour later Officer Sherwood arrested a man, who said he was William Lacey, because he had flecks of face powder all over his coat. Lacey was held on $100 bail.[32]

In New York City on March 26, 1929, Reena Blettel was described in the press as worn out from the exertion shattering three umbrellas over mashers' heads (the time frame involved was not stated). When a fourth would-be masher accosted her, she called a policeman. Later she explained to the judge that she had been too tired to hit him. As well, she was described in the press accounts, for no apparent reason, as a beauty contest prize winner. Perhaps that was included to indirectly reinforce the idea that only "pretty" women were harassed.[33]

8

Women Respond
Through a Protector

Mashers almost always harassed a woman when she was alone. Sometimes, though, a male relative or friend was on the scene, temporarily separated from his companion. In such cases it was often the male "protector" who stepped in and dealt with the masher. It was, of course, an article of conventional wisdom that a woman did not go about alone, especially at night, without a male "protector." While the protector could be a friend, a father, or a brother, it was most often the husband.

On a Sunday in July 1884 a masher had planted himself at a prominent point in Santa Monica, California. It was a point at which those walking along the beach had to pass. A news account described him as a "creature gotten up in the latest agony pantaloons, tight to bursting, with coat to match and flaming necktie." Standing at his chosen spot, he occupied himself by ogling and making remarks at women as they passed. One was married. On her first pass the masher insulted her. She returned to pass by again, only this time her husband was with her. He demanded an explanation; receiving none he deemed acceptable, the husband punched the masher once, knocking him down. Then he followed up by giving the masher "a thorough body beating." The unanimous verdict of the large crowd that had gathered was, reportedly, that his treatment "served him right."[1]

Charles H. M. Brooks was described as a leading society man in Chicago. On a night in March 1885 he took a young woman companion to a skating rink. As they skated around, a man tried to force his attentions on the woman. According to Brooks, the masher was not content with the usual methods but actually touched the woman several times as she skated by. Brooks approached the masher for an explanation, whereupon the masher struck Brooks a punch in the eye, which floored him. Learning the name of his assailant, Brooks swore out a warrant for assault and battery against W. N. Van Valkenberg, a clerk in the office of the Michigan Central Railroad. Ever the gentleman, Brooks said he hoped the case could be settled without the appearance in court of the woman who was the innocent cause of the affray.[2]

Near the corner of Douglas and Fourth Avenues in Wichita, Kansas, on the afternoon of February 15, 1886, Mrs. W. Williams and her sister were out for a stroll. Williams had her baby with her in a carriage. In front of Ned's shoe store and harness shop a man "caught" one of the ladies and made some "familiar remark." Mrs. Williams called her husband, who was but a short distance away, and who soon arrived on the scene and promptly punched him. Also not far away was Constable Doc Worrall, who rushed to the scene and hustled the masher off to jail. Several bystanders at the corner said the masher did not get enough punishment from Mr. Williams, and they told the reporter that they were sorry that Worrall did not stay away longer, until the masher had received his just deserts.[3]

Mrs. Dr. Hurd, wife of the well-known dentist in Saint Paul, Minnesota, had been out shopping in December 1887. Between 5 and 6 p.m. she started for home, going up Third Street toward her husband's office. Suddenly she noticed two men following her. They were close behind and made insulting remarks. Mrs. Hurd ran to her husband's office and up the stairs to the second floor. She told him (he was then working on a patient) what had happened, and he ran out into the hall where he came face to face with one of the two men. Once his wife had identified him as one of the mashers, Dr. Hurd's fist landed squarely in the man's face, and the forceps he still carried in his hand cut a long gash in the man's forehead. The blow knocked the masher off his feet, and he fell down the stairs. Dr. Hurd followed, delivering kicks and thumps as they went. Said Dr. Hurd, "It's getting so that a lady cannot go down the street on a shopping tour without meeting some such contemptible scoundrels."[4]

A masher was standing near an entrance to Pat Killen's saloon in St. Paul, Minnesota, in August 1888. Mrs. Killen and her sister came along, and as they turned in to speak to Pat, the masher made some remark to them. It was the second insult made to the women in two blocks (by different men). The women told Pat. He told them to go out, and if the masher repeated his harassment, Pat would tend to him. They did, and he did. Killen punched the masher hard enough to knock him out. Then Pat called in a policeman.[5]

At the end of October in 1888, on election eve in Saint Paul, a candidate on the Republican County ticket was at the city's Union Depot campaigning. While there he made an effort to mash the wife of a Fourth Street saloonkeeper.

The woman was angered enough to inform her husband, who laid a plan to punish the masher. The masher was induced to follow the woman up the street, where the husband was waiting for him. The husband jumped out, smashed the candidate about, and then kicked him into the gutter. As a souvenir of the event, the culprit ended up carrying around a badly damaged nose. The embarrassed candidate was afraid of the bad publicity right on the eve of an election, and, said a reporter, "by spending $50, succeeded in squaring everybody." However, his damaged nose made him readily identifiable.[6]

United States Congressman Amos Cummings (NY) discovered a handsome man paying "offensive attention" to Cummings' wife in Washington on May 2, 1892. The lady had been harassed for some time, and when Amos became aware of the situation he promptly administered corporal punishment to the masher. A friend of the masher declared that the masher would challenge Cummings to fight a duel and, in case the politician refused, would publicly horsewhip him.[7]

On May 15, 1892, in Fort Worth, Texas, Harry C. Robinson was killed and W. H. Coffman was seriously injured. Both were traveling salesmen. Mrs. Coffman claimed Robinson had "persecuted" her with his attentions. She and her husband went to Robinson's residence to make him apologize. However, Robinson would not do so, and the shooting commenced immediately, with the above mentioned results. It was reported that Mrs. Coffman claimed to have fired the shot that caused Robinson's death.[8]

Two "impudent" traveling salesmen got some good advice, a scare, and orders to leave town immediately at Louisa, Kentucky, one day in June 1892. J. Will Harm, a Cincinnati drummer, and Dr. N. B. Markoffsky, an optician from Louisville, were the men in question. Reportedly they "made impudent and insulting remarks to several ladies" in Louisa. The news of their antics reached the ears of some of the husbands and brothers of the women harassed, and those men waited for the mashers. When they found them, they delivered their advice. Those mashers, it was said, "barely escaped bodily harm."[9]

Just before dark on July 27, 1892, near Washington and Maricopa in Phoenix, Arizona, an incident took place. A well known merchant of the area was sitting with his wife on the sidewalk in front of his place of business when a man commonly known as "Frenchy" came along. As he passed the pair, although unacquainted with either of them, Frenchy raised his hat and saluted "impudently." He went on down the street but soon returned. The wife was then alone, as the husband was back in his store with a customer. Frenchy stopped and accosted the wife "familiarly." At that moment the husband returned to the sidewalk and heard some of the insulting remarks. Irate, the husband hit the masher in the jaw, knocking him down. When Frenchy got up, the husband flattened him again. Frenchy then got up and ran off. Said a journalist, "The incident is chiefly interesting on account of its exceeding rarity. The masher is a seldom seen bird in Phoenix and the dude by reason of his scarcity in the community is classified with Gila monsters brought in from the desert by the Indians, and other specimens of creation either nearly extinct or never abundant." He added, "There is probably no other place between the Atlantic and Pacific where a lady is so secure from insult as in Phoenix, and the outcome of this isolated instance will have the effect of discouraging similar episodes in the immediate future."[10]

Charles Hermany, son of the superintendent of the Louisville waterworks, and a society friend of his followed a theatrical party to a hotel after a performance in October 1892 and, "scorning the formality of an introduction," sent up a note inviting the leading lady, Lottie Williams (of the Ole-Olson theater group), to go out to supper with the pair of them. Ed R. Salter, manager of that theater company, answered the note in person and, said a news story, gave "the vulgar little beasts a severe drubbing before they could escape from the hotel parlor." The reporter commented, "Decent people should make it a point to patronize the company wherever it appears, as the best expression of their approval of the manager's praiseworthy punishment of ill-bred insolence."[11]

Chief Engineer Bennett of the telephone company in San Francisco was in the habit of working most nights until 9 p.m. in the telephone building on Bush Street, and his wife generally walked there to meet him about that time. For several nights she had been subjected to annoying remarks from a crowd of loafers who hung about the Standard Theater saloon as she passed that place on her way down Bush Street. One of those mashers had been particularly obnoxious to Mrs. Bennett, and on the evening of March 27, 1893, he had, said a report, "the audacity to address the lady boldly on the street." She informed her husband, and on the return trip she pointed him out to her spouse. Mr. Bennett blackened both his eyes and gave him a good thrashing. The policeman on the beat heard the disturbance and arrived on the scene just after Bennett "had succeeded in wiping the sidewalk with the repulsive insulter of women." Said the officer to Bennett, "I am glad of it. Go home, Mr. Bennett, and take your wife with you. I wish you would come around tomorrow and lick a few more of these loafers, for they well deserve it."[12]

For some months a well-known San Francisco masher named Charles E. Baseby had been in the habit of addressing a young woman "whose respectability and good family prevented her taking notice of the insulting conduct until driven to it by the masher's persistence," declared a journalist. Miss Gracie Worn, daughter of "prominent citizen" George Worn, was the subject of the harassment. She worked in the Postal Telegraph Company office, and in her daily trips back and forth to work she was frequently approached and addressed by Baseby. Finding his verbal approaches ignored, he wrote Gracie a letter, which she turned over, unread, to her father. As a result, Mr. Worn and his friends had an encounter with Baseby at the Sausalito ferry terminal, "thrashing that individual warmly and throwing him into the gutter." After that Baseby laid low and was not heard from until a day in the middle of April 1893 when he met Gracie on Kearney Street "and accosted her with his insolent remarks." As soon as she got home she told her parents, and Mr. Worn proceeded to get a warrant for his arrest on the charge of disturbing the peace, "as there was no other charge applicable." Masher Baseby was described in the piece as "one of the most confirmed of that obnoxious class to which he is happy to belong." Nothing more was reported on Baseby.[13]

George Baldwin was walking with a young lady on a San Francisco street in September 1893. When they reached a certain corner he left her alone for a minute on the sidewalk while he went into a store to buy a cigar. Just then John Duffy approached the woman and asked her to take a walk with him. He was persisting in his request when Baldwin returned and took in the situation. He landed several blows on Duffy before Officer T. J. Clisham came upon the scene and arrested both men for disturbing the peace. They were taken before Judge Campbell on September 5, and, after hearing the testimony of the woman and the policeman, he fined Baldwin $5 with no alternative, and Duffy $50 or 50 days in the county jail. A reporter covering the case declared that Baldwin's fine was equivalent to a discharge. A friend of Duffy paid the masher's fine in the afternoon.[14]

The Female Normal and High School (later renamed the Normal High School of the City of New York, and later still Hunter College) was originally organized in 1870. A reporter noted that "the doings of this tribe [mashers] were the cause of much annoyance [in 1892] to the Normal College girls." That "tribe" was back again in full force in the fall of 1893 as the school reconvened. One of the mashers followed 16-year-old student Mary as she left school, took an elevated car and then walked the rest of the way home. Finally, right at her door, as she was using her key, he spoke to her. She slammed the door in his face and ran upstairs. Mary told her father, who happened to be home at the time. The masher was still outside Mary's front door some 45 minutes later, trying to ogle the girl through the window. The father went outside and asked the man to leave, but he would not do so. In response, the father punched him out. Observed the reporter, "The neighbors wanted to finish up the masher in good old-fashioned style then ... but the old man wouldn't let them touch him. After the father gave the masher a piece of his mind he was allowed to leave."[15]

On the evening of October 26, 1895, at 9 p.m. a crowd in San Francisco witnessed the administration of corporal punishment to a masher by an angry husband. Osman Day (perhaps Dey) was the offender's name. The husband, who carried a cane, walked up to Day and struck him three rapid blows across the face with it, exclaiming, "You scoundrel, you would insult my wife, would you?" He made the blood flow from Day's nose. Day, after the third blow, ran off as fast as he could, followed by the jeers of the crowd.[16]

Maurice Butler, 16 and a masher, was taught a lesson by Miss Edith Hall, an actor about 30 years old. She was playing at an ocean resort near New York City in July 1897. She was a leading player in a company performing at Bergen Beach in Brooklyn. Butler sent her a bouquet of flowers in which was a note. That note contained a request for a meeting, with instructions to the actor that she was to wear the flowers if she consented to a meeting. Hall wore the flowers and afterwards met him at the specified place. However, she had four chorus girls and two men in ambush nearby. They fell upon Butler and ducked him in a pool. When he became penitent they caused his arrest. In the police court Dr. Butler (a physician and father of Maurice) pleaded with Hall to drop the case. She refused, and the case was put off for a day. Hall declared, "Never in the course of my experience has such a thing happened to me." The outcome was not reported.[17]

After visiting her mother, Mrs. David Williams took a car to ride to her home. She left the car at 9 p.m. to walk the remaining blocks home. This took place in Los Angeles in December 1898. As she walked along she noticed she was being followed. At her door the masher approached and said to her, "Hello, Birdie, can't I go in with you?" She was so angry she called inside to her son to bring down a revolver. Mr. Williams also happened to be home, and he hurried to the aid of his wife. When the masher saw Mr. Williams he took off running. However, Mr. Williams chased after him, ran him down and escorted him back to his house to Mrs. Williams, who promptly proceeded to rain punches on the man's face. The masher struggled to get loose but Mr. Williams held him fast. After Mrs. Williams tired of punching him, Mr. Williams kicked him several times "in the region of the trousers." Then they released the man.[18]

Masher Julius Rufus appeared in police court in San Francisco on November 21, 1899, to answer to the charge of insulting a young girl. Rufus was still suffering from the effects of a sound thrashing administered by the father of the victim. He had been arrested on a warrant sworn out by Daniel W. Saylor, owner of a restaurant at 10 Stockton Street. Testimony before Police Judge Graham showed that Myrtle Saylor, a high school student, was waiting for her sister on the corner of Bush and Stockton Streets on the afternoon of November 21, just after school ended. Rufus came up and jostled her. He insulted her, and when she moved away he followed her. Finally she ran to her father's restaurant and told some of the waiters. One went after Rufus, still standing on the corner looking for new prey, and taxed Rufus, who admitted his behavior but said he thought he knew the girl. When Mr. Saylor heard about the story he went in search of Rufus but did not find him until the next day when a waiter pointed him out. Mr. Saylor went and gave him a "good thrashing" and had him arrested. In court his excuse of mistaken identity did not go down well. The lawyer for Rufus said his client would not engage in such behavior again. "Not for the next ninety days," said the court. "There's too much of this thing of mashing going on. There's not a day that similar complaints are not made to the police. Women and girls can't go on the streets without being insulted by a lot of worthless bums that stand on corners and in front of cigar stores. There should be a stop to it."[19]

On the evening of April 13, 1900, George Gebhart was thrashed in front of the Waldorf-Astoria Hotel in New York City by George Holsworth after Gebhart had insulted his wife. In Jefferson Market Police Court the next day Mr. and Mrs. Holsworth were already in court when Gebhart was brought in by the officer who had arrested him the night before. As the pair passed by the couple, Holsworth stood up, leaned over, and punched Gebhart once again. Said Holsworth to the masher, as Holsworth was being restrained, "Just let me at him. I'd give $500 if they would let me whip you again. That's all right boys. I'll pay the fine, no matter what it is, if you will let me mash him." Magistrate Brann convicted the masher and said to him, "Ten dollars fine. I've no use for such fellows as you." Holsworth waited outside the court building, hoping to have another shot at the masher, after Gebhart paid his fine. However, several policemen were detailed to see Gebhart out of the building and safely onto a streetcar. The original incident took place when Holsworth left his wife alone on

MRS. HOLSWORTH.

MR. GEORGE HOLSWORTH.

GEORGE GEBHART

In April 1900 George Gebhart mashed Mrs. Holsworth, only to be thrashed physically by Mr. Holsworth. He was not the only husband to beat up a masher before the man was arrested. In court husbands were usually applauded by judges for their efforts.

the street in front of the Waldorf-Astoria for a moment while he went inside to get a cigar. Gebhart came up and harassed Mrs. Holsworth. She moved away, but he followed her. Then Mr. Holsworth appeared.[20]

Miss Mildred Brown left her St. Louis home to go for a short walk on an April evening in 1900. A masher met her on the street and attempted to draw her into conversation. She repulsed every approach he made, but he persisted, so she turned back and went home. As soon as she reached her home she rushed in and informed her brother, Ben Brown, of what happened. He immediately left the house, came upon the masher and demanded an explanation from the fellow. He got none and so beat him severely, blackening both eyes and bloodying his nose. During the fight the masher drew a knife and unsuccessfully tried to cut Brown. "It is said that a number of young ladies of the neighborhood have recently been insulted in similar manner," noted a reporter.[21]

The only woman in a Wentworth streetcar in Chicago fell under the eyes of a masher as he entered that car in March 1901. He promptly moved in on her, as she evidently was alone, for the only man near her was reading a newspaper with his back half-turned toward the woman. Sitting down beside her, the masher tried to attract her attention. When she ignored him he gently pressed her foot with his. She edged away. He leaned closer and addressed her. She turned from him forcefully, causing the man with the newspaper to look around. Her blushes told him what was going on. He got up, walked over the masher, grasped the fellow by the throat, and with his right hand he planted a punch on his nose. Then the woman's husband calmly sat down and went back to his paper. At the next stop the masher fled, said a reporter, "amid the taunts of his fellow passengers, but the husband paid not the slightest attention."[22]

Another husband to the rescue of his wife, punching her harasser in the nose. This took place on a transit car in Chicago in March 1901.

Actor Blanche Alexander (the stage name of Blanche Beckendorff), 22, was a native of St. Louis. In New York on a March evening in 1901 she vanquished a masher and had him thrown down four flights of stairs, according to her brother Oliver Beckendorff. Oliver said Blanche usually got rid of mashers—those that were "impertinent"—by having no words with the masher but by dismissing him after agreeing to a meeting, which she never kept. On the day in question she had been shopping and was annoyed by a well-dressed young man. He followed her home to her apartment. He stepped up and introduced himself, giving his name as that of a well-known Harlem dentist. When he asked for an appointment, Blanche told him she would dine with him and for him to call for her at 6 p.m. at her apartment on the fourth floor. He called at the scheduled hour and was met at the door by Blanche. Then she said to a man inside the apartment that was standing beside her, "This is the man who insulted me this afternoon." The friend beside Blanche stepped forward and punched the masher down the first flight of stairs and then kicked him down the remaining flights. Blanche had started acting four years earlier, in a stock company, and since then had starred in vaudeville and was then with the Charles Frohman company in New York.[23]

Mr. and Mrs. Arthur Kennedy were returning to their Chicago home from the theater when they passed a quartet of well-dressed young men on an evening in January 1902. One of those men addressed Mrs. Kennedy. In reply, her husband knocked him down with a punch. The couple continued on their journey, but the masher followed the pair and stabbed Mr. Kennedy in the back. When Kennedy turned around he was stabbed a second time, in the abdomen. His assailant fled. It was reported that Arthur Kennedy was expected to die. Nothing more was reported on this incident.[24]

A group of men were loitering on a street corner in Salt Lake City on a day in July 1903, drinking wine. One told his companions he would kiss the next woman that came by. Then a couple appeared and walked by. The masher leapt forward and kissed the woman. Just as quickly her companion decked the man with a punch to the jaw, knocking him unconscious. No identities were ascertained.[25]

Another assault by mashers on a man who dared defend a woman he was with against their insults occurred in Brooklyn early on the morning of July 31, 1903. Thomas Ford was escorting his fiancée, Miss Tillie McGuire, home from Coney Island on an open Smith Street car. They had seats on the front platform with the motorman. Two young men sat on an inside seat with their backs to the couple. Tillie suddenly felt her arm squeezed. She told Ford. He noticed one of the men had his arm hanging back there and told him to take it away. The two men then decided to make trouble by giving hisses and cat-calls, followed by insulting remarks. Ford had barely spoken when the window behind him was smashed and he felt a stinging pain in his back. He had been stabbed. His wound was not serious, but it kept him home in bed for a day.[26]

In Harlem, New York City, "mashers' corner" was the name given to West 125th Street and Seventh Avenue. According to a newspaper story, a young woman was walking past that corner when one of the mashers made an idle remark about her. She ignored him, blushed, and walked on. She went home and told her brother. They laid a trap and returned to the corner some days later. The same masher insulted her again. Then the brother appeared, grabbed the masher and took him to a lonely boathouse at 146th Street where he was tied securely to a post. Then the sister stepped forward and administered 30 lashes to him. For several days the masher stayed away from the corner and then complained to a lawyer that he had been assaulted and had been threatened with another thrashing if he ever showed up at that corner again. The lawyer told his client it was best for him to swallow his indignation and stay away from the corner. Many complaints had been made to Captain McGlynn of the West 125th Street police station about offensive conduct by young men on that corner toward passing women. Reportedly he was planning to station additional policemen in the area.[27]

Joseph Burke of Philadelphia saw Mrs. Hattie Fields, also of Philadelphia, sitting in the station in Atlantic City, New Jersey, as she was about to board a train for home. "Are you from Philadelphia?" he boldly inquired. He received no reply. "Say," he continued, "do you know I would like awfully to see you in a bathing suit." Hattie screamed loudly, and Mr. Fields sprang to her side. He beat Burke badly. Later, Recorder Babcock fined him $10 and commended Mr. Fields for his part in the affair.[28]

United States Congressman Timothy D. Sullivan (NY) and a woman were on their way to the New York Theater on the evening of November 10, 1904, in New York City. Sullivan stepped aside to buy a newspaper. A young man, one of three who were together and all in evening dress, spoke to the woman, who, said an account, "resented the affront." Without a word Sullivan punched the masher in the nose. The man fell to the ground. His two companions carried him away to a drugstore where he was revived. Then they bundled him into a cab and took off. Sullivan was a New York politician who controlled Manhattan's Bowery and Lower East Side districts as a prominent figure within Tammany Hall. He served one term in the U.S. Congress (1903–1906). Most of his political life was spent in the New York State Assembly and the New York State Senate.[29]

Leroy Stevens, 24, was horsewhipped on a Saturday in February 1905 in Chicago by Dr. Robert H. Harvey, a practicing South Side physician. For the previous several days Stevens had been annoying women in the neighborhood of Calumet Avenue and 21st Street. On the Saturday in question he was harassing Mrs. Harvey near the family home. Dr. Harvey was returning home in his buggy and saw the harassment. Taking his whip, he approached the masher from behind. Suddenly he commenced to whip Stevens. Again and again he applied the lash. Then smoke began to curl around the body of Stevens, and it was seen that his clothing was on fire. In applying the lash Harvey had ignited a match in the masher's pocket, and in a few moments his clothes were ablaze. Stevens was painfully but not seriously burned. Later in court Stevens was sentenced to three months in jail.[30]

Walter Christie was a trainer at the University of California and former manager of the Salt Lake baseball team. One day in December 1905, while he was holding a baseball practice with the Berkeley team, his wife came running up to him saying she had been insulted by a masher. Christie then set out after the offender, chased him for several blocks and finally caught him. "He then proceeded to give Mr. Masher one of the worst beatings a human being ever had and finally threw him into a muddy creek," recounted a reporter. Later in the day the matter was reported to the police, and it was found that the masher had been in trouble before over the same charge. At last account the police were looking for him.[31]

Frederick Dickinson and his wife got on a crowded Broadway car in New York City in August 1906. Louis Strauss boarded at the same stop and sat down beside Mrs. Dickinson. It was alleged that he tried to engage in conversation with the woman. She appealed to her husband, who was standing up in the car. Frederick slapped Louis in the face. Then Strauss had Dickinson arrested. In Jefferson Market Court, Magistrate Finelite held that Dickinson had no right to strike Strauss and fined him $5. That case was noteworthy in that it was one of the very, very few in which a male "protector" of a woman being mashed, and who had then physically repulsed the masher, was punished in any way. It was more usual for a magistrate presiding over such cases to congratulate the protector.[32]

At close to midnight on March 8, 1910, Donald Macdowell, 18, was struck down by two knife blows, barely escaping death, and was then lying in a hospital bed. At the time of the assault he was escorting Miss Myrtle Woodcock, 16, to her home in Seattle. A man tried to flirt with her as the couple exited a streetcar. A man got in their way and harassed her. Donald pushed him aside, and the pair exited the car. However, the masher got off and followed them. As the pair walked along, the man stabbed Donald twice. Macdowell's mother initially blamed the girl, saying her son "was dying in the hospital and she [Myrtle] was the cause of it." His wounds, however, were not that serious, and his life was not in danger. Myrtle exclaimed, "I am not to blame, for I did not know the man, except that he tried to flirt with me before and I would have nothing to do with him."[33]

In Grand Junction, Colorado, in May 1910, supporting the unwritten law giving a man the right to defend his wife's honor at all times, Tom Rogers was acquitted of assault on John West. Rogers claimed that West accosted his wife while passing her on the road, saying, "Come ride with me, Birdie." When Rogers heard of this he hunted for West, found him, and thrashed him.[34]

Three married couples dined on the evening of June 22, 1911, at the Café Republique in Washington, D.C., and then walked over to the E Street office of the Postal Telegraph Company. The three women walked together, somewhat in advance of the three men. Three mashers accosted the women at a street corner and then followed them into the telegraph office. The women complained to their husbands, who had arrived at the office by then. The six men squared off, and when it was over the three mashers had a black eye apiece, except for the one man who had two black eyes. The fight ended with the ejection from the telegraph office of the masher trio. It was reported that complaints of ogling of women after nightfall were being made with regularity to police headquarters in Washington.[35]

On a Friday night in July 1914 in El Paso, Texas, Detective George Harold delivered a severe rebuke to an alleged masher when he knocked the man down twice, following an insulting remark addressed to the detective's wife and niece. The three were walking along the street when the incident took place. When the masher arose the second time, he ran off. A bystander told Harold that the man had been making remarks about numerous women who had passed that spot during the evening.[36]

9

Bystanders Respond

Sometimes when a woman alone was being sexually harassed, one or more bystanders came to her assistance. They were as unknown to her as the masher. It was, though, accepted as a given that under the code of chivalry no decent man, no gentleman, would fail to come to the aid of a lady in distress.

On the evening of January 15, 1883, in St. Louis, Fire Marshal Sexton detected a masher at work on the streets of his city. Just after that masher had insulted the fifth lady he had met, and while she was running away from him, the veteran fireman leaped from his buggy and gave the fellow what was described as a "terrible horsewhipping." When the members of the Merchants' Exchange heard of this the next day they took up a collection and bought Sexton the article they felt was most appropriate—a "gold-mounted whip." Sexton was sent for and received an ovation from the assembled businessmen. After he was presented with the gift he made a little speech in which he joked that he found he was not just good at putting out fires, "but now I find that I can also make myself useful thrashing these scoundrels they call mashers." He added, "And I tell you that wherever I see one of these fellows insulting ladies I'm going to collar him and wear my whip out on him, and this is what every man here should do. There are too many of these scoundrels in this city insulting our wives and daughters, and we've got to run them out if we have to send them to _____."[1]

George Jones worked as a conductor on the streetcars in Oakland, California. On the evening of October 7, 1897, the streetcar he was on was coming in from east Oakland with just one passenger. Then a man boarded and at once began to act offensively toward that female passenger. She called Jones' attention to the man's impudence, and the conductor threatened to throw him off the car if he did not behave himself. Jones had formerly been one of the

101

best-known boxers of the Sacramento Athletic Club, and when the man challenged him he accepted. There was a scuffle that lasted perhaps 45 seconds, at the end of which the car had stopped, the masher was lying in the road swearing, and Jones was readjusting his cap.[2]

A well-dressed man got on the train at White Plains, New York, in July 1900, and although there were plenty of empty seats he sat down beside a "prominent" married woman of Unionville, New York. He tried to kiss and hug her. The woman called the conductor, who yanked the masher out of his seat. A farmer of Mount Kisco, New York, a passenger on the train, grabbed the masher by the throat and punched him in the face six times. The masher tried to escape to the smoker, but he was captured by other passengers who pummeled him until Mount Vernon was reached, when the masher jumped off the train and made his escape before the police could be summoned.[3]

A man who gave his name as Hugh M. Bragg, 40, was fined $10 by Magistrate Brann in the Jefferson Market Police Court in New York City on November 13, 1900, on the charge that he had annoyed Mrs. Grace McIntyre. She had been standing at the corner of 19th Street and Broadway on the previous night waiting for her husband, who was in one of the Broadway stores, when Bragg insulted her. She had to call a passerby for protection until a policeman arrived. Bragg pled guilty, saying he had been drinking and did not know what he was doing.[4]

W. White, who hailed from Newbern, Tennessee, formed an incorrect estimate of Kentucky females. His mistake cost him a $200 fine and a doctor's bill. According to a news story, "It will be months before White can wear clothes, sit down or even move with comfort. He was almost cut to pieces with whips wielded by irate young Kentuckians." It all took place in April 1901 in Fulton, Kentucky. White approached Ruby Baird in that community and got "a bit too fresh." Baird screamed and ran into a nearby store. Soon a police officer and angry citizens were chasing the fleeing White. The police caught him, got him away from the threatening crowd, and hustled him into police court where he was fined $200 on the spot. He paid his fine. However, a mob had formed in the street. When White emerged from police custody the mob grabbed him and tore his clothes off. He was tied over a barrel. Bob Baird (brother of Ruby) and another man wielded the whips. Before a large crowd, with White screaming at every stroke, they whipped away. When the mob was finished they released him. White had been taken from the police while they were escorting him to the railroad station.[5]

On the afternoon of November 21, 1901, while Miss Britonette Coombs was walking on Broadway in St. Louis, she was accosted by a stranger. She repulsed him, but he was persistent, and Coombs uttered a cry for help. Thomas Farrell was nearby and came to her assistance. He knocked the masher down with a single punch. As the villain tried to rise, Farrell rained more blows down upon him. The crowd which had gathered cheered when the masher finally ran off. Coombs thanked him and asked his name. He told her, and she recognized it as being the name of the winner of a cake-walk [dance] competition a year earlier. The couple had a talk and later attended a matinee and then had a meal together. They met on the following day and decided to get married. They married quickly, apparently before December 1, 1901.[6]

In New York City's Jefferson Market Court on August 4, 1902, Magistrate Cornell congratulated Henry Crow, a blacksmith, because Crow had punched Henry King in the jaw. According to the story, a girl of 17 was standing at West Third and Thompson Streets when she was approached by King. Just what was said was unknown, but the girl screamed. Several men ran forward, one being Crow. Crow decked King with a single blow to the jaw—King was unconscious for about 10 minutes. Policeman Campbell arrested King for disorderly conduct after he revived him. He also took Crow to the police station. Cornell fined King $5. He discharged Crow after he had extended his congratulations to the man.[7]

For weeks at the end of 1902 and into early 1903 a masher who came to be called "Jack the Hugger" terrorized the female residents of the fashionable sections of Jersey City and Hoboken, New Jersey. Miss Minnie Kloproph of Jersey City was walking home after visiting her sister when she noticed a man following her. As he came nearer she started to run, but he caught her, grabbed her and kissed her several times. The terrified girl screamed and struck him over the head. Then she broke away and ran off down the street, but he followed. Two men, R. G. Weaver and Charles Swartz, happened by and intervened. The masher ran off, with the two men in pursuit. The fleeing masher ran into the arms of another passerby, Thomas G. Lennon. They held him and summoned the police, who arrived and arrested him. Another struggle ensued before the masher submitted to arrest. When he was arraigned before Justice Murphy in the Oakland Avenue Court on January 27, 1903, the prisoner said he was Joseph Mills, 50, a laborer. Weaver's two daughters testified they had also been accosted by the hugger. Several other women came forward and identified Mills as the man who had insulted them in various neighborhoods in the area. Mills was sentenced to six months in jail.[8]

Solomon Siegelbohm, a traveling salesman from New York, spent part of April 8, 1903, in a police cell at the Chestnut Street police station in St. Louis, charged with trying to flirt with Mrs. R. H. Dreyer of St. Louis, who struck him and gave him a black eye. Solomon was locked up on a complaint from Dreyer, who accused him of disturbing her peace. He said he had never particularly noticed Dreyer until she struck him in the face. According to Dreyer, she was shopping on the day in question at a Broadway department store when a strange man attracted her attention by his peculiar actions. When she left the store she noticed he was following her. As she walked along, Solomon, on several occasions, walked directly in front of her, "rudely star-ing" and attempting to enter into a conversation with her. Finally he did it once too often, and she shot out her fist and hit him just below his right eye. It was at 4 p.m. when Fourth Street was crowded with bankers and brokers leaving their offices for the day, and a crowd gathered. Solo-mon was seized by half a dozen men who held him until a policeman ar-rived. Dreyer was upset and almost hysterical. She told the officer her story and was sent home. Her husband, Mr. R. H. Dreyer, rushed to the police station when he heard what happened

Mrs. Dreyer punched her harasser in the face, giving him a black eye. Then a crowd gathered and several men seized the masher and held him until the police arrived. Later Mr. Dreyer charged into the police station where the masher was being held and unsuccessfully tried to get close enough to beat him up.

and had to be restrained from entering Solomon's cell to attack him. The masher was a representative of a New York clothing house, and on this trip he had been in St. Louis for four days. No more was reported about this case.[9]

Scores of infuriated women beat John Nulty, recently discharged from the navy, "into insensibility" in Madison Square, New York City, in September 1903 because he attempted to hug Fortunito Lorito, 14. Lorito, with her two sisters, was listening to the band playing in the park when Nulty came along. "I'm going to kiss you," he said to her and then grabbed her in his arms. She screamed for help. Instantly scores of women, all in the park for the band con-cert, rushed to her aid and rained blows down on Nulty until he was felled. "He was kicked on all sides and his face was torn by sharp fingernails, and handfuls of hair were torn from his head," wrote a reporter. Men tried to join in and participate in the beating, but the women waved them back. By the time the police arrived, Nulty was unconscious. He was carried to the station house and locked up. No more was reported on the case.[10]

D'Antonie Attilio, civil engineer, was arraigned on September 1, 1905, in the Adams Street Court, Brooklyn, New York, charged by Miss Helen George, 17, with having followed her and forced his attentions on her. Attilio stood before Magistrate Steers with a broken nose and torn clothes, sans cravat and collar, his eyes blackened and cheeks cut. On the day before, George was returning to her job at the offices of a custom-house broker after her lunch break when she first noticed Attilio. The man ogled her, frightening her, and she ran back to her employer's offices. When she left work at 7 p.m. Attilio stood outside waiting for her. She boarded a car that ran on Adams Street only to find Attilio was with her. He took a seat near her and continued the smiling and ogling. Others on the car noticed the girl's discomfort, and when she got off several men followed. Attilio got off too and followed. George ran all the way home and became hysterical with her mother. Mrs. George went out to see Attilio. "What do you mean?" she asked. "I mean I want to know that pretty girl," said Attilio. Mrs. George threatened to have him arrested. Attilio then hurried off. But Robert George (Helen's brother) chased and caught him, and set upon him. At that point the other men who had alighted from the car joined him, and the group beat Attilio "unmercifully." The crowd grew to such an extent that the police reserves had to be called out from the Adams Street station. Order was eventually restored, and the police arrested Attilio. In court Steers asked Helen if she wanted the masher sent to prison. She said no, she just wanted him warned. "He seems to have been punished a good deal," remarked Steers. Then he turned to Attilio and said, "I will hold you in $100 bail for six months. If I ever hear of you mashing again, I will send you to prison." Helen remarked to a reporter, "Things have become so horrible now that a girl can't venture out night or day without being approached."[11]

When William H. Payne was arraigned in court in New York City in December 1906, charged with mashing on a Broadway streetcar, his frock coat was in shreds, one leg of his trousers was completely gone, and the upper parts of his trousers had been sewed into "respectability" by a court worker. As well, he had two black eyes and facial contusions. Two of his teeth were missing, and half of his mustache had been ripped off his face. According to the story, he had entered that streetcar and sat beside Miss May Shoobs, 15. He said to her she was so cute he would "chuck" her under the chin. Despite her protests, he did so. Then he turned and insulted Mrs. Charles Meyers. Her husband said to leave his wife alone. Payne told him where to go. The two men started to fight at that point. Soon much of the car joined in the affray, passing the masher around as he was beaten and pummeled by the passengers in turn. Even women joined in the fight, ripping out bits of hair, and scratching and clawing at him. The conductor had been shouting for the police, who finally arrived.

It took four policemen to pry Payne loose and take him away. After he was revived and patched up to some extent, he was taken to court and convicted of disorderly conduct. The magistrate fined him $10 "after lecturing him severely."[12]

While he was standing at a downtown street corner in Portland, Oregon, on the night of September 7, 1907, at about 9 p.m., a man going by the name of Frank Seals accosted two women. What was said was unknown, but at the end of the remarks Seals struck one of the women. Hardly had he landed the blow when a man from the passing crowd stepped forward and stretched out Seals with one punch. A policeman soon arrived on the scene to collect the unconscious Seals, but the bystander had, by then, vanished.[13]

Told that a young man had been insulting young women on their way to work in the vicinity of Seventh and Pine Streets in Camden, New Jersey, policeman Donovan, in plain clothes, went to the area to stake it out in September 1907. He had hardly reached the area when he saw a youth being given a "sound thrashing" by a man who then turned the masher over to Donovan. That masher called himself Cosmic Gulic and was covered with blood, caused by a sound blow to the nose. Emma Keith and Clara Adams later told police that Gulic had insulted them separately on several occasions. In Camden police court, Recorder Stackhouse sent Gulic to jail for a term of three months.[14]

Harry A. Stewart, salesman, who was rescued from a crowd of infuriated bystanders on West 34th Street in New York on January 12, 1909, after he struck Mrs. Catherine Shaw and knocked her to the ground, was released from custody the following day in Jefferson Market court when no complainant appeared against him. W. A. Shaw (husband) said his wife did not want any notoriety. Mrs. Shaw had a child that was just three weeks old. According to the woman's landlady, the injured woman's face was badly bruised and six of her teeth were knocked out. A policeman was called to the scene, who managed to drag Stewart from the midst of a dozen men who were kicking and thumping him. Mrs. Shaw urged her avengers on. "The rat," she exclaimed, "he accosted me and I called him a dirty loafer and told him I didn't know him. I was waiting for my husband." And then he struck her.[15]

Actor Rose Coghlan was approached by a masher as she was leaving the Van Ness Theatre in San Francisco on the evening of May 27, 1909. He accosted Rose and made repeated approaches. Colonel Bill Thomson, a well-known theatrical manager, happened to pass by, and he saw that Rose was annoyed. Thomson punched the masher in the nose. The masher punched back, but Bill landed another blow, drawing blood. Stumbling to his feet, the harasser ran off. Thomson did not know Coghlan, and as soon as the masher fled he hurried off himself, "in true knightly fashion, not waiting to be thanked," observed a reporter.[16]

In Thomasville, Georgia, in November 1909, Mrs. A. M. Bride was a passenger on a Coast train when a man persisted in pressing his attentions on her. She called Conductor Lewis, who confronted the man. Lewis said to McBride, "Now, madam, slap him in the face just as hard as you can. Kick him, too, if you like." That suggestion was acted upon vigorously by McBride, who slapped her annoyer's face until it was crimson. "I guess that'll do, Mr. Conductor. Thank you," she said, going back to her seat while, it was reported, the other passengers applauded.[17]

Two women were standing at a corner on Main Street in Salt Lake City waiting for a streetcar in December 1909. They were insulted by two mashers. They brushed up close to the women, then stopped, leered, smirked, and one said, "Oh, see who's here." The next instant they were collared by L. T. Cooper, described as the eastern millionaire medicine maker. Cooper bumped their heads together, whirled them around and then kicked them down the street. He had been visiting in Salt Lake City for about one month.[18]

Mrs. Mary Feldman and her 18-year-old son John were on an elevated train in New York City on the evening of December 13, 1910, when a masher annoyed her so persistently, on the Third Avenue line, that her son had to push him away. The man kept it up, and some of the other passengers went for him. Policeman John O'Brien got on at a station in response to the motorman's siren, and while the car was stopped the offender jumped the gate and tried to escape. When the gates were opened there was a rush of passengers, some armed with straps and pieces of wood torn from the car, others with knives. In the meantime, O'Brien had chased down and captured the masher, who gave his name as Rafaele Capuel. It took the police some five minutes to persuade the crowd not to molest their prisoner.[19]

Miss Agnes E. Smith, a music teacher, was plainly embarrassed in court in June 1915 in New York City as she told Magistrate Nolan how a man had seated himself next to her in a local train, and how he nudged her and finally placed his arm around her waist. The hug that accompanied that action made her scream. That brought action from the men on the car. The masher was dragged from his seat by the crowd and by the time Patrolman Hanley reached him his suit was in bad shape, his hat wrecked, and his face bore the marks of numerous punches. Magistrate Nolan did not believe masher Harry Kachadonia's story of being jammed against Smith accidentally by the motion of the train. Nolan reprimanded him and sentenced him to 90 days in the Workhouse.[20]

Sitting in a cinema in the fall of 1916, Percy Holland tried to kiss the woman (unknown to him) in the seat beside him. Christina Moore responded by slapping his face and crying out, "Help, Help!" Holland was roughed up by many of the men in the theater audience before the police arrive to rescue him and drag him off. Percy, 22, was sentenced to a term of 10 days in the Workhouse.[21]

On a Monday night in June 1921 in Houston, Texas, a lawyer by the name of W. J. Boyd was taken outside by a bunch of masked men and given a severe whipping with a blacksnake whip, and then admonished to leave town at once. Boyd declined to prefer charges against those who had lashed him. Boyd had been twice arrested in the area for "annoying girls in public," said a report.[22]

Esteban Sierro, 28, arrested and convicted of being a subway masher in New York City, was unable to pay the $50 fine imposed by Magistrate Ewald in Essex Market Court on March 12, 1928, and took the alternative sentence of 10 days in the Workhouse. Sierro, married and the father of two, was arrested a few days earlier after he had been beaten by passengers in an east side subway train, on the complaint of Marie Blaeser, 18, who said he had harassed her. When she protested against his advances, Sierro struck her. And then other passengers on the train came to her aid.[23]

An infuriated crowd followed Patrolman Frank Kelly from the Times Square subway station in New York City to the West 30th Street police station on April 15, 1930, threatening to attack his prisoner, who had already been mauled in the subway for harassing two school girls. Pedro Areipe, 27, was later sentenced to three months in the Workhouse when he was found guilty of disorderly conduct by Magistrate Earl Smith in Jefferson Market Court. Although Areipe said he had never been arrested before, police records showed this was his third conviction for a similar offense and the second time he had been found guilty by Magistrate Smith. The girls harassed were Eleanor Buckley and Lillian De Pascale, both 14 years old.[24]

10

Laws

Sometimes laws were introduced to deal with the sexual harassment of women in public places in America. Sometimes those laws were enforced and sometimes not. Generally, though, there were no laws in place that specifically dealt with the mashing of women. Usually cases against offenders were proceeded against by charging the man with disorderly conduct or with disturbing the peace. The problem with using the former charge was that the harassment had to be visible and vocal enough to attract attention. The latter charge was the one most usually used. It that case it was interpreted to mean that the harasser had, by mashing the woman, disturbed the peace of Jane Doe.

Another charge that was used, very infrequently, in the early years was that of vagrancy. It was reported in July 1891 that the new vagrancy law was to be tested in San Francisco courts. In one case William Dean Miller was called for sentence before Judge Rix. According to a news story, "Miller is a notorious Market-street masher of the cigar-store type—a corner statue of which decent women have long stood in fear." The article went on to declare that the masher was then pervasive. "It needs but a passing stroll on Market and Kearney streets between the hours of 4 and 6 o'clock in the evening to show how entirely the decent section of the community have been placed at the mercy of a worthless set of loafers and hoodlums in fine clothes, who esteem it a disgrace to labor and an honor to earn even the recognition of a disgust from a respectable woman." The journalist went on to argue that the rowdiest and most disreputable of the mashers gave the police the most trouble. "The mere fact of being ogled by silly dudes and accosted by well-dressed adventurers is bad enough, but the very glance of these reptiles is pollution. Unfortunately, it is hard to secure their conviction." It was the need for an efficient law to control the mashers that was the problem, the article remarked.

The vagrancy law had been enacted, at least in part, to try and deal with the sexual harassers.[1]

A couple of days later William Dean Miller, the "troublesome cigar-stand statue, masher and vagrant" who had recently been arrested for insulting ladies on Market Street and been convicted of vagrancy, was sentenced by Judge Rix to four months in jail.[2]

A day later an editorial appeared in a California newspaper regarding the conviction of Miller on a vagrancy charge. In full agreement with the outcome of the case, the editor declared, "The gentry who stand about to stare at our women, follow them, take opportunities to speak to them, and attempt low flirtations that are insults, need a taste of prison life to convince them that the meanest wretch on earth is the bestial fellow who posts himself to stare insultingly at our wives and daughters, and to crowd himself upon their attention on the street cars and in public assemblies." His method of operation was to strike an attitude at a street corner, or in front of a cigar store or a theater or a lecture hall, "and, with a half dozen of his kind, ogle the women as they pass." He was well-dressed, and when he was handcuffed and taken to prison he protested loudly the "outrage on a gentleman." The Miller case, continued the editor, was the first in San Francisco under the new vagrancy law, "but should not be the last until our women are as free to walk the streets of our cities without insult as to move in their own homes. Unfortunately, there is quite a large class of men who frequent the streets who have no idea of womanly purity." He added, "To these mashers all women are impure, vain, and are but waiting the opportu-

Two sketches showing what the situation was like for women in the downtown area of San Francisco in the summer of 1891. That is, mashers were all over the area.

nity to have their vanity flattered by the attention of the masher. The whole tribe should be exterminated, if it could be done lawfully." As far as the editor was concerned, under the law a very large class of mashers could not be pursued since they were not "loiterers around public places" as defined by the law. Hence, for those there was the new vagrancy law. Perhaps the editor worried that the new law would not work out, because he went on to tout another remedy—"the law that the stout brother and indignant husband make unto themselves, and we do not recall the record of a solitary case in which anyone has been severely mulcted [fined] for thrashing one of this order of men—in fact, it is worth the dollars and cents of a good round fine to chastise a masher as he deserves."[3]

With respect to William Dean Miller, another article noted the masher claimed to be worth $50,000 and was employed as a drummer for a liquor house. His real offense, said the reporter, was persistent loitering on certain streets and attempting to force his attentions on passing women. It got to be a nuisance. One man thrashed him while another had him arrested. But the establishment had difficulty in obtaining convictions against him, as no law seemed to apply efficiently; the ones used often tended to be too vague to secure regular convictions. Thus, Miller was sent away for vagrancy. However, vagrancy laws were little used for mashers, as they too were found to be too vague by higher courts.[4]

A report in April 1893 noted that Ohio Governor McKinley had not yet signed the "masher" bill, which provided a fine of $100 to $300 or imprisonment for a term from six months to two years as the penalty upon conviction of any married man who represents himself to be unmarried and repeatedly calls upon a female in that capacity. The Ohio Senate attached an amendment to that bill under which the measure was made applicable to married women representing themselves to young men as being single. This proposed bill was not really directed against mashers in the strict sense—men harassing women that were wholly unknown to them—but it was widely presented in the media as a "masher bill."[5]

A journalist observed in the fall of 1894 in Richmond, Virginia, that as the mashers of that city paused in their idle strolls before the building on Tenth and Marshall Streets, occupied by the Woman's College of Richmond, and cast lingering looks at the women therein, "they violate a city ordinance and are nabbed by a bluecoat, hauled up before the Police Justice, and fined not less than $1 nor more than $10." That recent municipal ordinance was enforced for the first time in the early part of October 1894. A male medical student by the name of Holley Williams stopped in front of that school, smiled at the women therein, twirled the ends of his mustache and struck a pose, described as an attitude of "satisfaction." Said the arresting policeman, "That settled it. He was a stranger and I took him in." On the following morning the Police Justice fined him $2.50 and costs. Williams said to the judge, "Students never have money; you can't get blood out of a turnip, your Honor." Replied the judge, "I can put a turnip in jail, though." Williams then suddenly found the money and paid his fine. Dr. Nelson, the president of the college, became gravely alarmed when he heard the verdict and that publication of the facts of the case would defeat the very object for which the ordinance was passed. He made a tour of the local newspaper offices and unsuccessfully lobbied to have the item suppressed. Thus the Richmond general public became aware of the case, and Nelson fretted that this would only draw in more mashers. It all came about in the following fashion. About 18 months earlier the Board of Directors of what was then called the Richmond Female Institute came to realize that this "time-honored Vassar of the South" was not flourishing as of old and began to look for a new president. Finally they settled on the Rev. James Agamemnon Nelson. As well, the institute was renamed, and it reportedly began to flourish anew. However, to Nelson's horror he discovered the young men of Richmond, especially the medical students (their college was nearby), were in the habit of loitering near the building, especially around dusk, to see the women, and smile, and twirl their mustaches, and strike poses, and so forth. Nelson tried to shoo the mashers away, but nothing worked, as they kept returning. Then things got worse. Nelson caught three men who had scaled the back wall to the extent they could hang over the edge, look into the back garden, and talk to the girls there. Nelson chased them away. For his next step in his personal war on the mashers he appeared before the Richmond City fathers and, after an appeal on behalf of Southern maidens, secured the passage of this ordinance:

> Be it ordained by the Council of the city of Richmond, that no person, under pretext of exercising his right to be on the public streets, shall loiter near the premises of the said institution for the purpose of prying therein or holding surreptitious communication with any of the inmates thereof; nor that any one accompany or follow the pupils of said institution on the public streets without the permission of the teacher in charge of said pupils or otherwise interfere with or annoy said pupils. Any person guilty of the offence or offenses herein mentioned, upon being duly convicted thereof, shall be fined not less than one dollar nor more than ten dollars for each offence.

It was the duty of the city police to enforce the ordinance.[6]

Richmond, Virginia, was the site of more legislative action a few years later. At the start of 1898, state senator McCone's anti-flirting bill, which, said a reporter, had heretofore been regarded as the joke of the Legislative session, took a more serious turn, and this reporter then believed it had a good chance of becoming law. The bill was considered on January 14, 1898, before the committee on public institutions and schools, and the testimony in letters from principals of girls' schools was so impressive that the members of the committee, who had heretofore treated the matter as a laugh, declared themselves in favor of the measure. That measure was designed to protect schoolgirls from the annoyance, and the loitering around girls' schools, by men "of objectionable character." The need for such a law was said to be so strong in Richmond that when the Legislature had failed to consider such a bill two years earlier the Richmond City Council passed an ordinance that effectively broke up the attention of young mashers to schoolgirls. Several arrests had reportedly been made under that ordinance, and no more trouble had been experienced in Richmond. Presumably that referred to the ordinance mentioned above that Nelson initiated.[7]

C. G. Jones, a legislator from Oklahoma County (OK), introduced a bill against mashers in the Oklahoma Legislature early in 1899. He had felt, he explained, the need of "some repressive hand on the foul mouth of the street-corner loafer...." He added, "Most of the situations of this kind will go no farther than words, lacking even the element of boldness. But when a loafing masher becomes so bold that he dares to approach a woman, then he ought to be taken in hand." The type of masher that Jones had in mind to punish was "the man who is bold enough to follow and petition, to address vulgarly." An editor for a Kansas newspaper thought Jones' initiative was doomed to fail because this type of masher "can not be reached through legislation. A good woman, who has been insulted by a masher, feels humiliation enough, without giving publicity to her humiliation. She would cringe from publicity, from an appearance in court, as all women do." According to the editor, there was only one remedy—"a good, sound thrashing for the masher. Pugilism is despicable in all save this, that the use of the fists comes in nobly in punishment of mashers. Violence is always to be deprecated save when it is exercised by some father or brother against an insinuating, lying cur who defames pure women." He thought Jones should introduce a bill holding brothers and fathers blameless when they beat up a masher. In conclusion, the editor exclaimed, "Legislation will not reach the leering Lothario of the western street corner. A good right-hand punch, full arm movement will, and it should be encouraged."[8]

In a message to the New York State Legislature at the start of 1900, Governor Theodore Roosevelt tried to impress upon the minds of the current lawmakers "the necessity of a law providing for the arrest and punishment of the most detestable type of human being that can be found in any community," wrote a reporter. Roosevelt was arguing for a law to punish pimps and not just prostitutes (in such circumstances the women involved were punished but the men were not). An unnamed public official who commented added that in connection with this matter it would be good if the reporter would call the attention of the public and Governor Roosevelt "to the shameful fact that there is no law in the state under which a masher can be arrested and punished. The law provides that a woman who accosts a man upon the street can be arrested and punished, but a loafer, well dressed or otherwise, who accosts a woman cannot be dealt with by our police magistrates, because there is no law providing for the loafer's punishment." He cited instances of magistrates reluctantly discharging such men and of the effect such discharge had on other mashers. "The police are now unable to arrest them, without stretching their authority, and you will find complaints against that class of offenders all over." They used to be arrested, explained the official, under a city ordinance against loitering and lounging, but then a judge decided that the ordinance referred only to obstructing the thoroughfare. Then he added that if the mashers were made disorderly persons they could be summarily arrested and summarily punished. According to this official, though, Section 899 of the Code of Criminal Procedure dealt with disorderly persons yet did not reach the masher. Disorderly conduct defined by the New York City consolidation act, Chapter 410, read this way: 1.—subsection to deal with muzzling a dog. 2. "Every common prostitute or night walker loitering or being in any thoroughfare or public place for the purpose of prostitution or solicitation, to the annoyance of the inhabitants or passers by." 3. "Every person who shall use any threatening, abusive or insulting behavior with intent to provoke a breach of the peace or whereby a breach of the peach may be occasioned." Police magistrates had held that section 3 did not warrant the fine or imprisonment of any man who may quietly step up to a woman's side and address her as if she were an old friend or acquaintance.[9]

This unnamed official felt the problem could be resolved by adding the following section to the law: 4. "Every person who stands in a public place, or in any thoroughfare, who willfully and wrongly annoys women therein or thereupon, by accosting them shall be deemed guilty of disorderly conduct."

The *Brooklyn Eagle* newspaper urged city officials to adopt such a law:

> For the masher has long been in evidence as a public and exasperating nuisance. Lusty men have caned, thumped and spat upon him; he had had his nose pulled and kicks have bruised his vile anatomy, yet he continues in evidence upon our thoroughfares, in theaters, cars and even in the churches. Unprotected women are continually subjected to his bows, his smirks and his feigned mistakes in pretending to recognize acquaintances.

Even though other males sometimes stepped in to beat him, added the editor, "yet the nuisance continues to offend. It is high time that the police and police magistrates should be invested with the authority which will enable them to deal with the Masher severely and effectively."[10]

An article published at the end of September 1903 declared that Toledo, Ohio, would have an anti-flirting ordinance on its books. The ordinance was introduced by request of the Board of Public Safety "to protect women from the masher nuisance," and was drafted by the City Solicitor and approved by the County Committee on the night of September 30. It provided that "any person who shall unlawfully follow, pursue or otherwise molest or insult any female shall be fined, not to exceed $50 and costs."[11]

As of September 1905, the making of "goo-goo eyes" was a misdemeanor in Houston, Texas. The law had just been enacted by the city council as follows:

> Section 1. That hereafter any male person in the city of Houston who shall stare at, or make what is commonly called goo-goo eyes at, or in any other manner look at or make remarks to or concerning, or cough or whistle at, or do any other act to attract the attention of any female person upon the streets of Houston, with the intent or in a manner calculated to annoy, or to attempt to flirt with any such female person, shall be deemed guilty of a misdemeanor and upon conviction thereof in the Corporation Court be fined any sum not to exceed $100.

The police in Houston had been instructed to see that the provisions of the law were strictly enforced.[12]

The LeRoy, Kansas, City Council began a crusade in October 1905 against what was described as "too socially inclined" traveling men. An ordinance making it a misdemeanor for traveling men to make goo-goo eyes or carry on flirtations with young women "is being considered and will pass," remarked a journalist. The penalty was to be a $100 fine. According to the story, "Most of the drummers are married men, and a possible expose of their conduct by being fined for flirting is the most effective way to stop the practice."[13]

According to a new District Code in Washington, D.C., "any man who smiles at a woman passing him on the public streets, or who makes grimaces of a flirting or insulting nature such as to incur the displeasure of the woman in question" was subject to arrest and a fine not exceeding $25, as of the end of 1905. That law, wrote a reporter, "was designed to protect unescorted women from insult by men such as are termed 'mashers' and 'curbstone Johnnies' who loaf on street corners or along the sidewalks and make remarks to women as they pass." The reporter added the law was not enacted for fun or as a joke, and was enforced by the police in the most active manner. In the future it was expected to be enforced with even more zeal, since Police Commissioner Sylvester declared he was determined that women would not be subjected to insults while walking on the streets of the nation's capital. Said Sylvester, "It is most essential that this law should be rightly executed, and I take pride in saying that there is less of this outrageous conduct in Washington than in most of the other large cities at the present time." That law stated:

That it shall not be lawful for any person or persons within the District of Columbia to congregate and assemble in any street, avenue, alley, road, or highway, or in or around any public building or inclosure, or any park or reservation, or at the entrance of any private building or inclosure and engage in loud and boisterous talking or other disorderly conduct, or to insult or make rude or obscene gestures or comments or observations on persons passing by, or in their hearing, or to crowd, obstruct, or incommode the free use of any such street, avenue, alley, road, highway, or any of the foot pavements thereof, or the free entrance into any public or private building or inclosure; that it shall not be lawful for any person or persons to curse, swear or make use of any profane language or indecent or obscene words, or engage in any disorderly conduct in any street, avenue, alley, road, highway, public park or inclosure, public building, church or assembly room or in any other public place, or in any place wherefrom the same may be heard in any street, avenue, alley, road, highway, public park or inclosure, or other building or in any premises other than those where the offense was committed, under a penalty of not more than $25 for each and every such offense.[14]

At a meeting held on November 26, 1912, by the Racine Wisconsin city council finance committee, it was said that "flagrant mashing" prevailed upon the public streets in the city of Racine, according to the evidence produced by Miss Petersen and Attorney C. C. Gittings of the Central Association. And as a result, it was reported that the committee would recommend an anti-mashing ordinance be adopted by Racine, similar to the one said to be in force then in Milwaukee. During that meeting Petersen cited some "flagrant" cases of mashing she had witnessed on the streets of the city. For example, two men were on a streetcar who whistled at high school girls and called out to them, "Oh you kid." That was kept up for many blocks. "The men were 40 years old and should have known better," Petersen said. Other examples were given where boys stood in front of places and made remarks to passing females. Some girls accosted were said to be not over 15. Fumed Petersen, "This is not fair, girls 15 years old ought to be allowed to walk upon the streets without being molested." She added, "Many of the girls who have been insulted by these mashers have told me that they would like to call a policeman when accosted but were afraid they would have to appear in court and their names be published in the papers." Gittings told the committee that some months earlier the matter of mashing came to the attention of the board of directors of his group, the Central Association. They had no idea such things were going on, and when they investigated, the group found that such allegations were more than true. He told of a crowd of mashers in front of a saloon who tried to catch girls and make remarks to them. He cited other evidence of places where he had seen males trying to grab girls. It all led him and his group to conclude that an anti-mashing ordinance should be enacted. After evidence had been taken, the two witnesses left the committee room. The three aldermen on that committee then discussed the matter, and all agreed they were in favor of such a measure. Therefore they moved and passed a motion to instruct the city attorney to draw up an ordinance similar to the Milwaukee measure. First, though, the matter had to be taken up by the full city council. Nothing more was reported of the proposed measure.[15]

In Phoenix, Arizona, the Civic League, an organization of women said to exert a great deal of influence in civic affairs, decided in March of 1914 to push for a law against flirting. Miss Alice Mathews, a policewoman from Kalamazoo, Michigan, who was then in Phoenix on a visit, turned the attention of the League in the direction of mashing. She declared that crime and vice often resulted from flirtations begun on the streets. The penalty for such flirting could not be made too drastic, she declared. Her own city of Kalamazoo, she explained to the women of Phoenix, had a fairly good anti-mashing ordinance, but she recommended the even stricter ordinance of Chicago. Therefore the Civic League sent for a copy of the Chicago ordinance and was determined to ask that it be adopted by the Phoenix City Council.[16]

The Massachusetts State Senate, by a vote of 18 to nothing, passed to a third reading, on June 23, 1914, the so-called Masher's Bill, which would punish with six months imprisonment any man who accosted on the street a woman or girl with whom he was not acquainted.[17]

In April 1929 it was reported that Abilene, Texas, had just introduced "the first anti-flirting ordinance in the United States." It read: "It shall be unlawful for any person to idle and loiter on any street, thoroughfare, sidewalk, alley, or in any store, theatre, moving picture show, business house or in the entrance or doorway of any such place within the corporate limits of the City of Abilene, for the purpose of plying the avocation of flirt or masher."[18]

11

Courts, Actions and Reactions

Three ladies were riding in a streetcar in August 1880 with a Mr. Degnan. On the pretense of not being able to sit comfortably with his back to the horses, he placed himself opposite the ladies, and, said a reporter, "by a series of vulgar winks, grins and grimaces, endeavored to impress them with his personal beauty, good manners and fascinations." He "grossly insulted three respectable young women with his vulgar attentions," at which point the conductor intervened to give Degnan the alternative of ceasing his mashing or getting off the car. Degnan responded with bad language and by striking the conductor. Those activities resulted in his arrest. Appearing before Justice Walsh, Degnan received the heavy fine of $30. It was a reminder, said the account, that the people of Brooklyn had long ago made up their minds that a streetcar would be just as safe for women and children as their own homes. It was hoped, commented the article, that Walsh and his fellow police justices would make a rule and widely advertise it that streetcar mashers who annoyed ladies would have no mercy shown to them; then, perhaps, "this breed of animal will be taught to reserve its exhibitions of blackguardism for its own circle of acquaintance where, perhaps, they will be welcome."[1]

An editor with the *Brooklyn Eagle* declared in the summer of 1884 that "the masher's chief peculiarity is a profound faith in his dominion over the other sex." He warned that some of them were harmless and could be safely ignored, but others could not be so treated. The day before, in a New York City court, three publishers and a printer had been taken into custody on a charge of disorderly conduct. The ladies receiving the unwanted attentions appealed for protection to a passerby, and the police were called. In Judge Duffy's court, one was fined $10 and the other three were fined $5 each. However, he added, "women who might otherwise be willing to do society some service by going into a police court deserve the encouragement which the distinguished Duffy failed to grant." In court an effort had been made to "blacken the character of one of the victims," but it met with no success. But for the editor, that was not the point. "The woman who resents insult, however doubtful be her antecedents, is entitled to as much protection as any of her sex." When evidence was contradictory, said the editor, the character of the complainant may become a legitimate subject of inquiry, "but in the presence of uncontroverted facts, it was as gratuitous for his Honor to permit such a diversion as it would have been to try the prisoners on a charge of smuggling." In conclusion, he stated, "Insult in the street is added to injury in court, and the dude carries off his gold headed cane and diamonds with a sentence meaning almost literally nothing. There is, we are glad to say, more than one magistrate in Brooklyn who would have made it rather warm for blackguards of this stripe."[2]

A masher appeared in Minneapolis police court on October 14, 1884. A day or so earlier he approached a couple of women on Seventh Street and called them "la-las," and invited them to walk around the block with him. About that time a cab came along, and the women sought protection from him. The masher, who gave his name as Cook, was arrested, convicted and sentenced to 30 days in jail.[3]

The 18-year-old daughter of John H. Salts left her New York City home on a shopping trip on the afternoon of April 27, 1886. While walking up Broadway on her return journey, she noticed a well dressed young man with black hair and a mustache following her. He kept in her wake until she was at her father's door, when he approached closer and accosted her. She resented his insults, but he continued his attentions. The girl became increasingly frightened, and, as it happened, police officer Sandlands came by. He took the masher into custody. At the police station the culprit said he was John Tonsporn. A charge of intoxication was laid against him. The following morning he appeared before Justice Kenna, who "severely lectured" him before sending him to jail for 29 days.[4]

A Recorder in Galveston, Texas, fined a masher $50 and costs, or a sentence of 60 days in jail, in the spring of 1886 as punishment after being convicted of disorderly conduct. The fine was paid, and, said a reporter, "it is hoped it will prove a wholesome lesson to others of his genus who attempt street flirtations."[5]

Redmond G. Gillbarry was a masher and "insulter of ladies" on a crosstown car on Atlantic Avenue in New York City one day in October 1887, and was then, said a reporter, "thoroughly battered" by a young man on the car. He was then ejected from the car by passengers and arrested. When Gillbarry was arraigned before Justice Massey for trial, he said he wished to plead guilty.

"I am satisfied that I acted unwisely," he told the judge. "Now if your Honor will deal leniently with me, considering what I have suffered both mentally and physically, and let me off with a fine, I will take care that I am never mixed up in such an affair again." Massey said to him, "I'm disposed to let you go. But I consider that insulting ladies in a street car is about the meanest misdemeanor in the category." He fined him $5, on a Friday. Gillbarry asked for his bond to hold until Monday, as he did not have the money with him, promising to bring the $5 in on the coming Monday. Massey agreed to this, but Gillbarry did not show up on Monday. His bondsman was John Kelly—to the tune of $200. Massey issued a warrant for the masher's arrest. It was reported that Gillbarry spent an hour on Friday afternoon hunting up newspapermen and begging them not to put his name in the paper. It was said he was employed in a New York City dry goods establishment.[6]

Two young women on West 14th Street in New York City told policeman Edward Costa that a man had insulted them as they passed by. Costa watched him for a time and then saw him poke his umbrella into the sides of two other women, who hurried out of his way. As the officer approached him, the masher ran off, but Costa chased him down and arrested him. When the masher appeared at the Jefferson Market police court on September 11, 1888, he identified himself as John Sickenberger, 39, a designer for the Edison Electric Light Company. He told Justice Gorman he thought he knew the two women. Gorman fined him $10.[7]

Charles J. Moody, an employee of a railroad company, accosted a woman on Third Street in St. Paul, Minnesota, in March 1889. He followed her for several blocks and addressed her, said a journalist, "in a most insulting manner." Moody was arrested and appeared before Judge Cory, who sentenced him to a fine of $100 or 90 days in jail. The prisoner had about $30 on his person and a gold watch and chain, but no one to advance the amount of his fine, so he was taken to the workhouse and chained to a common drunk. It was said that he resided in Minneapolis and was a married man.[8]

The Moody case prompted an editorial in a St. Paul, Minnesota, newspaper. Starting off, the editor thanked the judge and the police officer, and said they were entitled to the thanks of the community "for their efforts in suppressing that pestiferous animal commonly known as the street masher." He hoped the sentence would have a healthy deterrent effect upon the mashers who congregated on street corners "for no other purpose than imposing their insulting attentions upon the females who pass by. It had come to pass that a respectable woman dreaded to go on some of the streets in this city for fear of encountering the mashers. The difficulty heretofore in bringing the scoundrels to justice was in the indisposition of ladies to appear in public as prosecutors." With respect to the penalty imposed on Moody, the editor thought it was not a harsh one. "The only regret is that the law does not fix the penalty for such offenses at three years in the state prison instead of the three months in the workhouse." Since the police had made a start in ridding the streets of mashers, the newspaper "urges them to go forward in the good work until any lady can feel free to go upon any street in the city at any hour of the day or night, without fear of molestation or insult."[9]

When 18-year-old Nellie Havemeyer was walking home alone on Friday evening, May 24, 1889, from the Novelty Theater on Driggs Street in Brooklyn, Frank Little began to follow her and tried to accost her. His actions became very annoying to her, and she informed a passing policeman, who arrested the man. Little was an employee of the Pennsylvania Railroad and appeared in court on May 25. Little told Justice Goetting that the woman spoke to him first. Goetting convicted the man and fined him $10. Little's wife was present in court, and she paid the fine.[10]

The case of Angelo Moropolus, the Greek who had frequently figured in the local courts in Los Angeles for attempting to mash young women on the streets of that city, was up again before Judge Smith on July 15, 1892. He had been harassing Jesusita Lopez off and on for two years. Deputy District Attorney Diehl said in court, "Moropolus is five parts masher and five parts conceit. He walks about the street ogling and following young women. He belongs to the most despicable class of men in this community, and it is time such men were rebuked." Diehl added, "It is time that the people of Los Angeles should know whether their wives, daughters and sisters shall be protected from the importunings and brazen impertinences of these profession mashers." It took the jury just 10 minutes to register a guilty verdict.[11]

When Angelo appeared for sentencing the next day he started to try and explain his actions, but Judge Smith interrupted him to tell him not to add perjury to his other crimes. He had been convicted of disturbing the peace of Lopez. Smith declared, "Ordinarily this is not a grave offense, but the circumstances connected with this case are of the most detestable character. Every person under our law has the right to be protected in their person from the interference, intrusion and insolence of others. The person of each is sacred, and no one has a right to interfere with the lawful freedom of that person." Smith continued, "You have been following and pressing your attentions upon this young lady when you knew from the first that your presence and your attentions were exceedingly distasteful to her. It seems almost incredible that a persecution of this kind could go on for two years in the very face of our society, and in our city, and no remedy be found." Smith went on to declare that Angelo belonged to a class of beings who made a business of insulting ladies as they passed on the streets "by lecherous stares, having nothing but impure thoughts, and those continually." The judge said the prisoner's conduct demanded the severest punishment, as the safety of the wives, mothers, and daughters of Los Angeles required that the masher be made an example of. The maximum penalty that Judge Smith could impose was a fine of $200 and 90 days in jail. Smith sentenced Moropolus to a fine of $200 and 90 days.[12]

Lewis Morris, a 29-year-old real estate broker in New York City, was required to post $500 bail for good behavior or spend six months in the jail on Blackwell's Island as punishment for mashing Mrs. Theodore Mundorf. He was sentenced in the Jefferson Market police court on September 24, 1892, by Justice Ryan. On the day before, Mrs. Mundorf was going downtown on a Broadway car. Morris was a passenger in the same car, holding a strap, standing in front of where she was seated. Said Mundorf in court, "He looked at me awful, and all the time he crowded up to me and tried to get my attention." He got off at the same spot as she did and followed her down the street, finally speaking to her. Mrs. Mundorf hit him with her umbrella at that point. She hit him several times before a passing policeman came along and arrested Morris. When he appeared in court, Morris was asked if he had anything to say. Morris said nothing but pointed to his lawyer. Attorney Steiner said, "It was all the result of a combination of circumstances. My client did not insult this woman." Then he told the judge that his client would apologize for the insult he hadn't offered. Steiner ended his plea by saying, "Mr. Morris has an undisputed reputation." Justice Ryan replied, "Lots of men have good reputations who oughtn't to have them. Six months, or $500 for good behavior."[13]

The case of Osman Day, alias the "Market-Street Masher," described as a "notorious character" in San Francisco, came up before Judge Seawell on June 16, 1893. Day had no visible means of support, despite the fact he was always well dressed and appeared to have plenty of money. However, because of "the complaints of several ladies, who said he was in the habit of insulting them on the street," Day had been brought up before Police Judge Conlan a little while previously and charged with being a common vagrant. Day had successfully beaten several similar cases before, but on that occasion he was not as fortunate, since Conlan, after hearing the testimony against him, found him guilty. After administering a "severe tongue-lashing," Conlan sentenced Day to six months imprisonment. Day appealed. His appeal was successful, on technical grounds, and on this day Seawell reversed the decision of the lower court and granted Day a new trial, this one to be held in Superior Court.[14]

In a case heard before Justice Haggerty in a Brooklyn Police Court in August 1894, Frank A. Ludwig was described as "something of a masher." Because of his mashing activities he had his nose "thumped" by William H. Cotte. In this particular court case Cotte was the defendant while Ludwig was the complainant. Ludwig testified that, without provocation, Cotte entered his house and smashed him in the nose. Cotte testified that while his wife was at Coney Island one day, Ludwig wrote an insulting letter to her. When his wife told him about the incident Cotte went around to Ludwig's house and avenged the insult. The wives of both men appeared in court, and both testified. Justice Haggerty declared that Cotte had acted "perfectly right"—that Ludwig had acted like a scoundrel and the judge was sorry Cotte had not administered a heavier beating to Ludwig.[15]

Charles Parker, a black masher, was in the county jail in Stafford, Arizona, in June 1895, destined, said a reporter, to spend not less than 10 years in the penitentiary "unless a half dozen indignant citizens who could be easily wrought up to the point of doing it, should make a colored corpse of him before the next grand jury can take notice of him." Complaints had been made against Parker in the previous couple of weeks by a "score" of girls and young women who had been frightened by his conduct. Sometimes he would walk behind a woman and stroke her hair; sometimes he would lay his hand on her shoulder or attempt to put his arm around her. At other times he would meet women on the street and horrify them with "an exposure of person," exclaiming, "Ah my darling." Parker was finally arrested, and at his arraignment he was given a change of venue. Nothing more was reported on this case.[16]

Charles E. Watson was arrested for insulting a lady in Washington, D.C., on the evening of September 13, 1895, by policeman Hodges. On the following day Watson was tried and convicted in police court. The evidence was said to be "strong" against him, and he was fined $25. Judge Kimball declared from the bench that he intended "to protect the ladies of Washington in all such cases."[17]

Joseph Bush appeared in Judge Conlan's court in San Francisco on January 26, 1897, to answer the charge of vagrancy. Two police officers testified that he had been hanging around in front of a department store for some weeks, and complaints had been made to the police that women had been insulted by him. Carrie Epstein testified that Bush had accosted her on Market Street. He asked to escort her home, and she said she felt indignant and told Bush she did not know him. Epstein walked away, but he followed her up Powell Street and again spoke to her. She ignored him and walked along, but he continued to follow her. Finally she ran into a policeman and had Bush arrested. Bush told the judge that he had no intention of insulting the woman, claiming he was a plumber by trade and a married man. Conlan convicted him of vagrancy. A day later Bush appeared before the judge again for sentencing. Conlan gave him "a deserved scorching" and sent Bush to the county jail for six months.[18]

A man giving the name of F. H. Brim, who claimed to be a representative of one of the leading insurance companies, was fined $40 in police court in

Kansas City, Missouri, on November 17, 1897, on a charge of disturbing the peace. Brim was a masher. He had arrived in Kansas City about a month earlier, and for the previous two weeks he had been harassing schoolgirls by following them from the schools to their homes. In one instance he so badly frightened a girl that she refused to go to school and finally told her parents the reason. Brim was unable to pay his fine and was thus committed to "the city rock-pile."[19]

The police said he was a masher; Walter Devoe said he was not. In any event, he was, said a reporter, "in a cell at Central police station, curly locks, winning smile, russet shoes and all." The account went on to say, "His dress is that of a typical masher. When on parade a white Fedora surmounts his curly ringlets, a stylish brown suit encloses his stalwart frame, and russet shoes, toothpick style, are in evidence. Walter believes that a blue percale shirt with buttons of pearl, and a bow tie of material in the national colors, are also the proper caper." Devoe was from Osawatomie, Kansas, and was being held in jail in Kansas City, Missouri, in June of 1898. When a reporter on a Kansas City newspaper visited Walter in his jail cell Walter denied he was a masher. When he was asked if he was in the habit of making a practice of mashing, he replied, "Not altogether." Asked to explain that, he elaborated, "I mean not all the time." Then the reporter asked him if it was not true that he flirted with the ladies as they passed by. "Well, yes, I do if I know them; but I never do with strange ladies," he insisted. Devoe said he came to Kansas City from Osawatomie on a Saturday in June in search of work. He claimed he was a baker and was estimated, by the reporter, to be about 30 years old. Devoe was promptly arrested and charged with disorderly conduct. Police did not believe his story that he was a baker who arrived in Kansas City on June 4. Rather, they said he was a substitute bartender and had worked for short periods of time in that capacity in several of the leading hotels of the city. According to the article, "The war against mashers is yet in its infancy." When Walter Devoe appeared before Judge Burnham in police court on June 11 he admitted that he had a predilection for smiling at the ladies. Burnham wasted no words on him and curtly fined him $25. Apparently Devoe could not pay the fine and was sentenced to the alternative— 50 days in the workhouse.[20]

Walter Devoe was convicted of being a masher in Kansas City, Missouri, in 1898. He was fined $25 but apparently could not pay the fine and so was sent to the workhouse for 50 days.

Mrs. Charles C. Lane knocked down Henry James on a day in December 1898 in New York City. James, who was a stranger to her, had harassed her by following her through the streets of the city. He had also further insulted her by speaking to her. After she knocked him down she went about her business (she was an entertainer—known as Mademoiselle Suzinetta—who juggled cannon balls and broke iron chains with her hands). James caused her to be summoned to the Yorkville Police Court to answer for assaulting him. Magistrate Meade not only let Mrs. Lane go free, but he congratulated her for having punched the head of James. In court James declared she lured him into her reach and then brutally assaulted him. Lane told the court he had been annoying her and speaking to her for two days. James had first seen her in the dime museum, where she performed on stage as Suzinetta with her husband. When James spoke to her and asked her if he could walk with her, Lane ran out of patience. She told the court, "I hit him." Meade declared, "I congratulate you. You are the woman this town has been looking for for a long time." He then dismissed the charge against her.[21]

Warren Shelton was fined $5 in police court in Kansas City, Missouri, on August 2, 1899, for his activities as a masher. Shelton followed two women down Walnut Street in Kansas City and tried to engage in a flirtation with them. They became angry and summoned Officer Halloran, who arrested him. In court Justice Spitz gave the prisoner what was described as a "deserved lecture" before he fined him. Shelton paid immediately.[22]

As she walked along Sixth Avenue in New York City on the evening of January 5, 1900, 20-year-old Clara Reilly (a recent convert to the Salvation Army) was accosted by a masher. Horace Butterworth followed her, accosted her, and addressed her. Frightened, she stopped a passing policeman, who arrested him. At the police station the masher refused to give his name, but a search revealed a transit pass in the name of Horace Butterworth. In Jefferson Market Police Court on January 6, Magistrate Pool asked Reilly, "Did you encourage him?" "I don't know what you mean sir," she answered, trembling. "I was on my way from the barracks, thinking what I could do to better mankind, when he took me by the arm and called me 'baby.'" Butterworth said he was married with several children and that he had been drinking. Magistrate Pool said to Butterworth, "You are entitled to no leniency. The severest punishment I can inflict is to put you under bonds of $500 for your good behavior for six months." The masher furnished the bond.[23]

Police Judge McAuley fined a married masher in Kansas City in June 1900 for harassing telephone operators as they left the company's premises after work. What was unusual was the amount of the fine levied against the unnamed masher—$500.[24]

Robert Cunningham, proprietor of the Cunningham Hotel in Kansas

City, Missouri, was in police court in that city on August 2, 1900, for mashing, with the technical charge against him being one of disorderly conduct. The particular charge against him was made by Miss Watson, of Lone Jack, Missouri, and Miss Emma Pryor, with whom Watson was visiting. Cunningham was 60 years old and had, reportedly, a long series of similar offenses behind him. He was convicted, and in passing sentence Judge McAuley said to Cunningham, "There is no excuse for you.... The women are entitled to protection and they have come to the right court to get it. Your fine is $500." He was the second masher in six weeks to receive such an astronomically high fine from Judge McAuley.[25]

Mrs. Mary Wood, the daughter of a well known law reporter by the name of Arthur Beckwith, was insulted on September 6, 1900, in Court Square, near Fulton Street in Brooklyn, by what was described by a reporter as "a well dressed loafer." Wood, who had been running errands, ran into the Court House and told her father, who in turn notified District Attorney Clarke, who told Detective Jerry Mahoney (all these people were in the Court House). The latter went outside to find the man, who was waiting at the same spot for more victims. Mahoney had Wood walk past him again. Again the masher insulted Wood and was promptly arrested. The group went immediately to the Butler Street court where a charge of disorderly conduct was made against Janson Slocum. Wood told her story, and Magistrate Steers promptly fined the man $10. Slocum had only $4 on him, but an acquaintance was found who supplied the other $6. In addition to giving officials his name, he told them he was an insurance broker whose office address was 186 Remsen Street, and that his home address was 552 Jefferson Ave. A reporter for the *Brooklyn Eagle* checked out his particulars and found the masher was not known by that name at any of the addresses he had given, nor was any man matching the masher's description known at any of the addresses given. That is, his name, address, and work particulars were all fictitious.[26]

Judge Wislizenus of the Dayton Street Police Court in St. Louis had a masher before him on July 1, 1901, and, said a reporter, "as a result issued a mandate which will strike terror into the hearts of those who have long made life a burden to the wives and daughters of respectable citizens in the public parks." Edward Brown was the masher, and he was fined $20 for attempting to get up a flirtation with a young woman in one of the public parks. The judge said to Brown, "Flirtation carried on by making goo-goo eyes or any other manner must be stopped, and the police have been instructed to arrest all offenders." Watchman Goldman, who had charge of the park, testified that Brown came there nightly, was dubbed the chief masher of Carr Park, and that more than one woman had complained of his "insolence."[27]

It was reported in September 1901 that the police at No. 3 precinct in

Washington, D.C. tried hard to hold for prosecution "an elderly, well dressed, and apparently refined gentleman" arrested for insulting Miss Frank Kell, 16, on a street corner at 8 p.m. on September 5. But James Kell, father of the girl, although anxious to prosecute, decided not to do so, and the man was released. It was said to be understood the masher was well known in Washington and held a prominent position in one of the government departments. The man "begged pitifully" to be let off, declaring it to be his first offense and entreating the police to release him "for the sake of his family." Kell decided not to prosecute "on account of the notoriety which would come to his daughter." In this story, "elderly" turned out to be "about 40 years of age." The masher spoke to the girl and asked her to take a stroll up the street with him. The girl suggested perhaps he should speak to her father, who was just across the street. The masher then hurried off. She went into a drugstore and told her father. Mr. Kell chased after the man and held him, despite the masher's resistance, until the police arrived. Miss Kell worked as a cashier in a drugstore.[28]

In St. Louis on January 15, 1902, Lester Hanover was fined $1,000 by Judge Pollard on charges of disturbing the peace of Mary Institute schoolgirls. Hanover was fined $500 on each of the two counts brought against him. That was the maximum penalty the judge was allowed to impose. Students who appeared in court testified that Hanover had stood on the corner of Beaumont and Locust Streets on several occasions and accosted them. He had appeared at the school nearly every day for a week and had gone so far as to walk beside some of the girls and engage them in conversation.[29]

On October 9, 1903, in Dallas, Texas, Claude Doyle received the heaviest penalty ever imposed in the Tarrant County Court, on a plea of guilty to a charge of insulting a woman during the Fort Worth street fair. Judge Milam sentenced him to pay a $2,000 fine and to serve four years in jail. Unless the fine was paid, Doyle would serve 15 years in prison. When he was arraigned, Doyle pled guilty and asked for mercy. Said Milam, "I shall impose upon you the maximum allowed by statute, and it is a matter of regret to me I cannot make it longer. I think the four years jail will give you an opportunity to think about this thing and that when you come out you will be prepared to take your hat off to women." He added, "The punishment I assess is no way incommensurate with the crime with which you are charged. It is reprehensible in the extreme, and I will give you the limit. It is necessary for the women of this country to be protected, and as far as this court can go it will give that protection."[30]

George Ross was arrested by the police at Union Station in St. Louis in April 1904 after he had made himself obnoxious to several ladies at the station by attempting to force his attentions on them. Ross, who said he was from Harrisburg, Kentucky, told the judge he was fond of children and had purchased candy and toys for them, and was amusing himself in that manner when he was arrested. Judge Tracy accepted the policeman's version of events and fined Ross $10 and costs. As the costs amounted to $3, the total fine was $13.[31]

Crushed because he had been fined and sentenced to the county jail as a masher, it was reported that Charles L. Morehead, a Louisville, Kentucky, barber, committed suicide by swallowing a quantity of morphine at the home of his mother in Louisville. The deadly dose was taken shortly before noon on a Saturday in July 1904. He lingered until 3 p.m., at which time he died. Morehead, 34, was survived by a widow and two small children. He had been a resident of Louisville for the previous 15 years and was said to have been "well known and respected." Morehead had never been in any trouble prior to his arrest on the charge of insulting Mary Hutti, 17.[32]

Two of Pittsburgh's leading brokers appeared before Magistrate Vichenstain in a police court in that city at the end of August in 1904. They were arrested for fighting on the street, and both men bore the scars of the melee. J. W. Arrott claimed that J. W. Hanley (both were said to be well known and wealthy) had insulted a lady he was walking with, and that he had physically rebuked Hanley. For his part, Hanley said he had not insulted the woman, claiming he knew her and, meeting her on the street, had spoken to her "as he thought was his privilege." He claimed to have been surprised when the woman called to Arrott, stating she had been insulted. During the street battle the woman made her escape in a cab. Vichenstain said to Arrott, "You did right to hit him, Mr. Arrott. I commend your action in defending a woman, and I wish other men would do as you have done with mashers." He discharged both men—Arrott because he found him blameless and Hanley because the woman had disappeared.[33]

When he was in police court in Minneapolis on October 12, 1904, Albert Hemrach was being tried on a charge of vagrancy. He was given the opportunity of leaving the city or going to the workhouse. He chose Chicago. He had been arrested the night before on the complaint of Rose Vose, a girl from Breckinridge, Minnesota, who claimed Hemrach harassed her on the street with improper proposals. Hemrach had been released from the workhouse, on a different matter, only on the previous morning, just hours before his arrest for mashing. It was said he had caused the police in Minneapolis a great deal of trouble in the previous six years.[34]

On the afternoon of February 1, 1905, at the corner of Main Street and Third Street South in Salt Lake City, a woman walking along the street was approached by a man who raised his hat and made some familiar remark. Instantly she became angry. Turning on the man, she gave him a severe tongue-lashing as to his egotism in thinking that any woman wished to make the acquaintance of a man such as him in that manner. Quickly a crowd gathered, and Patrolman Williams soon arrived. He said he would arrest the man if she would appear against him in police court. However, she declined to do that, and the man was released. It was reportedly the third or fourth time that particular man had harassed that woman over a period of time. And that was why she had reacted with such quick anger on this occasion—it was not the first time he had harassed her. The reporter who wrote the piece said that he put her refusal to appear in court against her harasser down to a "woman's modesty."[35]

In New York City on July 15, 1905, a six month prison sentence was imposed upon Benjamin F. Smith, from St. Louis, by Magistrate Steinert. On the previous evening Mrs. Grace M. Gamble was waiting for her husband at the Madison Avenue and 42nd Street subway entrance. Smith was passing and spoke to her. Gamble resented the insult, slapped Smith in the face and had him arrested. In court Gamble herself requested leniency; however, the magistrate imposed the heavy sentence and at the same time invited other women who suffered from mashers to act as had Gamble. When Smith first spoke to her she told him he had made a mistake and that he had better move on. He repeated his remarks, and then Gamble, insulted and angry, struck him in the face with her handbag. That did not drive him away, and then she slapped his face. Smith still persisted, and Gamble yelled out that her husband was nearby and would soon return. Policeman McDonnell came along and arrested him. In court Smith pleaded with Gamble not to disgrace him further, saying it had been a terrible punishment for him to be locked up in a cell. "I think he has been punished enough, your Honor," said Mrs. Gamble. "He comes of respectable people, I am told, and I think the night in a cell has been a lesson to him." A surprised Magistrate Steinert responded by saying, "What? You ask for his discharge after the way he treated you? He shall be punished as an example to others. The streets of New York must be made safe at night for respectable women." From the gallery Mr. Gamble added, "That's right, your Honor. Don't show him any leniency." And so Smith was sent to Blackwell's Island prison for six months.[36]

An editorial on the Gamble case appeared in a Salt Lake City newspaper in which the editor declared:

> Smith got exactly what he deserved. It is a pity that more men of his stripe are not similarly punished. There is altogether too much of that sort of thing in Salt Lake. Several prominent corners are rendezvous for beasts in trousers who ogle passing women and who try by all devices known to such animals to attract their attention. Often they are bold enough to accost women, often bold enough to persist in spite of rebuffs.

He noted that at times mashers had been dealt with by being "severely handled" by male relatives of the victims, and at other times severe sentences had been imposed, but the practice of mashing had not been stopped. "This is true because of the rarity of prosecutions," he thought, for the usual reasons that women were reluctant to be subjected to the notoriety involved in creating a scene on the street, calling in the police, lodging a complaint at the station-house, and prosecuting the case in court. Yet, grumbled the editor, the mashers should not feel safe, the way they did. To prosecute a masher was "a duty" that every woman owed to herself and to her sisters. "Every woman who prosecutes such a man may be sure of the most courteous, considerate treatment in court and in the newspapers. No blame attached to the woman who is approached and who discourages the attempted acquaintance. She does nothing to warrant the approach, and when the unpleasant event comes to pass she should resent it in the most effective manner possible—in the nearest court that has juris-diction."[37]

Ninety days on the chain-gang was "a righteous sentence" imposed in a Los Angeles Police Court in July 1905 for the offense of mashing. A newspaper editor thought it was the first time such a sentence had been imposed on "one of the class of contemptible curs who make a practice of posing on our leading street and ogling passing women." He added that his newspaper had frequently called attention to the "effrontery of the masher class of social vultures in Los Angeles." In conclusion, he declared, "Enough feminine pluck to cause the arrest of a masher, followed by that ninety-day treatment on the chain-gang, would soon stop the outrageous insults to which women are subjected occa-sionally by disreputable loafers who infest our prominent thoroughfares."[38]

Harry Peyton, who said he was a clerk in the general offices of the Mis-souri Pacific Railroad, was fined $300 by Judge Tracy in the First District Police Court in St. Louis on September 13, 1905, arraigned for having attempted to flirt with Mrs. A. W. Ecoff and for harassing her at Union Station earlier in the week. Ecoff told the court she had gone to the station to meet her husband. The masher accosted her twice, asking her to go over to Pine Street with him for a drink. She told him she was there to meet her husband and not to speak to her again, but, she said, "he persisted. He was very offen-sive." Peyton testified that Mrs. Ecoff had first accosted him, and that he had then lifted his hat to her and passed on.[39]

A masher was arrested in December 1905 for insulting Mrs. Bessie Keough while she was walking past the Pennsylvania Avenue entrance of the Willard Hotel in Washington, D.C. The masher refused to give police his name, so the authorities christened him "John Brown." When Bessie passed the masher he said to her, "Hello sweetheart, are you going home?" She said, "If I could find a policeman I would have you arrested." He replied, "You mean I'll have you arrested for walking alone at this hour with no escort." Finally, she found a policeman, and the man was arrested. Brown said to Officer Harry

Lohman, "Officer, this woman is mistaken, and I sincerely trust you will not take her word in preference to mine." When the officer did just that and arrested Brown, the prisoner became angry and abusive toward the policeman. According to the article, numerous complaints had been made over the previous few months to both the commissioners and the police concerning insults offered respectable women by men on Pennsylvania Avenue. Extra police attention to that area had resulted in many arrests of mashers, and complaints had decreased. In court Judge Mullowny convicted Brown and sentenced him to pay $15 or spend the next 45 days in the workhouse. As he did not pay, he was taken off to serve the time. Before Brown was taken away, Mullowny said to him, with respect to the jail time, that "possibly a little time to reflect will teach you to have more respect for women in the future."[40]

Two male passengers on a trolley car bound for Hackensack, New Jersey, at the end of July 1906 tried to mash two women on that car as it traveled through North Bergen, New Jersey. They winked and smiled at the women, and then addressed them. Justice of the Peace Joseph Kennell of North Bergen was also on that car and noticed the embarrassment of the two women. He suggested quietly to the two men that they should behave themselves. They told him where to go. Kennell then jumped up from his seat and grabbed the men by the collars. One punched him. Then Kennell roughed up the pair and quickly subdued them. Then he arrested them. Later he arraigned them before himself at his office, convicted each of them of disorderly conduct, and fined them $10 each. Kennell did not let them go until they apologized to the women they had insulted. The pair said their names were George Morton and Frank Decker.[41]

Speaking from the bench on August 27, 1906, in San Francisco, Police Judge Mogan said, "The women of this city must be protected from the insults of rowdies and the advances of mashers," after finding four men out of four (separate incidents and cases) guilty of "insulting unprotected women." James Gaynor, Thomas Barrett, Lawrence Crain, and Charles Laigi were the men involved. Their mashing conduct took place in different parts of the city. Craig accosted two women and forced them into a doorway. Their screams brought a local merchant, who beat up Craig and held him for the police. Barrett entered a candy store where he made several insulting remarks to a female clerk. A call brought the police. Gaynor tried to force himself into a buggy containing two women. He got in and made himself objectionable to them until a passing policeman arrested him. Laigi had persistently followed a 14-year-old girl around, frightening her and causing her to call for the police. Mogan said, to all four after convictions were registered, "It is seldom that I have four men before me accused of the same base offense. The women of this city must be protected from rowdies and the advances of mashers. When this court convenes tomorrow I think that I can teach each of you something about chivalry and the respect that is due our women. At least I can give you time to reflect on your conduct." The sentences were not reported.[42]

Albert Callais, described as a "flagrant" offender of the masher class, found himself appearing before Judge Conlan in San Francisco on January 31, 1907, charged with following Mattie Moore and forcing his unwelcome attentions on her. To set an example of Callais, and to show he meant to display no mercy to mashers, Conlan had the man arraigned on two separate charges, one for disturbing the peace and the other for battery. He did this because the maximum penalty under either charge was six months of jail time. On two separate occasions Callais had followed the girl along the street. The first time he kept close to her and called out to her persistently until she turned into a nearby store for protection. On the second occasion, after pursuing her for several blocks, he attempted to take hold of her arm and force his attentions on her—hence the battery charge. Callais had been locked up, with bail set at $500. After the masher was found guilty on both charges, Conlan sentenced him to the maximum of six months in jail on each charge, with all 12 months to be served. Conlan remarked, "A man of his kind should be kicked from one end of the street to the other.... I have given him the full penalty that the law allows. I am sorry that he could not have been made to answer to a more serious charge." He added he would deal just as severely with all mashers in the future.[43]

Charles Billington, 60, was arrested in Oakland, California, in July 1907 for annoying women on the street by mashing them and presenting cards to them on which was printed a request to meet him later. On July 27 Police Judge Samuels sentenced him to the city prison for a term of 60 days. The technical charge was that of disturbing the peace, to which he pled guilty. He pled guilty only after having twice faked deafness in court and declaring he was unable to read the complaint against him. One of the jailers at the city prison reported to the court that he had heard Billington conversing with another prisoner and that there was nothing wrong with his hearing.[44]

An article published on May 12, 1908, was about the problem of mashers on the streets of Ogden, Utah. It argued that the mashers who visited the city and committed mashing offenses were punished, while the local mashers were not. It was said that several cases showed what the situation was like, and "the strangers get it and the local product go unpunished. There is not a night but what unattended ladies passing along the street, particularly Twenty-fifth street, are the objects of the abuse of unprincipled ingrates who happen to come from old families and have 'a pull' with the administration."[45]

Otto Marine, the accused masher, failed to appear in Police Judge Conlan's court on July 18, 1908, to receive his sentence for disturbing the peace in following and harassing Mildred Rueff, 13, by following her home about a week earlier. The judge forfeited the $10 bail put up by Mrs. Carter (Marine's mother) and issued a bench warrant for his arrest, fixing his bonds at $1,000 or $500 cash. Mrs. Daisy Marine, the separated wife of the masher, voluntarily came to court to testify against her husband. She had read of the case in the newspapers and came forward. She told Conlan she had been forced to leave her husband owing to his flirtatious behavior toward young girls. He had not contributed one cent to her support but had lived off her money. She had paid his expenses and put him through barber college. Daisy called Otto a "loafer," and said that he had spent "all his time in flirting with young girls instead of working."[46]

"Insulting women on the streets of Salt Lake must be stopped, and I am going to make an example of you," declared Judge J. M. Bowman in police court on October 27, 1909. He imposed a fine of $25 on William Frances when it was shown he had followed and accosted Miss Lucy Hutchings and Miss Lucille Player, employees of the Sparks Candy Company. The women testified he had followed them on two different occasions. Said Bowman, "It is time a stop was put to the practice of insulting women. It has come to the point where the women of the city must be protected. More cases of this character will draw prison sentences." According to the article, from time to time it had been brought to the attention of the police that women were not safe from insult even during the early hours of the evening on the downtown streets of the city. "Vulgar and profane remarks are directed at any woman who chances to be alone, and the practice is not confined to the night hours alone. The practice, it is stated, is not alone among the rougher class of men, but includes well dressed and supposedly respectable youths of the city who have become intolerant mashers."[47]

A masher was standing at the corner of Jefferson and First Avenue in Phoenix in December 1909 when a lady he did not know passed by. He "addressed her lightly by an endearing title" and asked her if she would not take a walk with him. Instead she turned back and walked in the direction from whence she had come, to where two men were standing. One was her husband and one was Deputy Sheriff McCann. When she recounted the insult, the officer said he would handle it. He put the masher under arrest and took him before Judge Johnstone. The man admitted to the story told by the officer. Neither the lady nor her husband had come to court, but that was unnecessary, as the man pled guilty. The justice said it was his inclination to give the man 100 days, but he would not impose that sentence. He would commit the man to jail, and later, after having talked with the woman who had been insulted, he would name the number of days of the sentence; it would be left entirely to her. Said the reporter, "There had been no complaint and there was no formal commitment. The man was locked up and left in jail overnight. That was it as far as the justice was concerned, the matter was dismissed; it had never been on the docket." A few days later the justice learned that the prisoner was free, and that the officer involved had taken him before the lady where "he made an abject apology and promised to have more sense in the future."[48]

An employee of the Milwaukee Railroad by the name of W. S. Gorman accosted a woman on the street in Tacoma, Washington, in June 1910, saying, as he grabbed her by the arm, "Hold on dearie." She told him to go away. He persisted. She tried to go around him, but he blocked her way. Then she hit him a solid punch to the face that sent him sprawling. Appearing before Judge Arntson, Gorman was fined a total of $165 ($15 in costs added to the $150 fine). Being unable to pay, Gorman was sent off to jail for 83 days.[49]

Two men charged with following Mrs. Alice Tackaberry from a subway station to her home in Harlem, New York, in August 1910 were convicted by Magistrate Appleton and sent to the workhouse for 30 days each. That sentence came about under a new law in New York State that allowed the magistrate to give the accused and convicted no alternative sentence of a fine but a direct trip to a term in the Blackwell's Island jail.[50]

Mrs. Agnes Bush was waiting for a car in New York City at 67th Street and Third Avenue in January 1911 when Arthur Foggin approached her and said, "Hello, dearie." He tried to put his arm around her, but Bush pushed him away. Then a car came along and she got on. However, he followed on board and again forced his attentions on her. Police Officer Berger, who had also boarded the same car, witnessed the harassment and took Foggin into custody. When Foggin was arraigned in Yorkville Court on February 1, Magistrate O'Connor declared, "The women of New York City must be protected. It matters not what hour of the day or night they happen to be out, the streets must be made safe for them." He added that it was lucky for Foggin that he was intoxicated at the time of the harassment, "or I would have sent you to the workhouse for six months. You stand committed for thirty days without bail."[51]

After several complaints had been made by women in Pullman, Washington, to the effect that they had been followed by a man, and in several instances remarks had been addressed to them by the masher, Marshal Hooper, police arrested a man fitting the description given by the women in October 1911. However, City Attorney Dow was of the opinion that no law had been violated, and the young man, noted a reporter, "after listening to a severe lecture and being warned not to repeat the offense," was released.[52]

Whether a "friendly smile" accompanying a "sly wink" represented the meaning of mashing in the eyes of the law or was just ordinary sociability was a question that Justice Anderson took under advisement in November 1911 in Sacramento, California, in the case of I. Down, who was charged with insulting

Mrs. C. B. Trott. As a result of Down's alleged mashing, he and Mr. Trott came to blows, and Dow was arrested. No more was reported on this case.[53]

Mashers who believed they could make such remarks to women as "Oh, you beautiful doll," "Oh, you kid," "chicken," and "baby" were warned, in July 1912, to stay out of Chicago. If such mashers were caught in that city they would stay at least 30 days, and if they had any spare change they would drop that into the public coffers, said a news story. Judge Newcomer assessed one youth $50 and costs for addressing a woman as "chicken." Judge Bietler freed a man who took the law into his own hands when a masher called his wife "baby." The masher was whipped by the husband and fined by the court. Judge Caverly, while admitting that "Oh, you beautiful doll" was a compliment, declared that the only man who could use it and get away free had to address that phrase only to his own wife.[54]

Also in Chicago in July 1912, Judge Scully started his own war on mashers in South Chicago. He set out a list of fines that would be levied for specific behaviors. For a kiss by a masher the fine would be $100; for a wink $40; for each additional wink $25; for a covert glance $10; for an additional covert glance accompanied by a "good afternoon" $50. Scully explained that there were doubtless other mashing behaviors not then on his schedule, but they would be added as they came to his notice. The schedule was prepared by Scully after he had heard evidence in the case of Michael Relinski.[55]

John Hernandez, 38, who gave his occupation as "artist painter," was sentenced to 10 days in the workhouse by Magistrate Krotel in the Essex Market Court on August 8, 1912, in New York City, for annoying Mrs. Mary Wilson. She said Hernandez rode downtown on the same elevated train from Harlem as she did and tried to attract her attention, even going so far as to press her foot with his. He followed her off the train, trailed her for a block and then tried to speak to her. She tried to shake him off, but he persisted in walking by her side and talking to her. She called Patrolman Stackhouse over and had the man arrested, charged with disorderly conduct. Hernandez admitted "that although he did not know this woman he had spoken to her." Said Magistrate Krotel, "Well, you are old enough to know better than to speak to women with whom you are not acquainted on the street. Ten days in the Workhouse."[56]

In Portland, Oregon, Municipal Judge Taxwell announced in the summer of 1912 that he would fine mashers $10 for each word uttered to a woman the masher was forcing his attentions on. On the evening of August 29, Mrs. Paul Correll was waiting in front of Steve Lambert's shoe shine parlor, and when Lambert approached her and accosted her she called Patrolman Richards over to arrest Lambert. On the following morning, when Lambert appeared before Taxwell, the judge kept his promise by fining the masher $20 for saying "hello cutie" to Correll.[57]

Mrs. Grace M. Martin was on her way home from the theater in October 1912 with her daughter when Harry Halle, 32, who described himself as "an attorney from Buffalo," approached the pair and said to the daughter, "Why are you so shy?" The women ignored him and walked on to their hotel. A witness named Edmund Bartley stepped forward at the hotel to say he had seen the harassment and was willing to be a witness. Martin decided to make an example of him, and they found a cop and had Halle arrested. In Night Court Bartley corroborated Martin's story, stating, "I was with a friend. I said to him, 'Isn't it an outrage that apparently decent and respectable women cannot walk in the streets of this city without being insulted.' I came here because I think an example should be made of this man's conduct." Halle told the court he was not practicing law "just now." He argued he thought he recognized a woman he knew but realized too late he had made a mistake. Magistrate House did not believe him. In sentencing him he said, "Here is an instance of two very respectable persons—a mother and her daughter—walking in one of our principal thoroughfares and insulted by a person unknown to either of them." He added, "Respectable women must be protected both night and day when they are abroad in the streets of this city." Halle was sentenced to 30 days in the workhouse. Just before he tried the Halle case, Magistrate House heard another case involving a masher. That one involved William Hofer, 19. Mrs. Mary Hausworth was walking along Third Avenue with a neighbor, Mrs. Nora Gilbert, when Hofer took hold of Mary's arm and said, "Hello, kid, how be you?" Both women ignored him, but he followed them and spoke to them again. Then both women slapped his face, and he ran away. They were so mad they waited around for two hours for Hofer to resurface in the area. When he did they went at him again and finally had him arrested. In sentencing Hofer to 30 days in the workhouse, House said, "We can't stop the mashers in New York, but I am going to do my best to do it. The trouble is that the women are afraid to take the men to court. I compliment you women for this."[58]

Also in New York that month, Daniel Kennedy, 33, was held by Magistrate Krotel in the West Side Court on a charge of disorderly conduct, preferred by Marcella Farman. She alleged Kennedy accosted her in the street with vile names, and when she repulsed him he struck her in the eye. She was standing on a street corner with a friend at 11 p.m., waiting for her fiancé. Both the friend and the fiancé backed up her story. After he had insulted her repeatedly and had been repulsed, he still did not leave. Then he punched her, after which he went across the street and into a bar. The first policeman Farman appealed to for help told her to forget about the incident. However, she found another officer, who went into the bar and arrested Kennedy. When he was asked in court for his side of the story, Kennedy said the woman had solicited him, and when he ignored her she became furious and struck him. In pushing her away,

Kennedy allowed, he might have inflicted the bruises on her cheek and eye. In this case, for unreported reasons, Krotel ordered an investigation. That report from Probate Officer Patrick Shelley to Magistrate Krotel, said a reporter, changed completely the Kennedy case. Officer Shelley found the girl's mother, and she admitted to Shelley that her daughter Marcella was "beyond her control." After lecturing the young woman, Krotel said he was going to have her character further investigated. He fined Kennedy $5.[59]

On the evening of November 12, 1912, Miss Maude Stafford, 19, was walking along the street around 11 p.m. when John Carroll stopped her and asked her where she was going. She told him to mind his own business. Then he stopped her again and told her he was a cop. He put his hand on her shoulder and told her to follow him into a darker area of the street. At that point she screamed. A real policeman responded to the noise and heard the stories. Then he arrested the sham cop. When the magistrate sentenced that man to 30 days in jail, he remarked, "This is but another instance of a respectable young woman being insulted on her way home. It is an outrage."[60]

Blaine Starner was arraigned in court in Hagerstown, Maryland, in January 1913, accused of being a masher after he called a woman in the street "a chicken." The testimony was all against Starner, and it looked as if he would be punished as a masher, when the magistrate asked him what he had to say for himself. Said Starner, "I think I was entirely within my rights when I called her chicken. Look in Webster's dictionary, you'll find I'm right." The magistrate looked it up, and he found that the definition read as follows: "Chicken—a young person; a child: especially a young woman." Said the magistrate, "I guess you're right. Discharged." That was a bizarre ruling at the time because the fact that a man spoke in the street to a woman he did not know made it a mashing offense; what the words were mattered not at all, except perhaps to make the offense more egregious.[61]

During the day on February 7, 1913, in New York City, Mrs. Nora Thompson, a 30-year-old mother of three (one being a nursing baby), was downtown shopping. She was standing at a counter in a store on 14th Street when she suddenly turned and drove her fist into the face of a well-dressed man past middle age who was standing behind her. The first blow broke his glasses, and the second knocked a cigarette from his mouth. A crowd assembled. The man started to back away as the crowd became more and more threatening. So hostile had the crowd become that when Patrolman Abdell arrived he had difficulty in protecting the man from violence. In the crowd was a witness, Samuel Kinysons, who said he witnessed the affair, and that the man tried to flirt with the woman. He flicked his glove at her and he winked. Thompson said that was exactly what he had done. The arrested man, 60-year-old Joseph M. Voss, denied everything, saying he had never seen the woman in his life and never winked or flirted at her. "It was she who winked at me and I ignored her," he claimed. At the police station Lieutenant Finn told her if she made a complaint she would have to go to Night Court. Thompson said she couldn't, as her baby needed her. When Voss made the same claim at the station that it was Thompson who had done the winking, she got so mad that she rushed at Voss and had to be held back by an officer. At that point Kinysons spoke up, saying he saw the whole thing and was in a position to make, and press, the complaint, if the police would entertain his complaint. They would. Nothing more was reported on this affair.[62]

The idea of assigning a specific fine to specific mashing behaviors caught on, to a small extent, during this time. Judge Charles E. Foster, who presided over an Omaha, Nebraska, police court, drew up his "Masher Schedule" in May 1913. He declared the following schedule of fines would hold good in his court, regardless of who the mashers were and what their social standing was; for calling a woman a "chicken" the fine would be $5; "honey-bunch" $10; "turtle-dove" $15; "baby doll" $20; "Little cutie" $25. His schedule went into effect there following the result of a street encounter when a woman was followed from a railroad station by a masher. He caught up to her, grabbed her by the arm and told her she was "some cute chicken." The girl jabbed him several times with a hatpin. Foster punished that masher with a $5 fine. From the bench Foster declared, "Whenever it comes to a point that respectable women can't go about their shopping without being annoyed by some pussy-footing masher, it will be because the police haven't followed my instructions to fetch in all the street corner male beauties who, if their guilt is proven beyond a reasonable doubt, will find that this court is here to see that good women can be upon the downtown streets without being annoyed."[63]

At the police court in Wailuku, Hawaii, on August 15, 1913, Judge McKay gave a Filipino a "well-deserved" jail sentence of six months under the vagrancy act. That man had been hanging around the home of a well-known Wailuku man and been trying to get a young daughter that lived there to speak to him. He had even written notes to the girl, trying for a meeting. The father of the 12-year-old girl was told of the matter and immediately had the police arrest the man. The daughter had been afraid to go outside her home for some weeks by that time.[64]

Having attempted to curb the habits of Atlanta, Georgia, mashers by having three of them arrested in one week (separately) in January 1914 for harassing her on the street, Mrs. Jay H. Pickel had asked for a permit to carry a gun to protect herself. "A woman as pretty as you are is too good looking to be walking around alone," was the comment of the police judge, who thought that her pretty face furnished a good explanation, if not a good excuse, for the attentions of the mashers.[65]

Something similar took place in Los Angeles in March of 1914. A judge there declared that Reatha Watson, 20, was "too pretty to remain in the city unattended." The court gave her the choice of going back to her family or having a guardianship appointed. She returned to her people. Watson had complained that she was constantly being annoyed by mashers, and it was when she hauled one of the more persistent ones into police court that the judge took official cognizance of her attractiveness.[66]

In the Centre Street police court in New York City on July 23, 1914, Magistrate House sent Salvatore Le Verdi, a bank clerk, to the workhouse for 10 days. He was accused of harassing Anna Molnar, a stenographer, on the Third Avenue L line. According to Molnar, the masher had been annoying her for several days. Each morning, she said, he waited for her at the elevated station she used and smiled at her. "He tried to force his attentions on me, lifting his hat, smirking at me and in other ways," she told Magistrate House. Officer Lavender saw Le Verdi following Anna on the morning in question and observed his behavior. He warned him off, but Le Verdi told the officer to mind his own business. Lavender responded by arresting him. Said Le Verdi to House, "I am an honorable man and I wanted to meet this young lady. She is handsome and I am attracted by her. I have seen her often and I love her."[67]

Jim Mendoza was arrested on the night of February 25, 1915, in Albuquerque, New Mexico, on the complaint of a woman who said he accosted her and followed her. The next morning Mendoza was sentenced to 30 days in jail by Judge Craig in city court. According to the girl, she was walking home on East Central Avenue when Mendoza brushed up to her and asked her if he could take her home. She

Judge Charles Foster of Omaha, Nebraska, decided, in 1913, he would fine mashers partly on the basis of what language they had used on the women they had harassed. For example, if the masher called a woman a "chicken" the fine was $5; if he called her a "little cutie" the fine was $25.

repulsed him, but he persisted in his attentions. He asked her for her address; she refused to answer him. He said he would follow her home and started to do so. The woman ran to the office of Dr. Shorile for safety. That doctor called the police, who came and arrested Mendoza.[68]

Frank J. Bishop had once been a private detective employed by the W. J. Burns Detective Agency. He was fined $50 in Judge Prindiville's court in Chicago for annoying Agatha Nash in May 1915. Nash, a stenographer, said Bishop had followed her for weeks, trying to force his attentions on her and trying to get friends of hers to introduce him to her. He used to wait for her at the L station and ride home on the same car as she did, trying to mash all the way. Bishop was arrested at the Madison and Wabash L station on her complaint.[69]

In March 1916 in Little Rock, Arkansas, the State Supreme Court ruled a woman was justified in inflicting corporal punishment upon a masher who annoyed her, and affirmed the $250 in damages which a lower court had awarded Mrs. Nettie Trussell of Hot Springs. She was a school teacher who had sued the Memphis, Dallas and Gulf Railroad. A male passenger on the train stood in the center of the car in which Trussell was riding and winked and threw kisses at her. Trussell broke her umbrella over his head in response. The Supreme Court, in its opinion, ruled that not only was Trussell justified in her action on the train, but was entitled to damages for the annoyance and humiliation to which she was subjected.[70]

It was announced in August 1916 that in New York City the authorities had adopted a new method of handling the masher. In that city a woman had recently caused the arrest of two mashers. The magistrate who heard the case agreed to give them a suspended sentence, but not before he had ordered their fingerprints be taken. According to this piece, "It is a very proper plan to make mashers realize that their actions are regarded seriously by the authorities." Fingerprinting of criminals in America was introduced by the NYPD in 1906. The use of fingerprinting of convicted mashers went a long way in combating the difficulties all authorities faced in that so many charged with a misdemeanor gave a fictitious name, and the courts usually had neither the time nor inclination to confirm identities.[71]

Henry Pike, a masher arrested early in October 1916 for harassing Miss Ruth Stanton, was sentenced to three months in the workhouse by Magistrate Nolan in the Men's Night Court. A probation officer detailed to investigate the case reported Pike's real name as Harry Pike, and that the address he gave— 216 West 18th Street—was false. The masher had five aliases and a long prison record. In imposing the sentence, Nolan declared, "The street must be made safe for unescorted women both day and night."[72]

When Anna Tyle appeared in Adams Street Police Court in Brooklyn on August 22, 1917, she sat in judgment on the man who accosted her on the night of July 15 when she left home to mail a letter. Joseph Biandino, the masher, was to spend 10 days in the Blackwell's Island jail. As she was returning home from the mailbox, Biandino accosted her by saying, "Hello, bird." She did not respond, but he followed her. Meeting a policeman on the way, she had the man arrested. In court Biandino threw himself on the mercy of the court, but the magistrate left it to Tyle. "Shall I fine him or send him to jail?" he asked her. She replied, "He should be sent to jail. He insulted me, and his friends have offered me money to drop the case."[73]

Mrs. Eva Turner and her husband went to the movies at the Crown Theater in New London, Connecticut, on the evening of October 2, 1919. H. B. Haywood sat beside her. During the show he rubbed against her. She drew away from him, but he persisted. After a time he tried to hold her hand. Then she asked her husband to change seats with her, not giving the reason. Afterwards she told him what had happened, and the couple had Hayward arrested. On the following morning in police court the masher was fined $50 and costs after being found guilty of insulting her. Judge Colt said that in the future all such offenses would receive a very severe sentence. He also commended Mrs. Turner for her courage in bringing the man to trial.[74]

Miss Elizabeth Hart was riding downtown in the subway during New York City's rush hour in February 1921. A swarthy man who smelled of garlic persisted in ogling her and rubbing against her. The woman would have normally fought her way to another car to get away from him, but a headline in the *Evening World* newspaper advising that mashers be lured to the vicinity of a policeman came to her mind. When Hart left the car at her stop the garlic man followed her. She saw a policeman on duty at the corner and called him over. The masher started to run but did not get far. In Jefferson Market Police Court he gave the name of Sergio Caldoletti. When told he could choose between a $50 fine and 10 days in jail, he paid from a wad of bills said to amount to $2,000.[75]

On August 6, 1921, Sam Young, 21, appeared in Essex Market Court in New York City. The taxi driver was sentenced to five days in the workhouse after being convicted of mashing. Magistrate Francis X. Mancuso declared, "We've got rid of the Broadway lounge lizards, and now we are going to clean up the new species, the taxicab and motor lizards." Mrs. Frances Knapp was at a street corner on a Friday evening waiting for her husband when Young drove up in his taxi, stopped in front of her, and said, "Say, Cutey, how about a long ride?" She ignored him. He jumped from his cab and embraced her, saying, "Come on in, dearie." A friend of the woman happened along and gave Young a beating. That thrashing was still underway when a passing police officer intervened to arrest Young.[76]

Presiding in West Hoboken, New Jersey, Recorder Caesar Walter imposed a 30-day jail sentence on August Schneberger in January 1922 for harassing women in that community. The masher's wife and three children appeared in court and pleaded so earnestly for him on the ground that if he was imprisoned for an extensive term they would be in danger of starvation that it caused Walter to alter the sentence. Walter told Schneberger that he could serve his sentence on weekends of 1.5 days per week, from Saturday noon until Monday mornings. The masher readily agreed.[77]

Judge Felix Robertson of Dallas, Texas, corporation court stated from the bench in June 1922 that he had only one fault to find with the law covering mashers, as he was fining H. B. Williamson $100 for harassing a woman. Robertson said, "I only wish that I had the power to fine you twice as much."[78]

George Duvall was charged with having harassed a woman in a cinema in Washington, D.C. in September 1923. After being convicted he was fined $100 by Judge Schuldt in police court on a charge of assault and battery. As he could not pay the fine he had to serve 60 days in jail. Duvall offered no explanation for his behavior except to say he placed his hand on the woman to attract her attention and was slapped by her in response. He was arrested a few minutes later on the street.[79]

Moses Greenberg received a two-day sentence in the City Prison in New York City from Magistrate Edward Weil in the Tombs Court on March 24, 1928, because Miss Rae Sachs, an 18-year-old stenographer who had accused Greenberg of annoying her in the subway, had, at the court's suggestion, fixed the term. When Sachs suggested the two-day sentence to Weil, she added that she believed he should be punished as a protection for other girls. Weil commended the girl for her courage in causing Greenberg's arrest and in prosecuting him.[80]

Two mashers found themselves in Ames, Iowa, police court on the morning of May 21, 1928. Gerald Cummings and J. M. Griffith were convicted, and each fined $5 and costs, by Mayor F. H. Schleiter for molesting girls on the streets of Ames. The pair had been arrested about 9 p.m. on May 19 after they had accosted some girls and asked them to go riding.[81]

Four mashers were arrested in September 1928 in Berkeley, California, by Officer Ipsen after they attempted to pick up females on University Avenue. Three of them were 17 years old, and they were all released after being reprimanded by police officers. Oscar Zeigler, 31, was arraigned before Judge Oliver Youngs Jr. on a charge of disturbing the peace, convicted, and fined $25. Zeigler had pulled up beside two 16-year-old girls and asked them to go for a ride. They complained to Officer Ipsen, who promptly arrested the man.[82]

At the start of 1929, Magistrate Gottlieb in New York City announced he was starting a campaign "to make the theaters safe for decent girls and women." He kicked off that campaign by sentencing John Juno, 34, who had been arraigned and pled guilty in Night Court on a charge of disorderly conduct, to 30 days in the workhouse. He had been arrested on the complaint of Mrs. Pauline Klapp, 34. She told Gottlieb that she went to the Chaloner Theatre in New York, and that Juno tried to flirt with her. To escape his attentions she changed her seat, but Juno persisted and moved to an adjoining seat. She then had the masher arrested. After Juno pled guilty, he told the court he had touched Klapp accidentally. Said Gottlieb, "I don't believe it was an accident. I mean to see to it that the theaters are made safe for decent girls and women if I have to send every theater and movie masher arraigned before me to jail. If fines don't stop them, maybe jail sentences will."[83]

Walter Tedford, 20, and Erwin Cox, 21, were found guilty of disorderly conduct in April 1929 in municipal court in Hamilton, Ohio, and were fined $25 each and costs. Charges of harassment were filed by Mrs. Mary Pennington of Hamilton, who alleged the men called her insulting names after they had tried to make a date with her.[84]

Convicted of disorderly conduct and of reckless driving as the result of paying unwelcome attentions to a young woman, Morris Gass was fined a total of $50 in police court. Mrs. Mary Hawken, 21, testified that Gass, who was in an automobile, annoyed her one evening in June 1929 as she walked along a street, until Policeman C. L. Smith happened along. Judge Gus A. Schuldt rebuked Gass and fined him $25 for disorderly conduct. Gass was then taken before Judge Ralph Given, and the rest of the story was told. Officer Smith said that when he approached the masher, Gass drove away, and a 45-mile-an-hour chase resulted. Given imposed a $25 fine for reckless driving.[85]

On a day in August 1929 in Fargo, North Dakota, F. A. Leonard, police magistrate, explained that sentences calling for fines up to $100 and up to 90 days in jail could be imposed upon mashers. The city ordinance made it optional with the court to decide upon the severity of the punishment. Fines could be imposed for the crime, the judge said, and prison sentences were given at the discretion of the court, either with a fine or without. A number of complaints from females that they were unable to walk downtown and back home without being accosted by would-be mashers had come to police headquarters, the judge added, before saying that his action of giving one man a fine of $25 that week was intended to be a lesson to all who might be inclined to attempt to mash. "And another thing," declared Leonard, "if any man feels that he should blacken the eye of a masher who has accosted his daughter, I don't know but that I should be very, very lenient with the fistic minded gentleman."[86]

12

Remedies

Over time, various individuals came up with their own remedies for the problem of being harassed in the street. These were remedies touted by their proponents as being ones that virtually all women could use in the streets and at other public places. Some were perhaps sensible, others not so much.

One remedy put forward came in the spring of 1882 from the *Baltimore American* newspaper (reprinted in various other papers). It was a humorous, tongue-in-cheek explanation of how ladies could paralyze a masher. "The lady has only to cast her eyes modestly down and fix her gaze intently on the feet of the masher. The glance at the feet should be concentrated, yet full of pity," the article explained. Such action would shake the self-confidence of the masher—the stare made him worry his shoes were not of the latest style, that they were dirty or muddy, or that something was wrong with the lower part of his trousers. This would cause the masher to rush to a quiet corner of the streetcar to inspect himself. But even when he found out he was okay he could not regain his self-confidence. In conclusion, the article said, "To prevent a hog from rooting, slit its nose; to keep a jackass from braying, weigh down its tail; to keep a masher from mashing, gaze sadly at his feet."[1]

Most remedies, though, were serious. A March 1898 piece that originated in the *Pittsburgh Leader* was also reprinted in many other papers. That piece started with a reprint of a small classified ad: "Mashers Fooled—Ladies, protect yourselves from street insults; a sure remedy; particulars free. Address _____."

After that ad appeared in a Pittsburgh newspaper, one woman wrote off for information. She had been sorely troubled by mashers in front of the prominent hotels in downtown Pittsburgh and resolved to rid herself of the annoyance if, indeed, there was a cure. In response to her inquiry she received a picture and description of a "unique Yankee invention." It consisted of a pocket pistol designed by means of compressed air to discharge its barrels loaded with any old powder—from facial enamel to red pepper—with a force that would make the person into whose face it was shot feel the effect keenly, or so the ad said. It was also capable, reportedly, of discharging small shot or paper pellets. The woman in question sent away for one of these air pistols (cost not specified), and when she received it she loaded it with cockroach powder, the principal ingredient of which was cayenne pepper. Then she slipped it into her pocket and went out. A few days later a masher approached her and tried to speak to her. She ignored

FIRST MOVE TO CHECK EMBRACE.

THUG AT HER MERCY.

HE MAY GRASP THE SHOULDER.

TO · BREAK · SHOULDER · CLUTCH

This 1901 illustration showed women how to defend themselves from mashers by using jiu-jitsu moves from Japan. Reportedly, the author of the article was a police inspector from Nagasaki.

him and walked on. He followed and continued to harass her. At that point she turned and gave him a shot in the face, with the powder going up his nose, and into his mouth and eyes. He howled in agony.[2]

A January 1901 article by J. J. O'Brien, with accompanying photos, illustrated how a woman could defend herself. Reportedly the author was a police inspector at Nagasaki, Japan. He observed, "In older times a woman was only allowed to walk abroad under the guidance of some older or stronger person. A woman could never go unescorted into the streets at night." But all that had changed, with women working in shops and factories often forced to get there by going back and forth alone. Women, too, in the spirit of freedom, took walks on their own, he argued. It was the purpose of the article, the author declared, to teach women how to protect themselves from all manner of bad men—not just mashers, but others such as thugs and pickpockets. Then O'Brien offered detailed instructions on how to deal with the "dangerous" masher, such as one who came up from behind, made an insulting remark and tried to slip his arm around the woman's waist. If the woman was in a well-lit or crowded street it was simple enough to call for help. But often in a quiet or dark place other help was unavailable, so he advised women to use his instructions in judo holds and throws. A series of four photos showed various grips and holds to use on a would-be masher, with the article subhead referring to the method as Jiu-Jitsu.[3]

Mrs. Duke Cabanne was described as one of the leaders of the St. Louis "Smart Set." In April 1903 she came out with the idea that every society woman should carry a revolver. "Women are not protected as well as they should be. There are officers on every street of the principal American cities, but even then the women are not safe." She added that there were robbers at night and mashers in the daytime, and one was as bad as the other. "Personally, I have more respect for the robber. The police can't or won't rid the community of the evils," she concluded. "Therefore women ought to carry revolvers, and they ought by all means to practice so as to become efficient in using them."[4]

Five years after the first piece on jiu-jitsu appeared, it was reported that the young women of Los Angeles, following the footsteps of their sisters of the east and north, were organizing a jiu-jitsu society to protect themselves against mashers and other thugs. That group was said to be especially for women who were compelled to return to their homes after dark unescorted. One of the leaders of that movement was Miss Virgie Drox. She had recently returned home to Los Angeles from a visit to relatives in New York City, and her idea of organizing a society among her girl friends on the West Coast suggested itself to her when she visited the gymnasium of the New York Jiu-Jitsu club. "Why, the girls in New York who are members of the club never think of having an escort if they want to visit one another after dark," enthused Drox.[5]

As of June 1906 in Cincinnati, some 500 "Hello Girls" were reported to be practicing with the punching bags—that is, boxing. Those women were operators for the local telephone company. It was said the punching bags were being installed in all the branches of that telephone company. General manager of the firm, R. T. McComas, denied he had his sights set on the mashers who lined Vine Street and persistently annoyed the telephone girls of the main office on their way to and from work. He did, however, admit the punching bag lessons would have been put to good use if some phone girl did land a "knockout" on some masher.[6]

Bertha Pollock was, as of August 1906, a three-time champion woman fencer in America. She praised her sport for its exercise value, and for its ability to teach self-control and a command of the temper. She also argued that the art of fencing was also "a splendid feminine safeguard against attacks or insults. It gives a woman a command of her arms that is useful on the streets even though she is not armed with a rapier."[7]

Miss Mabel Bohle of Chicago was that city's champion female skater, and in 1910 she declared, "If a girl wants rosy cheeks, bodily strength and confidence in herself, let her skate. Any girl who is afraid of burglars, footpads [old term for a thief who specialized in pedestrians] or mashers will lose her timidity if she will take to ice skating."[8]

A minor stir arose in 1910 over the use of hatpins. Major Sylvester was the superintendent of police of the District of Columbia in Washington, and according to him, Washington women could jab hold-up men and mashers with long hatpins all they wanted and no one in Congress would rise up and cry "outrage." Sylvester pointed out—in discussing the agitation then underway against long hatpins—that in Washington there were 16,000 more women

WOMEN WHO FENCE ARE TERRORS TO MASHERS

Bertha Pollack was a champion fencer in America. In 1906 she advocated that women take up fencing as a sport. It was good exercise and kept women in shape. It was being in good physical condition that led women to be better able to repulse mashers, not the idea of carrying around a sword.

than men (the D.C. population in 1910 was 331,069). "Such predominance of the gentler sex can have but one result. Numbers of women are obliged to go about the streets at night without escorts, and numerous instances have come to the attention of this department where women assailed by marauders at night have used hatpins with telling effect."[9]

That issue of hatpins prompted a response from officials in other American cities. A statement made by Police Chief Samuel H. Barlow of Salt Lake City stated there would be no boycott against long hatpins in his city so long as the current "mammoth" type of headgear continued to be worn by women.

He saw no reason for the agitation that was then said to be sweeping over certain parts of the county and which had resulted in the Chicago City Council passing an ordinance making it a misdemeanor, punishable by a fine of $50, for a woman to wear a hatpin, the point of which protrudes more than half an inch from the crown of the hat. There was said to be little if any agitation in Salt Lake against the wearing of those long hatpins, and even if there were, Barlow said he could see no reason why they should be considered dangerous. Sylvester had also said, "Of course, there always will be isolated incidents of accidents, but it seems to me that when all is said and done on this subject, the hatpin's value as a weapon of defense to a woman so far outweighs all arguments as to its danger, that this department does not feel justified in issuing a restrictive order." And, added Sylvester, "as long as women must go about the streets, otherwise unarmed, so long will we feel reluctant to take from them a 'concealed weapon' that serves them so effectively."[10]

Continuing the hatpin debate was an article from Marion, Ohio, in which the reporter asked why wouldn't a hatpin be a good cure for some of the mashers "who disfigure the peaceful face of the Sunday evening streets" in Marion. The article went on to tell the story of a woman on her way to the post office on a Sunday night. She passed by mashers at separate places along her route. "You look lonesome, girlie," said one. Another said, "Say kid, like to take a ride," while still another said, "Oh you summer doll." When she glared at that one, he added, "Don't scratch, little one, give a guy a chance." Then she ran into yet another masher. "There were all the implements of warfare, from the latest extreme in fashionable tailoring to the lightest and most dove-like colored hat crushed down rakishly over one eye in an attempt to simulate a youth now some years past. Also there was the insane calf-quality smile, half simper and half leer." When that last masher approached the woman, she stopped, said not a word, and reached for her hat, "extracting therefrom a nice long business-like steel stiletto in the guise of a hatpin." It was enough that she drew it and brandished it—the masher quickly fled. This article concluded, "If a refined woman can't walk down the main street of a small city like Marion without being subjected to annoyances from amorous and vulgar loiterers ... how about the hatpin cure?"[11]

In its September 1910 issue, the Salvation Army publication *The War Cry* advised women to memorize a speech read by Bessie McCoy in the stage play *The Echo* at the Globe Theatre and use it whenever they were accosted by strange men. In an article on "Working Girls and Mashers," McCoy was quoted as follows:

> Yes, it's true that I am only a working girl, but I don't think myself above the job, and just because I am working is no excuse for you to think I'll let you talk to me. I don't know if there is a dance on tonight, and if there is I won't go with

you. That man standing over there is my big brother, and he weighs two hundred pounds. Last week he wiped up the floor with a fresh young man who tried to make a date with me. He is watching now because he knows men try to flirt with me, and unless you disappear there is going to be trouble. Don't hurry on my account, but it makes me nervous to see a fight. Goodbye.

Bessie McCoy was a hugely popular actor/singer of vaudeville and the legitimate stage. She was very popular in 1910. She opened in Charles Dillingham's latest musical comedy *The Echo* in August 1910 at a time when she was a leading singer/dancer on Broadway.[12]

In the summer of 1911 the police gave the following information to women on how to deal with mashers. "Make a show of the masher. Kick up a row on the street, in the car, wherever he annoys you. ... Call a policeman. If he won't act, arrest the masher yourself. The copper is then bound to lend a hand. ... Stay with the case in court. Don't let your indignation cool; keep it red-hot until after the trial." The piece, from a Tacoma, Washington, newspaper, did not sound as if it was issued by a police department.[13]

Miss Eunice Faley of Boston was so angry that so many women had been accosted on the streets of her city that in July 1912 she demanded that police headquarters establish a "new gallery of mashers." She wanted the pictures assembled of all persons arrested for mashing, declaring that only in that way could the practice be eliminated. Police officials said her request would be considered.[14]

Speaking from the pulpit in Minneapolis in August 1912, the Reverend G. L. Merrill, a prominent minister in that city, delivered a sermon titled "The Masher Mashed." He described a masher as "a biped who roosts on the corner and by look, gesture or speech takes familiar advantage of women who pass by." He added, "And if these fellows seem to want a hot time, girl," then "wallop him with your lung and then throw red pepper in his eyes." His remedy was in the form of an offer to any poor and bashful man in his audience who had fallen in love with some worthy woman and wanted "to meet her for a wife." Merrill promised to see the man was introduced, had a place to court, and to marry him free of charge, and even to pay for the man's marriage license if necessary.[15]

An article appeared in 1912 that was authored by Ethel Intrapodi, described as a young actress. She said she was not a suffragette, not even a suffragist, "but I do believe that a woman should be able to protect herself from that breed of brutes commonly known as mashers. These insufferable beings masquerading in the form of man have been on the increase, and there seems to be an epidemic of the craze, or disease, or whatever you may call it." She argued that the "clinging vine" type of woman runs screaming for a policeman, but the girl "of spunk and independence is able to take care of herself." That

SMASHING CURES MASHING—GET BUSY, GIRLS!

Ethel Intrapodi described herself as an actress. In 1912 she urged women to take up the sport of boxing for self-defense, and to use it in any encounters they might have with mashers.

is, she could if she could deliver some boxing blows. Intrapodi learned boxing—at one point taking lessons from Jimmy Walsh, the flyweight champion of England. She said that if every business woman would take up boxing she would save herself a great deal of annoyance. "When women take up boxing, the masher will be a thing of the past. He will slink away like the coward he is. A jab in the jaw will eliminate him entirely and he will be as rare as the dodo bird."[16]

Another member of the clergy who got involved in giving advice to young girls who were accosted on the street by mashers was the Reverend James S. Montgomery of the Metropolitan Episcopal Church in Washington, D.C. In a sermon he delivered in September 1912 he advised them, "Don't call a policeman." He advised the females of Washington and other cities to organize for their mutual protection against mashers, "and instead of subjecting themselves to the embarrassment of appealing to the arm of the law, to give a signal to other girls to come to their assistance and put the young men to flight." The title of his sermon was "The menace of F Street to our young women." Montgomery argued that mothers should take care that their daughters "are not permitted to walk the streets in the afternoon. They are subject to the flirtations of men who live on the street for the sole purpose of making the acquaintance of pretty girls and taking them to cafes." He argued further that the police were doing their best, "but you know how hard it is to prove that a young man has been flirting with a young woman. This makes it hard to convict when an arrest has been made." Thus, it made more sense to avoid the embarrassment of calling a policeman for a problematic result. But a woman could readily tell if a man was mashing and if he was persistent in forcing his attentions. "She should have some sign by which she can attract other girls and thereby get assistance." And that was the end of his vague suggested remedy.[17]

A remedy against mashers came out of Connersville, Indiana, in 1913, although no names were attached to it. Supposedly it was a new way to combat mashers. When a man was caught leering, ogling, or otherwise annoying women, a public notice containing his full description "as fool and moral idiot" was posted on billboards. That was said to be fully as effective as a coat of tar and feathers. The masher, it was said, never came back for a second dose.[18]

Marguerite Mooers Marshall (1857–1954) published 14 novels, as well as short stories, from 1911 to 1952. She was a columnist for two New York daily newspapers from 1922 to 1945. In a piece under her byline in August 1913 she weighed in on the masher issue. She profiled Viola Brophy and her physical assault on masher Irving Bonder. Viola gave him a black eye and had him arrested. When interviewed, she told Marshall, "Every woman who is insulted ought to do as I did." Added Brophy, "A decent woman who is followed or annoyed on the street should not hesitate to defend herself. She should use her fists or her fingernails or her hatpin or any weapon that's handy. She should strike and strike to hurt. And she should have her man arrested and appear against him in court." Whenever a man spoke to a woman offensively and she was too timid to treat him as he deserved, he was encouraged to annoy another decent woman. Even if a woman had the spunk to get a masher arrested, Brophy continued, she often acquired cold feet overnight and failed to appear in court against him. Then, of course, he was released and ready to begin his work again. Concluded Brophy, "The right sort of man makes friends through the medium of proper introductions. And to the wrong sort a woman's fist is the best answer."[19]

Caroline Josefson was a woman from Iceland who authored an article on self-defense that appeared in American newspapers in April 1914. It was an illustrated article designed to help women learn to use Glima, a form of self-defense used in Iceland. Glima was said to be an Old Norse word that covered

Caroline Josefson from Iceland urged women to use Glima to subdue harassers. It was described as a type of Scandinavian folk wrestling. It culminated in something called the "Curious Knee Grip" which was said to prevent the fallen masher from rising and was easily learned.

several types of Scandinavian folk wrestling. Caroline explained by saying, "If she knows Glima I can promise that mashing, the unwelcome kind, will vanish from your country when your women have learned the art of self-defense practiced by those of my country, Iceland." From the illustrations it looked to be some form of martial arts. A few lessons and two months of practice were said to be enough to make a woman fearless. The series of moves illustrated in the piece ended with the "Curious Knee Grip that prevents the fallen masher from rising and is easily learned."[20]

The problem of the masher in movie theaters was addressed in August 1914. "It's easy," said Mrs. S. M. Gregg, a prominent Cleveland clubwoman, "we'll segregate the sexes." To accomplish that end Gregg already had taken up the matter with the Cleveland Mothers Congress, of which she was a member. It was expected that, if that body acted, the city would be asked to frame an ordinance "which will put a fence in movie houses between unaccompanied women. Escorted women only would thus be allowed to talk to the men in the dim light."[21]

For the purpose of routing mashers, 50 Spokane, Washington, working women were taking special physical training sessions in December 1914 at an evening course conducted at the Lewis & Clark High School. It was run by Physical Director C. H. Hunt and Jack Carnahan, captain of the high school football team. At the request of the women enrolled, it was reported that everything known to the boxing and wrestling sciences, jiu-jitsu, and practical "sword" work with the umbrella would be taught. Carnahan said, "The girls contend that the police have failed to stop mashers. The girls believe that a couple of short hooks to the jaw, a jab from a skillfully handled umbrella, or a forced back flip on a hard pavement will do more than moral persuasion to repulse unwelcome attentions."[22]

Sharp spurs that would warn the masher on a crowded streetcar that he must beware of sitting too close to his female neighbor were invented by a Philadelphia woman. Those spurs were described in a 1915 bulletin of the patent office. "It is well known that rude and flirtatious youths and men, mashers, frequently avail themselves of the crowded condition of cars and other means of transportation to annoy and insult ladies next to whom they may happen to be seated by pressing a knee or thigh against the adjacent knee or thigh of their feminine neighbor, who, as often happens, is too timid or modest to create a disturbance by calling attention to the fact," said the patent applicant. That patent application went on the say the object of the invention was "to guard against undue familiarity of the character designated by the provision of means whereby the offender is automatically warned, punished, and deterred from persistent offense, and to this end my invention consists primarily of an elastic resilient spring arrayed in conjunction with a spur or prick and adapted to be attached to an underskirt in such manner that when subjected to extraneous pressure the sharp point will protrude." As well, it was pointed out that the device was simple and inexpensive, and adapted to be concealed and worn without inconvenience. "[I]f properly positioned on an undergarment, [it] will afford ample individual protection against misconduct of the character designated."[23]

Three young women were outside on State Street in Chicago in December 1915 modeling the periscope bonnet; it was reported to be a new invention. It carried an arrangement of mirrors by which the wearer could observe pursuing mashers without turning her head around to look at them. A tiny mirror was tucked into the bonnet at an appropriate angle. Thus alerted to a masher's coming from behind in preparation to mash (such behavior being reflected in the system of mirrors), the woman could elude him by ducking into a side street or by seeking the protection of a policeman.[24]

A newspaper photograph appeared early in 1918 that showed members of the NYPD holding sessions to teach women the art of self-defense, with the hope that at the end of the course most of those women attending would be able to repel attacks made upon them by mashers and pickpockets. That photo showed Police Sergeant Shore (male), a physical instructor with the NYPD, Miss Margaret Scudder (position not identified), and many women in the audience.[25]

Jiu-jitsu as a remedy against mashers was mentioned again in the press in the summer of 1918. Noted was the

This 1915 sketch shows an artist's rendition of what the periscope bonnet looked like. It was a real invention that supposedly allowed the wearer to see what or who was behind her without looking around. It was a way for a woman to prepare to flee from a masher who might be sneaking up behind her.

Teaching Girls How to Deal With Mashers

This 1918 photograph shows a large number of women attending a self-defense course. It was designed to help women deal with mashers, and any other undesirables she might encounter in the street, and was run by the New York City Police Department.

Don't Be Afraid of Mashers, Girls; Learn Jiu Jitsu

This photograph shows women at a 1918 class where jiu-jitsu was being taught. Once again that martial art was being touted to women as a good way to be prepared for run-ins with harassers.

fact that Uncle Sam was teaching jiu-jitsu to his soldiers for use against the Germans. A photo was shown of females at a jiu-jitsu class, and the article urged females to learn the technique "to salute the would-be masher with the very latest in jiu-jitsu."[26]

Another proposed remedy came out of Baltimore in 1925. It was reported that revoking the driving licenses of men who were proved to be "annoyers of women" was being considered in that city by Police Commissioner Charles D. Gaither and Motor Vehicle Commissioner E. Austin Baughman. The latter said he had the power, under the appropriate act, to revoke or suspend a license "for any cause which he may deem sufficient."[27]

Perhaps the most bizarre remedy came from Berlin, Germany, and was reported in the press in America in 1926. An anti-masher device that looked like a wrist watch and could knock out an assailant by means of a low amperage electric shock of 1,000 volts was being recommended to females by police-women in the area. Invented by Emil Pruess of Geisenkirchen, it was worn on a wrist in the usual way. Thin wires connected it with a tiny battery and induction coil carried in an invisible pocket of a dress or on the coat pocket of a woman. When needed, the wearer pressed a button, took a swipe at the masher so as to touch his body, and, said the report, "the fight is over."[28]

13

Crusades

Crusades were undertaken by groups, or sometimes individuals, that were well organized, or not so well organized. Sometimes they went into action, at least for a time; but often the crusade went nowhere, generating little publicity or notice and, seemingly, never really getting off the ground.

It was reported at the beginning of 1896 that a movement was then being discussed in New York City to work against "that particularly despicable creature, the New York masher.... A crusade against men who make insulting advances to women who appear in the streets without escorts is soon to be begun." It was said that the fight would be undertaken by women, and they proposed to fight what they considered to be a greater evil than the soliciting of men by women. These unnamed women saw their movement as a counter to the proposed plan of the City Vigilance League to encourage unfortunate women to make advances [that is, solicit as prostitutes] and then cause their arrest. One prominent female physician said her heart burned with indignation at that plan because "at the same time pass unnoticed the dozens—yes, scores—of men who insult women openly. Are women—the sisters, wives and mothers of New York's best citizens—to be left unprotected, while the men are hedged around and protected from the advances of designing women? It seems to me that it is a pretty weak-boned man who cannot take care of himself. Women, not men, need protection." She added that as the police seemed to care so little about making an organized effort to rid the streets of the mashers, "we women propose to take the matter in hand." At that moment the group was said to be being organized, but no details were given. This woman doctor thought the plan of the putative organization would involve sending some of "the strong-nerved women" in the group out on the streets, followed by a policeman or detective in plain clothes. "The first man who speaks to them, the policeman will arrest. She was of the opinion that a few expeditions of that sort would lead to the arrest of men in the "best social and financial circles. It would be a revelation to New Yorkers to know who these insulters are." When NYPD Captain Pickett was asked about the proposed crusade, he expressed support: "There is nothing that would give me more pleasure than to see such a thing undertaken." That was because "there is one great hindrance to our work in that line at the present time. This is the dread women have of appearing in a police station or, worse still, in a police court, as complainants."[1]

A letter to the editor of a Los Angeles newspaper in 1896 told of the mashers then infesting Eastlake Park in that city, describing one of them in particular as "the beast in human form that exposed his person to ladies in the park." He had managed to escape from a man with a shotgun. The letter writer warned that all mashers should give Eastlake Park a wide berth because "those living in the vicinity of the park are resolved to take the matter in their own hands inasmuch as they cannot get a watchman appointed to guard the property of the city and keep it clear of the denizens of the dives." Mashers were further warned not to be found in the park, and if they disregarded the warning they would be roughly dealt with. "Since the citizens in the neighborhood of the park are denied protection from the city, they will protect their families from insult by monstrosities, by meting out summary punishment to the offenders."[2]

In Gloucester City, New Jersey, in October 1902 it was reported that the girls employed at the Welsbach Light Works in that city had banded together to "trounce" the crowd of mashers who assembled on the street corners when the women worked until 10 p.m. "and pass insulting remarks as they return home. These young mashers are mostly from other cities." With respect to those women, it was also stated, "They have notified the police and say if the habit is not stopped they will take the matter in their hands."[3]

A report in April 1903 remarked that the masher nuisance in Brooklyn was to be suppressed, if possible, by the organization then being formed by Harry Dyruff, a real estate agent in the city. According to the article, "The police appear to be powerless to stop the annoyance of women by loafers on the streets and on the trolley cars and L trains." Dyruff's society had not then been named, but it was to be composed of 100 representative citizens of Brooklyn, all of whom were to be regularly sworn deputy sheriffs "empowered to make arrests only of men annoying women." It was said the members of the group would be so chosen that they would represent every part of Brooklyn. Dyruff has already been sworn in and had received his deputy sheriff's badge from Sheriff Melody, who was in full accord with the movement and its goals. The full compliment of 100 members was to be recruited within a "short time." According to Dyruff and other observers, the practice of annoying women had grown to be an intolerable nuisance in the borough of Brooklyn. The difficulty in controlling that class had been that modest women dreaded the notoriety that accompanied a trip to the police station or an appearance in court to prosecute men who had forced their attentions on them. This new society for the suppression of mashers was to eliminate that difficulty because the member of the society who made the arrest would be the one to attend to the court prosecution. Said Dyruff, "A few arrests, followed by sentences of fine or imprisonment, or both, will, I believe, go a long way toward driving this despicable class of persons from our streets and public conveyances."[4]

Several months later the above cited group was profiled again in the press. Dyruff was president of the Law and Order League, as of August 1903, and the members of which, having been duly appointed deputy sheriffs, and "equipped with badges, revolvers, billies and handcuffs, have been on the warpath for 2 weeks in an attempt to stop mashing and the gross insulting of women" on Coney Island cars. The group had a dramatic incident to report. It took place on an elevated train from Coney Island, at the foot of the elevated railroad stairs at the Union Street station at 3 a.m. on the morning of August 16. Present were Dyruff and four other members of his league, all wearing special deputy badges and "armed to the teeth." The other principals in the drama were six well-dressed and respectable looking young men, and two young women "said to be of good families." It started with a car on a crowded train bringing back a group of pleasure seekers from the shore over the Fifth Avenue line. Edward Hughes and Carl Holsten, members of the League, on duty, watched the "undignified and noisy conduct of the 6 men" who were taking liberties with the two young women in their group. A woman across the aisle remonstrated with one of the men for his conduct and language, and received an insulting reply. Special Deputy Sheriff Hughes stepped up, threw back his coat to show his badge, and warned the young man to stop. His efforts were met with derision. One of the other men of the six suggested it wouldn't be much trouble to take his badge and throw him off the train. When the train stopped at the Third Street station Dyruff and Special Deputy Sheriffs Theodore Hale and Frank Marshall entered the car. Hughes reported to his chief and a course of action was laid out. When the train arrived at the Union Street station the party of revelers got off, as did all the special deputies. At the bottom of the stairs Hughes and Holsten each grabbed one of the men (the ones who used the most insulting language) and declared them under arrest. The detainees took it as a joke. The other deputies showed their weapons. The other men in the group, not then detained, all ran off. The remaining two were said to have dropped to their knees and begged for mercy, claiming they meant no harm. After several minutes and a "sharp lecture" from Dyruff, the two remaining men were released. President Dyruff said that the various squads of special deputy sheriffs who were on duty on the Coney Island cars early on that same morning had administered in total 23 rebukes and warnings, although no arrests were made. He felt the "moral effect of the work being done is marked, and that there is less insulting language on the cars than formerly. The public understands that the league means business, and now it is seldom necessary to do more than warn offenders in order to quiet them."[5]

A couple of months after the above cited event, a newspaper editor discussed the Dyruff society. He remarked first that "every now and then some city makes a spasmodic effort to suppress the masher, but the objectionable creature, like the potato bug and the coddling moth, appears to survive all attempts at his eradication, and lives on in all his insolent effrontery." He then declared that Brooklyn was attacking the problem with new vigor, citing at length the Coney Island drama. Said the newsman, "There is a field for the operation of such a society in many other cities than Brooklyn, for the masher is a pest that is prevalent almost universally. These curs who insult women are not confined to any locality." And the masher would be very leery of plying "his detestable practices if he were assured that the particular form of punishment which his offense deserves were likely to be meted out to him."[6]

In Denver in October 1903 a news story reported that a crusade against mashing in the streets, and the more serious offenses to which young women were subjected in the offices in which they were employed, had been taken up by the Business Women's Club of Denver. It planned to push to the limit to achieve public prosecution and legal punishment for offenders, and every case of which the business women learned would be brought to the open courts, it was said.[7]

Miss Fannie M. Hardin, president of the Business Women's Club and editor of the *Business Women's Magazine* in Denver, declared, "There is to be no abatement of vigilance until we have located and exposed the business man who, in the despicable role of masher, insulted the wife of an honest citizen recently on the public streets." She said they would have women detectives appointed who would go about the streets in plainclothes and who would be chosen "from the most handsome and striking looking young ladies employed in the various stores." Hardin added they would also have some detectives among the stenographers, "and it will not hereafter be safe for any old hoary-headed sinner to offer his blandishments to the pretty girl who pounds the machine." Her group, she said, had inquiries from business women's clubs of Chicago, Milwaukee, and other cities asking how the Hardin group worked, "with a view to establishing the same sort of masher-catching bureau in their several cities." It was clear that the Hardin group planned to go after the sexual harassment of women in the streets and other public places, but also to try and tackle sexual harassment in the offices and other places of employment.[8]

An article later in November named Louisa Lee Hardin, president of the Denver Business Women's Club, and gave a little more detail of the group's ideas. The plan consisted first of a patrol of city streets by a score of young women who would keep an eye out for the street masher; when one was found he would be reported to the nearest policeman. In addition, Hardin planned to organize the young women in shops and offices on a mutual protection plan. "In this way when a girl has a complaint against her employer she can rely on the assistance of many of her fellow employees to prove her charges." It was said that details were still being worked out, and the group was expected to be fully operational before Christmas of that year.[9]

With respect to the sexual harassment of office workers, Hardin said, "No one woman will have to confront her employer in court, to be browbeaten and intimidated by lawyers and retire wilting under the abuse heaped upon her. She will have several witnesses of her own sex to substantiate her charges."[10]

An article on the Denver women that was published on Christmas day, 1903, observed that the young women of that city had formed an organization for the suppression of the masher. "These women have suffered long and patiently from the annoyances put upon them and following them on the streets. Arapahoe street, one of the principal thoroughfares of the city, has become a terror to the pretty girl when out shopping, and even the fashionable district on Capital Hill has not been free from the presence of male flirts." According to this piece the police were appealed to but failed to respond, as it was next to impossible to obtain the kind of evidence that would stand up in court. The victims were ready enough to complain "while burning under the immediate effects of the insult, but in nine cases out of ten no policeman was in sight and the man escaped." Even when the arrests were made, the female complainants failed to appear in court the next day. So a dozen young women decided to take matters into their own hands and make an organized effort to stamp out the nuisance. Hardin was the leader who came forward with the plan, with men being entirely left out of it—except for the policeman to make any necessary arrests. With respect to the proposed street patrols, wherever possible those women were to work in pairs (for evidence). They did not necessarily walk together in pairs, but they remained close enough to each other on the street for evidence corroboration. As to solving the problem of a policeman never being around when he was needed, these pairs of women were to enlist the aid of an officer beforehand so he would be nearby when the women were patrolling. Many volunteers for the group came forward, it was said. Hardin selected Miss Sheridan and Miss Athison as her chief aides, and, with other volunteers, the street patrols were started. According to the reporter, "Several arrests were made, and so overwhelming was the evidence against the prisoners that convictions were obtained in every case." Also mentioned was

Hardin's idea for workplace monitoring, but it was noted only in the vaguest of terms, and nothing along those lines seemed to have been organized.[11]

Somewhat of a "sensation" was caused in Norfolk, Virginia, in November 1903 when a number of girls employed in various shops in the city publicly appealed as a group to Mayor Riddick to protect them from mashers. Those mashers, said the women, congregated on the street corners and made comments on the appearances of the girls as they went home from work, "and often offer gross insult." In concluding their plea, the women said to Riddick, "My Lord, is there no protection for young girls who have to work for their living? For God's sake, save us from these men."[12]

A "war of extermination" on the masher was declared in October 1904 in Chicago by the State Street department and dry goods stores, according to a reporter. "The insults offered to respectable women, who come downtown on shopping trips have become so frequent and so gross, that the merchants have been forced to act in the absence of any willingness on the part of the police, to rid the street of the pests who ogle women at every turn," wrote the journalist. No specific details were provided, except that an invitation was to be extended to the proprietors of the leading downtown stores, especially those on State Street, to join in a systematic crusade for the protection of their women customers.[13]

Several prominent young women in Joplin, Missouri, it was reported in March 1905, were forming themselves into a club to protect themselves from mashers, "with which the town in overrun." The club was to have no name, and as the members were preparing to violate a city ordinance, they were trying to keep the whole affair a secret. That is, they intended to carry pistols when out at night unattended. The idea had come to the unnamed women after a recent incident in which a clerk going home on a Saturday night from work was forced to flee from a masher who followed her and accosted her with insulting remarks. Since then, several more such incidents occurred, and these women in Joplin were determined such things were to stop. Their club was said to be composed of females employed in stores, businesses, telephone offices, and other places, which were forced to be out late at night unescorted.[14]

Some of the best known and "most reputable" young men in Louisville, Kentucky, had reportedly formed a society for the promotion of chivalry and the smashing of mashers, in August 1905. For a long time the major streets of the city had been infested by mashers, said the account, "who have made life wretched for not only shop girls in particular but for all unattended women generally." Joseph D. Bradburn was the head of the movement to suppress the mashers, and the unwritten rule of his group was to beat up the mashers when they were caught, and then to have them prosecuted in court. It was said that in three recent cases in Louisville that was exactly what happened, with three mashers beaten up but no arrests made. All three of the beaten mashers were said to have declined to prosecute anyone. Bradburn, secretary of the Louisville Federation of Labor, said he had spoken with several young men before beginning his organization, and that each one had expressed a willingness to become a member. He stated, "There are various ways in which the club can operate, but I believe the most effective way would be to do a little judicious punching at places where the law does not reach."[15]

To rid the public parks in Minneapolis of loafers and mashers, and to make them safe and attractive to all people, was the purpose of a campaign started on a Sunday in June 1906 by the Reverend G. L. Morrill. After announcing his plan from the pulpit, he took his plan personally to Minneapolis Mayor David P. Jones. He thought that mashers discovered in the parks should be horsewhipped, while other miscreants, such as loafers, should be arrested. Just days before Morrill made his plea to Jones, it was said, the police and park officials in that city had discussed that very matter of mashers in the parks. Supposedly, the solution they had arrived at was to launch their own vigorous campaign during the summer months by stationing more regular police in the parks on Sundays, the busiest day of the week in those facilities, to help the understaffed park police. Morrill lived opposite one of the city parks and had, he told the mayor, "heard young women addressed in coarse, insulting language by members of tough gangs, or ogled at and stared out of countenance by mashers."[16]

Mashers would be jailed in Seattle, Washington, in the future if the April 1908 request by a delegation from the Humane Society was granted. Dr. Mary B. Martin, Mrs. Harry S. Stuff, and Mrs. Frederick Kruger called on Mayor Miller with an urgent request that Acting Police Chief Ward be directed to appoint two plainclothes men to wage war on mashers. Miller agreed with the delegation that mashers had to be suppressed. He said he would confer with Ward to achieve that result.[17]

The Roosevelt Club, an organization that had been active in former political campaigns in Minneapolis, was reorganized in this city as of August 1908. But it was not restructured for politics; rather, its members were pledged to "curb an epidemic of mashing which is on here, and they will, incidentally, beat up the captured mashers." In their former political activities, the Roosevelt Club men became proficient in taking women's part in amateur theatricals, it was reported. Now they were planning to put those skills to use by parading the streets in women's clothing at night, and would arrest and apply their "big stick" treatment to all mashers who approached them. Minneapolis Mayor Haynes was reported to have given his okay to the plan.[18]

Citizens of South Oak Park in Chicago organized a vigilance committee in September 1908 to put an end to the "terrorizing" of women and children by mashers and peeping Toms. Nine "prominent" members of the suburb, incensed by insults received by family members, volunteered to do police duty and walk beats in their neighborhood until the mashers and peeping Toms were driven from the community. They applied for badges and for the authority to make arrests. These were secured from J. E. Tristam, clerk of the village, and members of the vigilance committee went on duty for the first time in the middle of September. Those men were also provided with revolvers and flashlights, and were instructed to "shoot if necessary."[19]

It was reported in May 1909 that mashers were to be banished from State Street in Chicago. Shop girls in that area had organized the Anti-Mashers' Association, and they planned to "wage war on the street corner pests." Police Chief Shippy, in response to pressure from these women, had approved the appointment of a mashers' squad (from within the police) for State Street and the Loop district.[20]

Around the same time, young women of Covington Street in Youngstown, Ohio, had been patrolling that area for several nights in men's clothing in order to chastise a masher who had been insulting women in the area recently. The women planned to catch the man alone and give him what they believed he deserved. The police had been notified of this activity by the women, and a reporter observed, "It is not likely the young women will be permitted to carry out their plans without trouble." One of the women involved declared, "It is not a case where notoriety in police court would satisfy," and for that reason they wanted to take the law into their own hands.[21]

So incensed were the people of Richmond, Virginia, in February 1911 at what they perceived as Mayor Richardson's refusal to take appropriate actions to protect women from mashers that citizens had appealed to the police commission.[22]

Canes and whistles as protection against mashers were to be carried in Boston by members of the Women's Homestead Association, it was reported in the summer of 1913. The whistles were to be used to attract attention. The mayor's secretary informed the association that no law would be violated so long as the whistles were not blown, but the women declared they would blow them just as hard as they possibly could, and if any of their members were arrested for disturbing the peace the association would pay any resultant fine.[23]

One of the organizers of that Boston group was Mrs. Annie Ray, and in August 1913 she declared, "This thing has gone far enough—this masher business. The masher has got to go." Ray was at the head of a "police force" of five women, organized by the Women's Homestead Association to drive the masher off the street. The group has issued a bulletin advising every woman who was out after dark to carry a whistle. "If a man speaks to you," suggested the bulletin, "blow girls, blow, and one of the women police will be near to help you." Those five women carried canes and whistles. They had no official standing but were paid for their services by the Women's Homestead Association.[24]

Mrs. George Howe, niece by marriage of President Woodrow Wilson, followed up her action in New York City of October 20, 1914, when she had a masher sentenced to 10 days in jail, by declaring war on all Broadway mashers. Howe made her announcement on October 21 that her patience was at an end, and that in the future she would call a policeman every time one of the "Broadway battalion" of mashers spoke to her. She remarked to a reporter, "Just think. I have been in New York three years, studying elocution, and in that time I have been annoyed by no fewer than 500 mashers." With respect to the incident on the evening of October 20, she said, "I had that man arrested because I had promised [my husband] Dr. Howe to call a policeman the next time I was accosted on the street." Howe added, "I am a member of the Woman Suffrage party and the Political Equality League, and I shall try to get all my fellow members to join with me in correcting this mashing evil. And the women in these two organizations can tell you some amazing stories of the way women are annoyed on the streets of New York, particularly on Broadway." Mrs. Howe's husband, George, was a university professor and a nephew of Wilson. The masher she had prosecuted was Dr. Ernest C. White.[25] Dr. White began his 10-day sentence in the Workhouse on October 20. He was assigned to kitchen duty, and his first task was mashing potatoes for the prisoners' noon meal. Mrs. Howe came to New York City some three years earlier to try and embark on a stage career.[26]

Well known reporter Marguerite Mooers Marshall also discussed the matter at length. When Howe was walking home alone, the masher spoke to her on Broadway near 25th Street. Howe pointedly ignored him. It was only when he tried to follow her that she called a policeman and had the man arrested. In Night Court, Magistrate Breen convicted Dr. White and sentenced him to 10 days in the workhouse.

Marshall then spoke to Magistrate John J. Freschi, who gave the reporter the following advice as to how women could accomplish much in banishing the pest from the street:

> First, any woman who has to be out alone in the evening should dress quietly and strive to make her general appearance refined and inconspicuous. Secondly, if a man attempts to address her, she should promptly discourage him by glance, words and even action, if necessary. And finally, if a man persists in annoying a woman, after she has plainly shown him that she is annoyed, she should not hesitate to call an officer and press her charge in court.

Freschi added that in a city the size of New York many respectable women were compelled to go out in the evening without an escort. "It simply is not fair that they should be subjected to insult which they do not invite, subjected

This sketch from 1914 gives women a few hints about what not to do. That is, it illustrates some of the behavior patterns that would make females more vulnerable to the attentions of mashers. Don't loiter, discourage the masher, and don't be afraid to call a policeman.

to it even after severe discouragement on their part." With regard to those women not quite respectable, Freschi declared, "Even a woman who hasn't been all she might have been in the past has a right to walk our streets without molestation if it can be proved that she is going along quietly and minding her own business."[27]

All the publicity that was attracted by the Howe case caused a reporter in Washington, D.C., to ask Judge Alexander R. Mullowny of the District Police Court in that city about the prevalence of mashers in the nation's capital.

He said he did not have one such case a month, "and the offense in most cases has been committed while the man was under the influence of alcohol. I shall say that Washington is particularly free from any such types as the persistent masher ... the boldness which is required to approach and insult a woman in the street doesn't seem to be very prevalent in Washington from the infrequency with which I was called upon to hear cases of that kind." Mullowny declared, "If a woman avoids extremes of dress and discourages advances, she can always take care of herself in Washington. If the insult is so persistent as to require her to slap the masher's face and call a policeman, she should not hesitate to press the case in the Police Court."[28]

Mrs. Gertrude Gardner Eggleston, a civic worker and Suffragist in New York City, was out to eliminate mashing on the streetcars. She had long been planning such a crusade, but on January 25, 1916, she had her first opportunity to put that plan into action. She caused the arrest of Charles Roig on a charge of disorderly conduct after he had insulted her on a Ninth Avenue streetcar. Roig was fined $5 in the Men's Night Court. She explained that she was going to the streetcar companies that day to see what she could do to make riding the cars less dangerous for women. She meant to ask officers of these transit companies what they were prepared to do to bring about such a result. Eggleston said she also planned to ask city officials to help her organize what she termed a women's vigilance committee, each member of which would wear a small badge vesting her with the authority to arrest all men "who persist in displaying everything but graciousness to the women they encounter on street cars." In conclusion, Eggleston said, "I had been putting up with so many insults on the Ninth Avenue line, which is the most convenient for me, that I decided to act. This man I had arrested was only one of the many I have seen in the last few weeks, although his offense was the most glaring." She was a member of the Women's Political Union.[29]

On the first day of 1917 the Waldorf-Astoria Hotel in New York City announced that it was going to undertake to protect its female patrons from mashers by

This 1916 sketch shows a man sitting on one of the bench seats on an L car, edging closer and closer to a woman. That was a favorite method of attack by a harasser.

adding a corps of young and pretty women to its secret service staff to watch for mashers. Hereafter, Peacock Alley (a restaurant at the hotel), the new roof garden, and the skating rink would have a number of circulating women in the pay of the hotel to draw mashers. When one of these women was mashed she was expected to call one of the hotel's male detectives and have the man evicted from the hotel. Joseph Smith, superintendent of service at the Waldorf, refused to reveal the number of these women to be employed but did say they would range in age from 18 to 22. A. S. Crockett, an official with the hotel, told a reporter that at the present time the hotels of New York City were "infested" with the problem of mashers. He speculated it may have been due to many mashers having left Europe because of World War I and resettling in America, especially New York. The Waldorf-Astoria decided the only way it could tackle the masher problem was by using women.[30]

A crusade against cinema mashers was being urged on District authorities in Washington in the fall of 1920 by clubwomen and civic workers of that city. It was said that increasing numbers of complaints were being received from females being accosted and mashed in the D.C. cinemas. Said Mrs. Francis St. Clair, state regent of the District D.A.R., "The menace of the moving picture masher must be wiped out. The motion pictures are one of the nation's greatest educational agencies. They must be kept clean so they can serve their great purpose of uplift and progress." Mrs. George Barnett, clubwoman, noted that perhaps 90 percent of the girls and women of the United States went to the movies at regular intervals for recreation, and, "It is preposterous that any man or gangs of men should be allowed to offend the proprieties and decencies of the movies." Mrs. Howard L. Hodgkins, president of the District Federation of Women's Clubs, said, "What's the matter with the women police. They should supervise the behavior of patrons of motion picture houses as far as possible. A chaperon should be stationed in every motion picture house, whose duty would be to afford protection to the women and to prevent untoward incidents."[31]

On the evening of August 13, 1921, Mrs. Eleanor De Hart was in Night Court in New York City as the complainant in a mashing allegation against Joseph Zanarelli. She said she was walking through Central Park when Zanarelli followed her and tried to force his attentions on her. A policeman was summoned, and a charge of disorderly conduct was laid against him. He pled guilty in court and was sentenced to one day in the Workhouse. His sentence was lightened, reportedly, because of his war record. Magistrate Silberman said he thought he had seen De Hart in court as the complainant in similar cases in the past, and she admitted to him that she had been responsible for the arraignment of eight other mashers in recent years, with a conviction being registered in each of those cases. Silberman complimented her.[32]

Using Jiu Jitsu on Time and Mashers,
Mrs. De Hart Tells How to Master Pests
In Three-Minute Hot Weather Interview

MRS ELENA DE HART

A 1916 photograph of Eleanor De Hart, a woman described by the press as being on a one-woman crusade against mashers, any mashers and all mashers.

Eleanor De Hart was 30 years old, and her mission in life, it was reported, was to go after mashers. She declared war on mashers some five years earlier when her husband died. She had frequently been a victim of oglers, and, said the reporter, "She deliberately stalks her prey. Armed with a rubber-handled billy, she frequents the parks and when the masher sidles up to her and begins his tactics she swings on him with the warclub, with fists, teeth and claws." Said De Hart, "Every masher has a yellow streak. Any woman or girl will find it easy to whip these human skunks if she just sails into them. I rather enjoy my crusade. I always get them." This somewhat sensationalized account said she had beaten Zanarelli the other day, while other accounts mentioned no such event.[33]

A couple of days later the same sensationalizing newspaper ran a supposed interview with De Hart. According to the subhead, she was the "women who has laid low 40 or 50 so-called men...." According to this article, De Hart could not remember if the last masher she caught (Zanarelli) was her 40th or 50th harasser. When Zanarelli accosted her she did not have her club but used jiu-jitsu moves on him before the policeman arrived. With respect to the conversation she had in court with Magistrate Silberman, it was reported herein that "she admitted that she had arraigned many other flirters recently and obtained a conviction in each case." That was not true, but by leaving the number unspecified it allowed the newspaper to use the fiction of 40 or 50 mashers arraigned. The truth was that she had told Silberman she had caused the arraignment of eight others, plus Zanarelli (which, of course, would not have allowed this newspaper account to pretend the number was 40 to 50). De Hart was said to have told the reporter, "I am simply disgusted with these men who go about the city trying to force themselves upon women of all ages, young and old." Prior to this article, no mention had been made anywhere about De Hart using jiu-jitsu moves.[34]

"Jail the flirt" was to be the slogan of the Anti-Flirt Association, which was organized and launched at the Hotel Biltmore in New York City on November 20, 1922, to prosecute a campaign against the masher. The five male organizers claimed the streets, especially in the theatrical districts, were unsafe, from approaches and insults, for women. The association planned, through publicity, to educate public opinion to the point where a woman would consider it to be her duty to prosecute the mashers. The five organizers were Samuel Fenton, Richard Lindley, Wade Trumble, George Carroll, and James Madison.[35]

A couple of days later it was announced that a lizard pierced by a hatpin would be the logo adopted by the Anti-Flirt Association at its meeting in the Hotel Biltmore. That design was to be placed on buttons to be distributed to members and any persons willing to ally themselves with the group in the fight against the masher. The lizard was said to represent the common street variety of masher and would be depicted pinned to the ground and writhing, pierced by a hatpin wielded by an anti-flirt crusader.[36]

James Madison, described as the leader of the Anti-Flirt group, wanted an organization that had branches in every city in America and

A 1923 photograph of Alice Reighly, president of the Anti-Flirt Club in Washington, D.C.

This photograph from 1923 shows a member of the Anti-Flirt Club in Washington out on the street distributing information about anti-flirt week, which started on March 5 that year.

that would make all city streets in the United States safe for women. The group was to have no fees or dues, and was looking only for the "moral support of the whole American public."[37]

An editorial on the Anti-Flirt group declared:

> It is a movement which should be sponsored by decent people everywhere. It is natural for a nice woman to dread the publicity attendant upon bringing the offender to justice, but she should not hesitate. She is protecting herself and her sex when she aids in prosecuting the masher and will be admired rather than criticized for her courage. When she takes no step against him she leaves him free to annoy some person perhaps more defenseless than herself.[38]

At the end of February 1928 in Washington, D.C., it was announced that Washington's vast army of young women (mostly government workers) were about to combine in a general movement "against the cake eaters and curb-hounds who fairly choke the downtown streets just after the government work-

A 1923 photograph of the charter members of the Anti-Flirt Club in Washington, of which Reighly was the president.

ers get out of office at 4:30 p.m." The nucleus of the Anti-Flirt Club, as it was to be called, was said to have already been organized by that point and was ready to set out to rid the city of the male pest. (Cake eater was a 1920s slang term indicating a slick young Romeo, someone of the upper classes, a companion to the flapper.[39])

Former United States congressman Manuel Herrick (from Oklahoma—nicknamed the "Okie Jesus Congressman") addressed a meeting of the Anti-Flirt Club in Washington on March 5, 1923. He said, "When I read of your noble work of putting down the mashers I could not resist coming out here to talk to you...." On that same day at 12 noon, and from 3 to 5 p.m., the members of the organization inaugurated anti-flirt week by parading down F Street in Washington, pinning anti-flirt week buttons on all passersby. Young girls, middle-aged women, young men, and dignified businessmen were all invited to join the group.[40]

When he addressed the Anti-Flirt Club, Herrick declared, "I am a man who has never stepped from the straight and narrow path. I may be a nut, but I am a hard one to crack." The club's slogan was "We are out to get the mashers." Herrick had just retired after one term in Congress. He told the women that their fight was a high and noble one, and that it should be aided and abetted and commended.[41]

A week or so later a newspaper piece claimed that the whole Anti-Flirt Club business had been a publicity stunt for a film called *The Flirt* that had been orchestrated by Miss H. R. Merrill, the public relations person for a film company. "And now though the club still exists, [we] will get no action at all while the papers are attempting to recover from their embarrassment." There *was* a film by that title released in the United States some two months before the club was formed. The Anti-Flirt Club was not heard from again, but then most such groups (even when legitimate and well intentioned) suffered the same fate.[42]

14

The Police, Actions
and Reactions

A reporter with the *San Francisco Call* asked Police Officer Pat Mahoney in February 1893 about his dislike for mashers. Said Mahoney:

> I hate that kind of an animal so badly that I can't keep quiet when I'm near one. They didn't know that when I first went on this beat, and that's the reason they gave me so much trouble. But it's different now. There isn't a Market Street masher but knows me. He knows how I love his kind, and he has learned to lay low accordingly. They used to stand around on the street corners and insult every well-dressed woman who passed them. They don't do that any more; not on my beat.

Mahoney went on to elaborate on how he felt about mashers. "Well, I'd rather eat out of the same dish with a yellow dog than even have to see one of them. Thieves and garroters are gentlemen compared to mashers." He said the police had succeeded in breaking up most of the street corner congregations, and, while not completely eliminated, "they don't congregate any more and make the street absolutely impassable for modest women like they did a few years ago."[1]

That reporter also spoke to San Francisco Police Chief Crowley who confirmed his officer's reputation by stating, "They call Mahoney the terror of mashers, and I guess he deserves it." He did admit that "there are lots of that kind of animal left in the city, but we manage to keep them pretty quiet, I think…. We're not going to have the women of this city insulted if we can help it, and the police think they can." When asked how his force proceeded against mashers, Crowley said they arrested them on the charge of vagrancy. "There ought to be a law covering the case, but since there is none we find the vagrancy law pretty efficacious in most cases." He mentioned specifically the Miller case in which they drove a masher by that name off Kearney Street. "He made a regular business of standing about on the street corners and at the cigar-stands to insult women as they passed. We convicted him of vagrancy. He appealed to the higher courts and finally beat us; we worried him so much that he had to get out." Crowley admitted that if a man really had a home to go to, and some friends to come down and swear for him in court, the police could not make a vagrancy charge stick. "But we can keep on arresting him on appearances, and he soon gets tired of spending an occasional night in the City Prison." Again Crowley grumbled, "There ought to be some kind of a law that would distinctly cover the offense of insulting women. There are not greater nuisances in the city than those half-witted cattle who parade around in good clothes and do nothing but ogle women. And there's plenty of them who do that."[2]

Several years later, in July 1897, in New York City, it was reported that NYPD Captain Chapmen's men had turned their attention to what was called a "new nuisance" on Friday nights—the mashers of Broadway—and that two of that group had received their justice in Jefferson Market Court on July 31. When Magistrate Meade sat in Jefferson Market Court some weeks earlier, he first called attention to the loafer who insulted women on the street and in streetcars, and told Chapmen and his "woman hunters" (that is, officers after prostitutes) to use a part of their energies in bringing the masher class of men into court instead of expending it all in the rounding up of "unfortunate women." Magistrate Pool said much the same thing toward the end of July. Louis P. Singleton was arrested at Broadway and 26th Street on the last Friday night in July after a woman had complained to Officer Winters that Singleton was annoying her. He spoke to her and the women she was with "without being encouraged to do so," and when he persisted in forcing his attentions on them the pair complained. The complainant was Grace Roe, but she failed to appear and the case proceeded on the testimony of Winters. When Singleton was reluctant to state who he worked for, arguing it would do him great harm, Magistrate Pool said, "Not more harm than it does the hundreds of women who have been arraigned here for accosting men, and often without evidence." When Pool asked Singleton why he had spoken to the two women, the accused said he had probably drunk too much wine earlier in the evening. Said Pool, "You fellows are worse than the women of the streets, and no respectable woman is safe from you. I'll fine you $10, and I regret that I cannot make your punishment more severe." Singleton paid his fine and hurriedly left the courtroom. Policeman Leazenbee, whose actions, said a reporter, "in arresting women indiscriminately [for soliciting] became so notorious that Chapmen made him don a uniform and do patrol duty," had the other masher in charge. That prisoner said his name was Charles Johnson, but he refused to give his address. Leazenbee testified he saw the man accost four women (separately and at different times) on 34th Street on that Friday evening, and when he ordered him to cease, Johnson abused him verbally. He said the prisoner had been arraigned several weeks earlier for a similar offence and had been allowed to go with only a warning. Pool fined him $10 and said to the policeman, "I'm glad to see that you have let up on the women and are trying to rid the streets of these loafers." Johnson could not pay his fine and was locked up. When Singleton appeared, he finally told the court that he worked for a real estate firm, Frederick Southack and Company. It was learned, however, that Singleton was not known at the home address he had given police, nor was anyone by that name, or who answered to Singleton's description, known at the Southack firm.[3]

A girl aged about 15 was standing on a corner of East Broadway in New York City on the evening of December 20, 1897, when a well-dressed man came along, stopped, and began to ogle her. The girl walked a block away. He followed. The girl then walked to another street. He followed. She hailed a policeman and told him about the man. The masher slunk out of sight, only to reappear after the officer had apparently passed on. However, the officer had kept his eyes open and saw the masher re-emerge and start to follow the young girl again. The policeman dragged the masher away, threw him down in the mud and the slush, knocked him about, ripped his clothes, and finished up by kicking the masher hard. Said the officer, "There, he's been fined for disorderly conduct like this before. We'll see what corporal punishment will do for him."[4]

Mashers were to be eliminated from Troost Park in Kansas City, Missouri. Beginning on the first Sunday in July 1899, three additional policemen would be placed on duty at the popular park, and the men who ogled women would fare badly. The police had had trouble with mashers at Troost Park the previous summer, and Police Chief Hayes intended that it not continue in the summer of 1899. Half a dozen officers would be at the park on Sundays and at all other times when there were extra attractions that would draw large crowds to the park.[5]

An editorial in August 1899 explained that Pittsburgh was after the masher. It was said the police had received orders to drive him out of the city. "His smirks and his grimaces and insulting remarks to ladies on the street and in their presence are to be banished, and it is well." The editor added that smaller places than Pittsburgh suffer from this "animal," and "there are a few such animals in this place. Ostracize them."[6]

According to a July 1901 news account, the men who made a business of ogling women on the streets of Denver were not to be treated with any consideration by the police, "owing to the injecting of politics into the regulation of city affairs. The mayor has sided with the mashers who were recently arrested, and the women have been holding indignation meetings to express themselves." The women were backed by the chief of police and the police magistrate, who acted on all infractions of the city ordinances. It was thought even the federal government could become involved, as two of the "worst cases" of which the women especially complained occurred under the dome of the federal building in that city, "where the police have no authority and where the law provides no punishment for such offenses." A western police officer was said to have been beaten by well-dressed "hoodlums" whom he had detected insulting "decent women by taking liberties with them." He tried to arrest them and, when severely beaten, drew his revolver and succeeded in subduing his attackers. The next day the culprits were released by order of the mayor, "in accordance with a policy that has startled the women and rendered them hopeless of redress. Eight policemen bear evidence of bruises and wounds gained in the defense of women, but with the mayor against them very little can be done." Then the chief of police issued an order to his men that "they should take the law into their own hands and punish the offenders before the public without waiting for the mayor or any other person in authority to inter-fere.... In other words, mashers will be disfigured or branded for life at the first opportunity."

The trouble with mashers in Denver had been growing for some time, said a reporter, "until it is regarded as unsafe for women to venture into the shopping district." The most glaring of the outrages, the account continued, was committed on Sixteenth Street at 2 p.m. when a masher walked up to a woman, a perfect stranger, and, taking her by the arm, urged her to go down a side street. A cop witnessed the incident and arrested "the brute after a strong fight." The culprit was pardoned the next day by the mayor. "Emboldened by this result, the post office crowd renewed their addresses and boldly seized women by various parts of the body. Pardons were forthcoming again." Then Police Chief Armstrong issued his order and was personally congratulated "by one of the largest and most influential delegations of women that ever visited the city hall." The police chief of the city derived his power from the governor of Colorado, similar to the police magistrate, "but as the city jail is under the jurisdiction of the mayor, all efforts to secure jail sentences will be abandoned for the more direct and satisfactory dose of club juice."[7]

If an editorial that appeared on January 1, 1902, was to be believed, Kansas City, Missouri, "has set a commendable example to many other cities by instituting a vigorous and relentless war upon the professional street masher." That creature "is one who makes it his chief business to leer at ladies whom he meets on the sidewalks or at the entrances of theaters and other public places." According to the editor, there was no difficulty in spotting the masher. "He advertises himself by his disgusting boldness and his vulgar display of himself on all occasions. He stares at ladies in a manner that often impels them to invoke police protection. Sometimes he becomes so audacious that he actually pursues and speaks to them." Word had reportedly gone out in Kansas City that the masher must be suppressed. In that effort the police hurry him on when he is found loafing on street corners or hanging about in other favorite haunts. In conclusion, the editor stated, "The entire police force of Kansas City is engaged in a laudable attempt to teach insolent young men that when they appear on the streets or the public gathering places of that city they must have at least the semblance of respectability. It would be an excellent thing if similar instructions were administered in every other city in the land."[8]

With the summer (the height of the mashing season) well underway in 1902 in Washington, D.C., a news story observed that many years earlier the city was

> infested with self-satisfied men, both young and old, who had little to do other than to visit the parks or stroll on the fashionable thoroughfares, bringing all their fascinating powers to bear upon such members of the fair sex as chanced to pass their way. This practice gave the Police Department no end of trouble, as numerous complaints were made by women or girls to whom such attentions were odious. The result was that a crusade against the mashers was inaugurated, and to a large extent he was put out of business.

But not entirely so, as the reporter conceded, admitting that the National Capital still suffered, as did every other large city, from the existence of "this evil." In order to minimize the annoyance, Major Richard Sylvester, Superintendent of Police of the District, a pronounced anti-masher, had reiterated to the members of his force his instructions given long ago that flirting on the streets or about the public places of his city must be prevented. Of course, that had not completely stopped the masher, "but it has resulted in abating the nuisance, and conditions have improved." According to the journalist the police were always watching for mashers and the courts were tough on them. "The man who molests an innocent and inoffensive lady upon the streets of Washington is lucky, indeed, if he stops short of the workhouse." Sylvester said, with respect to the masher, "Washington has greatly improved in reference to the nuisance. There was a time when a lady hardly dared to go upon the streets of this city after dark, but now such is not the case. I do not mean to say the city is rid of the masher. He is still here, but is more guarded in his operations and is careful in the matter of selecting places where he may carry on his beloved practice." The police have instructions, Sylvester continued, to move people along who congregate on street corners, but with orders to use discretion, as some men may have a legitimate reason for waiting on a corner. He also said the situation in the public parks had improved, but admitted, "In one of the parks some time ago the masher became so objectionable and offensive that the benches were removed therefrom."[9]

When NYPD Captain Dillon moved from the Tenderloin station to the West 47th Street police station in the spring of 1903 he found the masher pest prevalent to an alarming degree. "They come out on matinee days like cockroaches out of a sink.... I have received lots of complaints and I realize that mashing is a hard thing to regulate, but with a few plain clothes men I am going to make a stagger at it and it will be a successful stagger too."[10]

A determined effort was said to have been launched in Chicago in June 1903 to rid the city of mashers. It was an effort in which the magistrates were said to be united. The reporter observed, "Until recently women showed a disposition to suffer annoyance in silence rather than bring notoriety upon themselves by open protest."[11]

A couple of months later in 1903 the Minister of the Interior in Germany directed the police president to organize special police, in plain clothes, to protect women and girls from the attentions on the streets of Berlin from mashers. "These daylight insults are probably practiced more in Berlin than in another continental city," said an account.[12]

Miss Kundert, secretary of a training college, aided NYPD detectives in arresting a masher who had been annoying girl students in the spring of 1904. Kundert, secretary of the Bible Teachers' Training College, assisted the police by acting as a decoy. Detective Edward Conroy of the NYPD arrested a man who said he was a barber in the Holland House hotel, and locked him up in a cell on a charge of disorderly conduct. That college was at 81–83 East 55th Street, New York City. It had been the custom of the young women studying there to walk in the avenues and streets each pleasant evening for exercise, but recently those walks had been shunned by many of the students because of the annoying attentions of a man. It was his practice to raise his hat or ogle them, and on several occasions he addressed remarks to them. Mrs. Dayton, president of the college, reported the problem to the police. Detective Conroy was dispatched to catch the masher. When Conroy told Dayton he would like to have one or two students to act as decoys, they all declined the duty. It fell to Kundert to act as decoy. At 8 p.m. one evening she went out for a walk. The masher approached her and not only raised his hat to her, he also spoke to her, asking if he could walk with her. At that point Conroy appeared and arrested the man. He said he was Ludwig Grotel, 29. When arraigned before Magistrate Crane in the Yorkville Court he said that he made a mistake, it being a dark place. He said he was on his way to see his girlfriend and mistook Kundert for her. Crane fined him $10 and added that if he repeated the offense he would receive a prison sentence.[13]

A report in a Salt Lake City newspaper on May 14, 1904, observed that mashing season had begun. It reported that a number of complaints had been received by the police of men making "goo-goo eyes" at women. Every police officer had been instructed to be on the lookout for mashers. Most complaints had been made regarding the number of young men standing on Main Street. The greatest concentration of them was said to be at the intersection of Main and Second Street South. "Around some of the corners they are getting thick as flies, but when they see an officer they are as quiet as lambs," said one policeman. "You can always tell a masher by the color of his socks and his general make-up. He wears clothes like a race horse tout, carries a dinky cane and has the smooth way of a con man. As soon as the warm weather sets in they infest the streets, but not this year. They will receive a cold reception this year from the police."[14]

It was reported in September 1905 that "Curbstone Johnnies" and mashers on Seventh Street along Pennsylvania Avenue in Washington, D.C., who had been "a great source of annoyance to the police and respectable persons," got a jolt the other night. All of the reserves and all of section B of the First precinct—in all, about 25 police officers—marched upon the area with strict orders to clear the streets of such persons and anyone found loafing on the corners or sidewalks. That crusade was the result of many complaints that had been sent to the commissioners and to Major Sylvester from persons claiming they or their wives or members of their family had been insulted while walking along the public streets by men who congregated along the downtown sidewalks and corners. "So great was the number of complaints, not only to the police but to the press, that Major Sylvester issued orders for Lieut. Amiss to bring a termination to the nuisance," wrote a journalist. At the 8 p.m. roll call at the First Precinct on September 28, Amiss read the order from Sylvester to the men and further instructed them "to clear the streets and arrest any man caught in the act of ogling or insulting women passing, or any one who refused to keep moving." Amiss said, "Arrest any one, regardless of their station or appearance, whom you think guilty of unlawful assembly." That "little army" of police marched to the area with "drawn clubs." The men then went to work, and in the course of two hours the designated areas were said to have been cleared of congregating males. No arrests were made. Many of those told to "move along" went to the station and complained they had been roughly handled, grossly insulted, and so forth, all to no avail.[15]

An editorial in the *Washington Times* the day after the police action declared that Sylvester was to be congratulated on his move to clear the streets of Washington "of that most disgusting degradation of pseudomanhood, the street masher. There are too many specimens of that type of imbecility apparent on our thoroughfares, and they are so weak in intellect that only the most repressive measures will ever make any impression on them." The editor advised the city to take care not to "mistake respectable persons waiting for the car," or it would bring the efforts of the department into disrepute and contempt. On the other hand, the decent citizen could aid the police by avoiding a display of virtuous indignation in case an officer should improperly request him to move on. In conclusion, the editor stated, "The streets of Washington should be free for any decent woman to walk, day or night, without the likelihood of insult by look or speech from any conceited puppy." Generally he felt those streets were safe, but some sections of the city were so infested by loafers "that it is uncomfortable for the most circumspect woman to run the gantlet of their brazen eyes."[16]

Just one week after the above editorial appeared in Washington, D.C., it was reported that two recent attacks by women upon men who had accosted them on city streets renewed the specter of mashers on the streets. But investigation revealed they were both the result of domestic disputes, not mash attempts. Sylvester commented that those stories would lead one to believe that mashers were realities in Washington when, as a matter of fact, they were "myths." He reiterated, "The police of every district have been ordered time and time again to spare no effort in stamping out mashing on the streets of Washington, and for months there has not been such a case in police court."[17]

A Mrs. Schaeffer was walking down Fourth Street in Minneapolis toward City Hall on September 27, 1905, when John Steele accosted her, attempting to strike up a conversation. She ignored him and kept on walking. He followed. When she stopped near police headquarters, the man stopped and disappeared. She went in and notified officers. They laid a trap. Schaeffer left the police building and continued her walking trip. Sergeant Tom Garvin stationed himself behind a billboard. As expected, Steele followed Schaeffer again, and as he passed the signboard Garvin collared him and locked him up on a charge of disorderly conduct. On September 28 Steele pled guilty in court and was fined $15. Steele said he was a hotel proprietor and was in the city on a visit.[18]

Due to the determination of NYPD Captain McDermott to stop mashing on East 14th Street in New York City, four men spent the night of September 29, 1905, in police cells and appeared the following morning in Yorkville Police Court, arraigned on charges of disorderly conduct. They were arrested by several different detectives who had been sent out by McDermott to bring in any man caught flirting on East 14th Street. Those men arrested were Emanuel Buck, John McCluskey, Harry Lee, and one other. They were arrested separately. In court all denied trying to mash women. McCluskey told Magistrate Wahle that he "didn't have to flirt" because he "got 'em without flirting." Wahle let the quartet off with a reprimand and a warning.[19]

A news story from the nation's capital on October 2, 1905, announced that, yet again, "War against the masher is now on at the Capital. Extra police-men have been detailed to watch fashionable thoroughfares by day and popular districts by night. There is to be no street corner loafing or dallying, but men must keep moving." That particular war came about because a few days earlier a lady in Washington smashed her umbrella over the heads of several men who had followed her about the streets until her patience became exhausted. According to the article, her experience was only what many other women underwent in silence. "Few women have the courage or become so exasperated that they inflict such highly deserved punishment as was given in this case." And, it was reported, "on F Street it is an occupation for some men, and they can be found there during the day hours as easily as the average man in his office.... It is the duty of the police to break up this practice, and they have set about doing it." With respect to the cited umbrella case, "the woman's name was thoroughly paraded in the papers, while they refrained from mentioning the men. It will probably be asking too much of the police to arrest, fine, and publish names."[20]

Two women were hurrying along the street, heading toward homes in Denver on the evening of December 10, 1905. Sergeant Joseph McIntyre of the Denver police department was not far behind (he was moving independently, walking his usual beat). A crowd of young men made remarks as the women passed them. Samuel Mason, a 23-year-old tailor, declared he would make the acquaintance of the women. Mason tipped his hat, followed the women and then made "improper" remarks to them. At that point McIntyre intervened and arrested Mason. Do you know these women, he asked Mason, who said no. Then the officer asked the women if they knew Mason, at which point the frightened women started to cry and said they had never seen him before. Mason then said he had been drinking a little. "Well," replied McIntyre, "I will knock the drink out of you." Then, said the reporter, "he proceeded to clean up the street with Mason." Then he arrested him.[21]

Philadelphia was in the middle of its crusade against mashers in the spring of 1906. Market Street had seen the arrival of the Police Reserve squad in force, in furtherance of the Bureau of Police's determination to rid the streets of annoyances. Forgetting the crusade of several weeks earlier, when scores of arrests were made, the mashers took courage and tried to revive their pastime. Reserve policeman Walsh saw four of them annoying young girls at the Reading Terminal and warned them, but said they kept up their "Hello, Lucy" and "Howd'y Susie" so long that he arrested them. Arraigned before Magistrate Eisenbrown on April 20, they gave their names as A. N. Brown (hotel clerk), C. C. Watts (messenger), John R. Shaw (chauffeur), and Lew Berg (machinist). The policeman declared they were a menace to respectability. The judge agreed, saying, "It's an outrage that this sort of thing is carried on. You have no business about the [train] station unless you are going away. I will let you go this time, but if you are ever brought before me again I shall send you to prison for a term long enough to make you sorry. You are discharged."[22]

Police authorities in Mankato, Minnesota, decided in June 1906 to clamp down in the case of mashers who accosted women in the streets of their community. Recently two of them had been given 90 days in jail with no alternative of a fine, and on June 25 Henry Mallen, 16, was given 10 days in jail for jostling two women he passed in the street one evening. A few days later Chauncey Jones, described as a member of a "prominent family" in Mankato, fell into the sweep against mashers and was accused of insulting three women on the street. His uncle paid his fine of $10 rather than see him go to jail for 30 days.[23]

On January 1, 1907, orders were issued to the police force in Alton, Illinois, by Police Chief Maxwell to shoot all mashers who annoyed women on the streets and attempted to escape arrest. The order followed an unsuccessful attempt by Maxwell to hit a masher at whom he fired. The chief chased him two blocks and, because he failed to obey a command to stop, fired two bullets at him, but both missed the mark. Maxwell then issued the general order and said he hoped his men would prove to be better marksmen than he had been. "Insulting of women on the streets by loafers and mashers must stop," Maxwell declared.[24]

Seven offenders, classed as mashers, were arrested during the first week of October 1907 in Washington, D.C., as a result of the determination on the part of Major Sylvester to break up the practice of loafing about the stage doors and entrances of theaters, and annoying female patrons and female actors. Lieutenant Hartley of the First Precinct said numerous complaints of that nature had been received by the police recently. Of the first five arrests made, three of the offenders forfeited their collateral, and the other two stood trial. Both were convicted and then fined. Said policeman Kleindienst, "It isn't only the youngsters that we have trouble with, for some of the offenders are possessors of patriarchical beards and bald heads, and have arrived at the age when their unsolicited attention to women is particularly offensive."[25]

On the evening of November 18, 1907, in Spokane, Washington, several women complained to the police about the boldness of mashers, who every evening could be found on Riverside where they "leer and insult women." Among the people complained to was Merchants Police Officer Flemming. One frightened woman tearfully told Flemming about some of the remarks made to her, which included, "Where do you room girlie?" "Let us walk home with you," "Bet she uses peroxide," and "Peach, ain't she?" So Flemming stationed himself at the corner of Riverside and Howard and caught two men (in separate incidents) who gave their names as J. A. Flanders and George Otto. Each was allowed to leave the station house after depositing cash bonds of $15 each—supposedly to guarantee they would appear in police court for trial.[26]

Also in November 1907 it was reported that mashers, "cigar store statues," loafers and the like had been ordered off the streets in Oakland, California. In an earlier court case, testimony as to the insults offered women pedestrians led to an order by Chief of Police Wilson to clear the streets "of ogling men and to keep the thoroughfares free from the pestiferous masher." Orders had then been issued by Wilson to all patrolmen to drive those objectionable characters off of the streets.[27]

In furtherance of a crusade to stop loafers and mashers in the vicinity of Seventh Street and Pennsylvania Avenue Northwest in Washington, D.C., 21 arrests were made on a Sunday night in September 1908 between 7 p.m. and 9:30 p.m. Officer Behrens said, "Some of these arrests inflicted a hardship, inasmuch as the prisoners were in no way misbehaving, although all of them were violating the park ordinances by loafing at this place. Some of the prisoners, however, were those who had been making a practice of ogling women and making insulting remarks to passersby, and this practice was what led to the determination to stop loafing in this neighborhood." F Street between 9th and 14th Streets was also to be targeted by police, as they said that every evening between the hours of 4 p.m. and 6 p.m. young men loitered about the corners and made it unpleasant for women who were passing.[28]

The ogling of women students at the University of California, Berkeley, was placed under a ban by Marshal August Vollmer of that city in the spring of 1909, and he had notified his patrolmen to take into custody all flirts and mashers seen on the streets. Flirting, he declared, was taboo. "Oh, you kid," was what Vollmer heard from the lips of Peter Olsen, said to three female university students, from his peddler's wagon on the street. "Oh, girls, have a cherry?" said C. A. Harens, a companion of Olsen. Those three women saw Vollmer, their police chief, and appealed to him for protection. Vollmer quickly took the two men into custody and took them to the police station where they were charged with disturbing the peace. However, the three women had by then disappeared, leaving no names and filing no formal complaint. In view of the fact there was no complaint, the two men were freed from custody with a warning that flirting had been placed under a ban in Berkeley.[29]

Five men were arrested on September 26, 1909, in Eastlake Park in Los Angeles, in separate mashing incidents. They were arrested as the result of a crusade instigated to rid the public parks of mashers. Two weeks earlier the edict went forth that the parks must be freed from Sunday mashers, and on the day in question a squad of plain clothes men were detailed to Eastlake to arrest any person annoying women. The five arrested were said to have "walked up to girls and women and made insulting remarks."[30]

Patrolman Edward McCormick caught C. D. Quistberg in the act of following two women who were trying to escape his attentions in November 1909 in Salt Lake City. He placed the masher under arrest, and both women stated he was a stranger to them. At that point Quistberg ostentatiously produced a note pad and pencil and proceeded to make a threat that he "would get the policeman" for interfering. When the pair reached the entrance to the jail, Quistberg pleaded to be released. Several of the masher's friends had followed the pair along. McCormick then insisted that Quistberg acknowledge publicly that he had accosted the women and make a public apology for his behavior. Then the officer released the sobbing Quistberg "on his solemn promise never again to accost a woman with whom he had no speaking acquaintance."[31]

A brief news story on March 24, 1910, observed that the police in Denver had declared war on mashers, and eight men had been jailed for that offense on the previous Sunday.[32]

The townspeople of Long Beach, California, commended Police Chief Moyer in May 1910 for his stand in instructing his men to nab, pinch, and hale before the courts each and every man, young or old, who was caught in the act of mashing in Long Beach that summer. The townspeople believed that action would result in more young women of attractive appearance visiting their city that summer.[33]

Back in Washington, D.C., Captain Tom Hollinberger of the First Precinct launched a summer crusade in July 1910 against mashers. It was said to have been launched some weeks earlier and had been pushed vigorously. During the "promenade hours" on F Street and Pennsylvania Avenue, two officers in plain clothes mingled with the crowds and "gently but firmly keep the street corner loafers on the move." Hollinberger declared the custom of annoying young girls and women with their remarks and stares had to be stopped, or he would know the reason why. Saturday evenings were one of the busiest times of the week for the masher squad, and on July 9 there were more than the usual number of plain clothes men on duty. For those arrested and brought to the station house, $20 had been set as the lowest amount of collateral to be accepted to release an offender before his court date. In special cases the desk sergeant had orders to raise that minimum to $50.[34]

Also in July 1910 Chief of Police Kingsley in Minneapolis issued an order to be circulated among his men directing his officers to stretch carefully over one knee any masher caught in the act, and apply with vigor the palm of a white-gloved hand. No arrests were to be made. Spankings, he ordered, were to be administered publicly. Warnings of the impending punishment were to be published in the local newspapers.[35]

Pennsylvania Avenue, between Ninth and Tenth Streets Northwest, in

Washington, D.C., was reported, in September 1910, to no longer be a mecca for mashers after 6 p.m. in the evenings. They had all departed, according to Police Captain Hollenberger of the First Precinct, who recently had received orders to clean up the Avenue. He said the Avenue was then as safe as any other street in the city for women at night. After many complaints had been received at headquarters, Major Sylvester gave orders to arrest all men who attempted to annoy women. Hollenberger detailed extra men in uniform to patrol the street in front of the theater entrances. The presence of those extra officers was said to have done the trick.[36]

During the spring of 1910 it was reported that ladies in Hibbing, Minnesota, had been annoyed on several occasions by being followed by men in the residential section of town at night. Several ladies were badly frightened when men caught up with them in the darker portions of the streets. During the summer, that abuse had grown worse "and of late has become quite serious." There were a number of mashers who made a practice of lurking in the alleys at night, making vile and insulting remarks when ladies passed by, and in some cases following ladies and "keeping up a volley of coarse remarks." In September the village council of Hibbing determined to do away with that abuse and planned to put enough police officers on duty to thoroughly watch all the streets, promising to deal with the mashers to the full extent of the law. It was also reported that the village authorities were likely to have some assistance in that matter from the men of the town, "and an informal vigilance committee will deal out summary chastisement to any Jack the Loafer that can be caught."[37]

Back in Washington, D.C., at the end of September 1910, it was noted that the "annual fall crusade on the mashers who patrol F Street, from Eleventh to Fourteenth Street, is on." Every year for the past four, numerous complaints had been received from merchants whose places of business were obstructed by men congregating in and around the doorways of those establishments. An officer on the beat remarked, "Many of the young men go along the street tipping their hats indiscriminately to young girls they don't know. This is a vulgar practice, and we have been trying to eliminate it for some time with some little success."[38]

In Marion, Ohio, Mayor Dr. Seiter's latest crusade, in October 1910, was against the masher who, said the mayor, was becoming a nuisance on the streets of the city. He intended to chase all the mashers off the streets of Marion by making examples of a few of them. Mayor Seiter said to a reporter of a local paper, "It is a disgrace to the city that women, unaccompanied, are unable to walk down the street without having loafers insult them and make remarks. I have had many complaints of late and know that the practice is quite general. It must be stopped or there will be arrests." He added that two women complained to him that very day that mashers not only addressed them but tried to take them by the arm and walk down the street with them. "I advised them that they should take their umbrellas and hit the mashers over the head with them; use their hat pins or anything else they found handy," said Seiter.[39]

Mayor Seiter's edict against mashers resulted in the arrest of William Boutwell on October 5, 1910. The complainant was Miss Leona Berridge, a 16-year-old domestic. Leona and a companion, Miss Eva May Stiffler, were homeward bound in the evening when Boutwell and two male friends overtook them. Boutwell made an insulting remark to Leona. She found a policeman, and Boutwell's arrest followed. On the following morning the two girls appeared in police court. Leona made an affidavit against Boutwell, and he pled guilty and was fined $5 and dismissed with a warning. Reportedly, Stiffler had been locked up before, and the two girls were both given "some pretty plain talk about the conduct thing." Mayor Seiter then instructed Police Chief Klinefelter to take the Berridge girl before the probate judge, who would inquire into her conduct during the past few weeks (she was a newcomer to town). None of this was explained by the reporter; Berridge was under some sort of suspicion and would be investigated, but the why was not given. Nothing more appeared in print about this girl.[40]

In Denver, in November 1910, it was observed that the government had decided to use a cameraman as a chief aid in its war on the post office masher in Denver. That announcement stated that as of the first of 1911, some "clever snapshot" man would be employed to get photos of habitual loafers who made the post office their hangout spot and from where they interfered with others, mainly by mashing women.[41]

Determined to exterminate mashers who flocked around moving picture shows in Washington, D.C., the police of the First Precinct started a crusade against them on July 18, 1911, and caught an alleged offender that very night. He gave his name as James Brown, age about 40. He spotted a woman on Pennsylvania Avenue and followed her. When she was between E and F Streets, he approached her and asked her if she would object to taking a walk with him. Miss Jessie Stedman did, and called a policeman.[42]

Charges that many mashers operated on Fourteenth Street between Fairmont Street and Park Road Northwest in Washington, D.C., were made in the form of many complaints to the Tenth Precinct, resulting in an investigation being launched. It was said that women and girls living in the area, in many cases, were afraid to walk along 14th Street in the vicinity of Park Road in the afternoon and evening. No woman walking in that section could feel sure she would not be annoyed by the mashers. "Oh, you beautiful doll," "Hello, baby," "Oh, you grizzly bear," and similar remarks met the unaccompanied female at nearly every turn. Groups of young "sports" loitered about the corners and near the entrances to the film theaters in the vicinity. They were said to even enter the theaters and "ogle girls and make remarks about their appearance."[43]

Aroused by all the complaints mentioned above, the police in Washington began, on July 19, 1912, "stringent" efforts to stop the practice, with the avowed intent of arresting any male caught mashing. Police said absolutely no flirting would be allowed in the area, described as "one of the most respectable sections of the city." On the evening of July 19 several uniformed officers and others in plain clothes kept watch, and quickly broke up any crowds of men that formed. Said Captain Elliott of the Tenth Precinct, "Absolutely no flirting along Fourteenth Street is allowed, and every precaution will be taken in the future to make it possible for women and girls to stay out on the streets just as late as they please and be secure in the feeling that they are as safe as they would be in their own homes."[44]

In order to help the police in Washington in their crusade cited above, clergymen and others had started a movement for the protection of women and girls. They had decided to be on the lookout themselves and report all mashers to the police. The Reverend C. H. Butler, pastor of the Columbian Heights Lutheran Church, said on July 20 that the activities of the mashers should not be tolerated for an instant. He said it was the duty of all parents to help banish the mashers from the neighborhood in order that the young girls may be protected from insults. "In a respectable neighborhood like Columbia Heights, where the great majority of girls are quiet and well behaved, it is most lamentable that ill-mannered boys and men should be allowed to offer insults on the street. Flirting should not be tolerated for an instant, and I hope the practice will be broken up," explained Butler.[45]

Superintendent of the Metropolitan Police Department in Washington, Major Richard Sylvester, was asked on May 26, 1913, whether or not he would sanction the wholesale thrashing of mashers by brothers and friends of women who were very often insulted on the street. He said, "I admire a man who will protect a woman." While Sylvester did not say it outright, the inference was, thought the reporter, that the police department would sympathize with the man who went to the aid of a woman who had been insulted by a masher.[46]

The State Street department stores in Chicago were to remain the happy hunting ground of the male flirt, or so a news account from September 1916 declared. Chief Justice Olson ended the newly-born crusade against flirting in those stores that had been initiated by several clubwomen. He announced that his scheduled conference with Police Chief Healey on the matter was cancelled. A couple of days earlier Olson announced that an anti-flirt campaign was to be started. Associate judges of the municipal court were to be called on to assist in stamping out the nuisance. Olson's main idea was to strike at the fellows who gave fictitious names to avoid publicity when arraigned in court. Olson had wanted the plan to be confined to mashers of the streets and cinemas, but several women's clubs, such as the Women's City Club and the Mothers' Congress, had wanted to go further and include the department store nuisance. At that point Olson's enthusiasm chilled considerably. Judges were said to be of the opinion that the worst mashing took place in the big department stores, but that only a few of the cases ever got to the police. Most women, opposed to publicity, paid no attention to the annoyances in the department stores, but if the insult was too great they had the privilege of calling a policeman. Clubwomen said that protection was not given to the underpaid shop girls, who could not complain to the police because the stores did not like the bad publicity of having anybody arrested in their establishments. Chief Healey expressed a willingness to cooperate with the clubwomen and Judge Olson in driving the flirts from the stores, but Olson would not have anything to do with that end of it.[47]

A few days later it was announced that in spite of complaints by department store owners, Chief Healey said his new anti-flirt squad would invade the State Street stores in search of mashers. When the cry against flirting in the Loop district was first raised, Chief Justice Olson of the municipal court promised to cooperate with the chief and several women's organizations to help end it. Then the women embarrassed the judge by trying to bring in department stores. Olson lost interest and cancelled a conference with Healey. However, Healey had already appointed four policewomen and six detective sergeants to the anti-flirt squad. Their duty was to patrol the downtown streets, the department stores and the cinemas to pick up all the mashers. Olson had agreed to cooperate with the police on one feature of the flirting situation. He would ask all associate judges to compel men arrested for flirting to give their real names when they appeared in court. "Chief Healey and the clubwomen say the fictitious identity protection is bad. They think they can curb flirting easier if the men arrested are forced to give their real names," said the journalist.[48]

Ed Cardigan arrived in Kalamazoo on February 22, 1917, from Kalkaska, Michigan, to contract to sell his father's potato crop. He did so and then went to a vaudeville show. Half an hour after the show he happened upon Alice Shar, a dancer from the show. He tipped his hat to her and spoke to her. She called a policeman. He asked her if he should take Cardigan to the police station. Shar said, "I'd rather give him a good paddling." The officer turned him over his knee and invited the performer to paddle. She did.[49]

In keeping with the changing times, crusades against auto mashers began to appear. In the summer of 1920 it was reported that mashers, especially those who drove autos to curbs and accosted females, would feel the heavy hand of the law in Ogden, Utah, according to County Attorney Joseph B. Bates. A masher was the sort of "human parasite" that Ogden could do without, he said, and a jail sentence would be their penalty when apprehended. Women had been reporting they were frightened by autos rushing up to the curb while they were out walking, with the occupants of those vehicles shouting to them to "come and take a ride." Bates urged people to report such men and such incidents to the police.[50]

At the same time, the summer of 1920, police in New York City were also getting complaints about auto mashers out cruising and pulling up to the curb, and scaring women. Police promised to crack down on the practice.[51]

A journalist enthused in August 1920 that the doom of the Broadway masher in New York City had been sealed by court and police edicts. The Masher Squad, a group of detectives, was under instructions to go after Broadway mashers—those who stand on Broadway corners at night and "make it hazardous for a woman to travel that thoroughfare without an escort." In the West Side Court just a day earlier, 24 alleged mashers were arraigned before Magistrate McGeehan. He told the prisoners just what they might expect if they ever appeared in that court again. McGeehan told them that it would be a stiff sentence in the workhouse, although apparently that time they got little or nothing. The police said the part of Broadway extending from 42nd Street to 50th Street "is infested nightly by hundreds of men who devote their time solely to insulting unprotected women who pass by." Those 24 mashers had been taken in raids on one night by the Masher Squad.[52]

Police in Washington, D.C., launched yet another campaign against mashers, this one in October 1920. They were doing it this time by using the anti-loitering law to break up "street corner flirting." Acting under orders from Major Harry L. Gessford, the police were said to be strictly enforcing the "move on law." F Street was, yet again, a prime target. Police in the streets were told that no loitering was to be tolerated. Extra officers were placed on duty, and all were told to be relentless in breaking up crowds and keeping them broken up. "The anti-mashing campaign, which is being conducted through promoting an anti-loitering campaign, and which was brought about as the result of public opinion expressed by various prominent Washington men and women in interviews in *The Times*, is creating more interest than any campaign that has been waged in Washington recently," said a journalist. One of the first to come out in favor of an anti-mashing campaign was Mrs. Sarah V. Farling, Washington's first policewoman, and Miss Gertrude McNally of the Federal Employees' Association. They felt women were not to blame, in contrast to the attitude displayed by Mrs. Mina C. Van Winkle, chief of the Women's Bureau of the Metropolitan Police, who had said that unescorted girls should not walk the streets at night, and "that the girls are to blame for the general flirting because of their immodest dress." Included in the article was an excerpt from a letter to the editor, a typical "man" letter. It was from David G. Hardy (his full address was given) who thought the answer to the masher problem was to pass a law against some of the current fashions: "I have never heard tell of a modestly dressed woman being approached when she conducted herself ladylike and minded her own business." He added, "A woman can dress to make herself pretty and attractive without leaving most of her clothes off, so why do they do it? There is only one answer; figure it out for yourself."[53]

Just three days after the this article, Mina C. Van Winkle was part of a group of officers who arrested four mashers as part of that police campaign. The four were in a car and stopped near three women walking along a street (Van Winkle and two policewomen). "Come on, let us take you for a ride," the occupants yelled. Sure, said Van Winkle and the three women got in. She then directed the driver to police headquarters, where one of the policewomen, Emily Steele, then arrested the four on a charge of disorderly conduct. They were released from custody on $25 bail each.[54]

Detectives in Philadelphia equipped with automobiles and motorcycles were sent out on the evening of October 25, 1920, by Superintendent of Police Mills in an effort to break up the "motor-mashing" habit that had infested the streets in the central section of Philadelphia during the previous six months. Many complaints had been made to the police from females who, after being invited to ride with strange men, were subjected to insults when they refused. With the police now being better equipped, the motor mashers would not be able to speed away with a taunting laugh at the appearance of a policeman, as they did when it was only an officer on foot.[55]

Another police drive against mashers was announced for Washington, D.C., in March 1924. This time it was to be against "drugstore cowboys" and mashers along F Street. Announcement of this drive was made by Commissioner Oyster. This campaign was decided on after complaints had been received from many women about being accosted. Several male officers were to be deployed in plain clothes as additional help for the regular beat officer.[56]

Sidney Smith, 27, was fined $50 on September 11, 1924, by Magistrate Louis Brodsky in Night Court in New York City when he was found guilty of annoying young women and girls on the subway. His accusers were Margaret B. Solen (policewoman) and William J. Jones (policeman), both of whom were attached to the subway masher squad. They testified they had seen Smith annoy several women and girls at the 42nd Street and 86th Street stations of the Lexington Avenue route. "I am not going to take your fingerprints nor incarcerate you because you are a young man," said Brodsky when he found Smith guilty. "You have an excellent position and reputation, which I shall take into consideration. But I want to impress on you that you had better change your ways. You have been found guilty of a serious offense, and I shall give you the limit fine."[57]

The warmer weather of spring 1926 reportedly brought out more mashers in Emporia, Kansas, and as a result the police in that community declared war on them. However, the police stated they could accomplish little without the cooperation of females, who were advised to call the authorities if they were harassed. Emporia Chief of Police Leroy Hurt urged women who were accosted by strange men to get the license numbers of their vehicles and immediately call the police. He said he'd like nothing better than to nab mashers, and "we'll give them the limit."[58]

Six months later in that same year it was reported that in Salt Lake City a squad of 12 men armed with sawed-off shotguns and riding in fast automobiles was pressed into service in that city's war against mashers. According to Chief of Police Joseph Burbridge, the officers had been ordered to "treat 'em rough and if necessary, shoot to kill."[59]

Also in September 1927 authorities in Fresno, California, declared themselves determined to "use the entire department if necessary" in their campaign against mashers. Chief of Police W. G. Walker declared publicly that the campaign had begun against the street harassers in Fresno, and that jail sentences would be asked for every harasser arrested. The campaign announcement followed the sentencing of George Rodgers and Fred Scheidt to 20 days and 10 days in jail, respectively, after they had accosted three women and hurled Roy McMinnville through a window when he tried to come to the aid of those women.[60]

In Concord, New Hampshire, Chief of Police George Kimball issued a warning to mashers in cars, at the start of 1919. Several complaints had been received by the police department from women who had been walking along city streets only to have harassers drive up beside them and invite them for rides. Kimball said those guilty of such actions would be severely punished.[61]

Two months later in Oakland, California, the police department launched a somewhat different campaign against mashers. On a Friday night, March 10, several of the most flagrant mashers were taken into custody. The new strategy was to phone the homes of these men to tell their mothers, wives, and girlfriends about their mashing activities. On Saturday morning the "women folk" of those in custody started to arrive at the jail to confront their men. The irate women led the men home.[62]

Not far away from Oakland, in Berkeley, California, one month later, in April 1929, Police Chief August Vollmer said that an aggressive campaign to rid the city of mashers and "grabbers" had been instituted, as a result of attacks during the previous few weeks on several University of California coeds.

Vollmer remarked that all persons jailed for molesting women would be prosecuted to the full extent of the law.[63]

Elbert Cole and Clarence Schrader were both residents of Sterling, Colorado. One day in August 1929 the pair drove to Greeley, Colorado, to engage, apparently, in sexual harassment. Police in Greeley caught them attempting to mash three females who were walking along a street. The men were following them in their car. The police of Greeley had the pair listed in their police records as "mashers" and dealt with them by escorting Cole and Schrader out of Greeley that same night.[64]

Mayor Ralph S. Bauer of Lynn, Massachusetts, announced on October 3, 1929, that he was going to stamp out auto mashers and flirting husbands. "I'm asking all women in this city to get the car number of any motorist who attempts to flirt with them. I'll publish it in the newspapers and report it to the Registrar of Motor Vehicles," he explained. Also, he announced he would appoint himself chief of police in a week when the present chief retired.[65]

In White Plains, New York, in October 1930 the wife of that city's chief of police, William Miller, was walking along a street in that town when she was annoyed by men in a passing auto who attempted to induce her to join them. As a result, the chief issued an order a few days later than any mashers discovered on the streets of White Plains should be summarily arrested.[66]

Denver police reportedly declared war on auto mashers in November 1930. Police Chief Reed issued orders to his force to halt and question every man seen to drive his auto to the curb near a woman. His action followed numerous complaints made by young girls and women about auto mashers. Assistant City Attorney George Bakke said every sidewalk or automobile harasser who was arrested would be prosecuted. The difficulty in prosecuting alleged offenders, he said, lay in the reluctance of their victims to testify in court.[67]

Policewomen

America got its first official policewoman in 1910—that was Alice Stebbins Wells, who was appointed to the post of policewoman in September of that year. She was the first woman in America to become a policewoman in the sense of being officially appointed by an authority such as a city, to be officially given that title, and to be fully paid for out of the police budget. Prior to that year many women affiliated with police forces were used by those forces in various ways. For example, police matrons, who were supposedly strictly attached to lock-ups to supervise and control female detainees, were often used by police forces in many other ways, often resembling, in very limited ways, the duties assigned to policemen. Sometimes even the wives of policemen were used in such capacities—unofficially, of course, but also unpaid and on a voluntary basis. Policewomen were ideally suited to work in a couple of areas that were difficult for male officers, such as in shoplifting situations and in mashing work.

In Pittsburgh in June 1908 it was reported that Police Superintendent McQuaide of that city had inaugurated a novel crusade. A half dozen women "who have had some detective experience were turned loose on the downtown streets as decoys for mashers." Each young woman had a plain clothes man within signaling distance. Said the account, "The behavior of all was modest, but they were not impossible to accost, and the harvest by the plain clothes men began before the matinee crowds were away from the theater section." Nearly a dozen arrests were made that first day before midnight, including "several prominent men about town."[68]

A report from Los Angeles on August 31, 1911, remarked that Miss Fay Evans, the "Flirt cop," was out of a job because Los Angeles Police Chief Sebastian did not like the clothes she wore. When Evans brought about the arrest of nine mashers, Chief Sebastian sent for her to inquire into her unusual success. When she reported to the chief, Evans wore, said a reporter, "a light colored lace dress, white shoes and stockings, black silk large-sleeved wrap lined with silk of brilliant red, and collar and cuffs of the same hue. This was topped with a tall black domino hat." Sebastian remarked, "It's all very plain to me now. That get-up would make most any man stare. You are discharged." Evans had been employed by the LAPD as a "flirt cop" to bring about the arrest of young men who made advances to women on the street.[69]

What had happened the day before in Los Angeles was that nine men accused of flirting with Evans, described in this account as the "volunteer official decoy" of the LAPD, had been arrested within 24 hours on August 30. The first four of those men to reach court all pled guilty and were each sentenced to pay a fine of $30 or spend 30 days in jail as an alternative. Reportedly Evans had offered her services to Sebastian several days earlier after she had complained that mashing should be banished in Los Angeles and that insults to women on the streets should be stopped.[70]

A young woman started walking down State Street in Chicago on September 1, 1911, accompanied by a Chicago police detective, at a distance, after her services as "city flirt" had been accepted. Captain Halpin, acting head of the detective bureau, gave the following instructions to the plain clothes man: "If a man only looks at the young lady or if he goes up to her, takes off his hat and asks if she isn't Miss So-and-so, and then passes on, well, that isn't exactly flirting. But if he sticks to her and asks her to walk with him and really gets offensive, well that's flirting and the man is a masher." After a two-hour stroll on State Street the woman returned to police headquarters without having encountered a single masher. She explained, "No one was rude to me, or attempted to speak to me."[71]

Official flirts seemed to be a trend, at least for a very brief time. A September 7, 1911, article reported that New York City might use official flirts if Commissioner Waldo continued to receive letters from women who volunteered their services as "beautifully plainclothes women" to the NYPD. Waldo was considering turning the letters over to his secretary, Mr. Sheehan, with a view to drawing up a set of qualifications for the position, such as physique, age, and so forth, in case the position of "official flirt" was to be adopted by the NYPD. It was said to be the report of the great success achieved by the official flirt in Los Angeles (this was before the word of her firing had spread) that was the catalyst for other forces, such as the NYPD, to consider establishing the post. Among all the letters from women writing to volunteer their services was one which stated, "I wish to be the first official flirt of Broadway. I possess a mysterious power which compels me to be ever on the lookout for danger from masculine skill and charm.... I would recognize sin if I saw it face to face." Another woman said, "I have a small magic face and my eyes are much swollen and red from weeping over what I have seen in Broadway. Nobody can help but look at me, as I radiate sadness and despair. Might I not be used as a decoy to attract the attention of sympathetic men?" Said a third letter, "My friends say I have the evil eye and all my husbands have endorsed the verdict. They are so superstitious where I am concerned they think it is a bad sign to pay me alimony and consequently I have developed into a practical business woman. I will catch and deliver mashers to you at $1 a head the first and second day, and then accept a regular salary as long as the mashers last. All men stare at me and follow me."[72]

Harry Gessford, a police inspector on the Washington, D.C., force, commented on the official flirt concept at that time by saying he thought it was unlikely that his force would resort to employing young women to decoy mashers. He did not think things were bad enough in Washington to warrant such a plan. "I don't think much of the plan. Some of the girls employed [in other cities] are so attractive that a man wouldn't be human who could pass by such a fairy creature without tipping her a wink."[73]

Still, in September 1911 a reporter for an El Paso, Texas, newspaper declared that his city needed an official flirt to work in connection with the plaza policeman. There was a masher at large in the San Jacinto Plaza, described as "a middle aged man of means who should know better." He walked through the plaza several times each day, ogled the women on the benches, and attempted to engage in conversation with them by sitting down beside them.[74]

At the beginning of 1912 Julius Harburger took office as Sheriff of the

County of New York. He was, said a report, a "friend of womankind who announced upon taking office that women are just as eligible as men to appointment as deputy sheriffs." He saw four reasons why women should be deputy sheriffs: (1) to protect young girls in dance halls; (2) to enforce the law forbidding the sale of liquor to children; (3) to obtain better conditions in factories; (4) to suppress mashers, not only in the street, but in the big hotels in New York. "Hereafter any woman possessing a deputy sheriff's badge will be empowered to arrest and take to the nearest station house any man who annoys her or another woman within the range of her observation." No uniform was to be worn by these women. Nor, it seems, were any appointed.[75]

William Gobrech, 24 and the married father of a two-year-old girl, was arrest on October 1912 by Alice Clement, a Chicago policewoman. Gobrech had been writing indecent letters to women. He used stationary from various city hotels to write mash notes and drop the letters into women's laps on streetcars, or hand them to them in the street, or leave them in the waiting rooms of department stores. All the letters sought appointments and told where he could be found. When complaints about these letters came to the Chicago police, the force detailed Clement to the case. She had him under arrest in a reported 15 minutes. At his home address Gobrech had not paid any rent for two months, and his wife was reported to be penniless.[76]

On June 5, 1913, in Joplin, Missouri, Miss Vernie Goff, that city's police matron, made her first arrest in a campaign she had started recently against street mashing. When Henry Miller of Monett, Missouri, accosted her on the street with the remark, "Hello, kid," Goff replied to him, "You are under arrest," and showed Miller her badge. "I'll just march you to jail." After she had taken him to the city jail, Miller asked the matron to mail a letter he had written to his wife. "I will do it," she said, "and I will write her a letter myself explaining how you happen to be here."[77]

In the summer of 1913 a reporter sought out two Chicago policewomen who were assigned to patrol the city's beaches, and asked them how the average Chicago woman should deal with a masher. They told the journalist that hatpins, clubs or whistles were not necessary to squelch mashers, a look would do it. "One substantial, wide-eyed look, with a touch of scorn in it, will send the boldest flirt about his business," they said. "All you have to do when a man speaks to you insultingly is to look at him, and he turns and runs," said Officer Mary Boyd. "I sometimes carry a little billy, but it's for dogs; men are scared to death of me." Said policewoman Emma Neukom, "Look a man over from hat to shoes and from shoes to hat and he will vanish.... I sometimes start talking in French or Greek to mashers, and they always run away. But a look is the best."[78]

Several policewomen were sworn in at Chicago early in August 1913.

They were soon dispatched to walk the streets in search of mashers. That same day a man had stationed himself on State Street in that city where he spent his time tipping his hat and smiling at passing women shoppers. Then someone tapped him on the shoulder and said, "Say, you beat it." He turned to the woman and asked who she was. "I am a member of the Chicago police department—a policewoman, to be exact. You are a masher, I take it, and have no business here. Now you just move on as fast as you can." He did so. The policewoman was Mrs. Alice Clement (perhaps Clements).[79]

Near the end of August 1913, when Chicago had had policewomen on its force for some three weeks, the chief of police announced that he wouldn't give up his female officers for anything. He said they had practically eliminated the masher from the shopping district.[80]

America's first official policewoman, Alice Stebbins Wells, was in New York City in February 1914 where she gave an interview to Nixola Greeley-Smith, a well-known woman reporter. Wells told the journalist she believed that policewomen would have a deterrent effect on the mashers of large cities. She reported to Nixola that her belief was only strengthened because a man had tried to mash her just a couple of days early while she was in New York City. She told the reporter she had stopped for a moment in the street to look at posters in front of a cinema, "when a man came up and asked ingratiatingly if I did not want to see the show, offering to take me. Now, I can readily imagine that if I had been a poor young girl without a nickel and worse yet, with the knowledge that I never would have a nickel to spare for such a treat, I might have accepted the man's offer and so possibly have taken the first step to ruin." Wells added that if the incident had occurred in Los Angeles she would have watched that man and that cinema to see that he did not repeat his performance with a younger and more ignorant woman.[81]

An article that was published in October 1915 profiled two Chicago policewomen, Misses Marie Crot and Marian Wrightman. They were in a train station depot, on duty watching for mashers, amongst other things. Those two women divided mashers into three types: (1) the obvious flirt; (2) the seductive flirt; and (3) the professional flirt. An obvious flirt was defined as one who dressed in fancy attire, seated himself across from a woman and who smiled knowingly. One of those made his unsuccessful attempt on Crot and then moved on the try his method on a 17-year-old girl who was waiting for a train. When he made a remark to the girl, Crot moved in and arrested him, after determining he had no train ticket (that is, he had no valid reason to be in the train station). After it was ascertained he had no ticket, the masher ran from the station, but Crot signaled to a male officer outside the station who ran the man down and arrested him. The next morning in police court he was fined $100. A seductive flirt, said the pair, was known for his charm—but the concept was not really explained. The professional flirt was the white slaver who, supposedly, grabbed naïve females and shipped them to parts unknown where they were forced into slavery.[82]

Mary Coney was an NYPD policewoman. On a Saturday night in May 1920 she was detailed to walk through Central Park and watch for mashers. She entered the park at 59th Street and, she said, was followed by a man. At the reservoir at 79th Street he took her by the arm and said, "Little girl, I like you. What's the chance of takin' you home?" She agreed with the suggestion, and together they walked until they were in front of the Arsenal police station. "Here we are," she said as she displayed her badge, "C'mon in and meet mother." He gave his name as Henry S. Miller. He did not meet mother, but he saw Magistrate Max S. Levine and paid a $10 fine for disorderly conduct.[83]

One month later New York City Deputy Police Commissioner Ellen O'Grady selected two of her policewomen and planted them in the Central Park monkey house as bait for mashers. Between 2 p.m. and 5 p.m. on their first day they captured five mashers. Two policemen who were stationed nearby made the actual arrests. All five of the men were charged with disorderly conduct. In Night Court one of the men was sent to the workhouse for five days, one was fined $5, and two were held for further examination.[84]

As of the spring of 1923 it was reported that the NYPD policewomen were engaged in a task to "eradicate the masher pest that infests the subways, the elevated roads, and some of the public squares, libraries, museums and picture houses." Large numbers of complaints were received daily at police headquarters. Mrs. Mary Hamilton, chief of the NYPD women's squad, said, "It is a serious situation." She mentioned that it remained difficult to get women to testify against mashers, but said it was a little easier now than in the past. That task that so many women regarded as unpleasant had been made a little easier because the hearing was held privately in the judge's chambers, "partly to protect the accused in case of exaggeration or misrepresentation, and partly to protect the accuser." Publicity for such cases, Hamilton said, was avoided. The police subway squad that pursued mashers often did not need to have the female who was harassed go to court to testify. It was a male officer who arrested the man who mashed the policewoman, thus those two alone could bring about a conviction in court. Said Hamilton, "Sentences of six months in prison for men caught annoying women in public places are not uncommon. The cases are seldom reported in the press, though there are many of them." Hamilton did admit that in the past it had sometimes been difficult for a harassed woman to get the police to take her complaint seriously, and that sometimes a male officer, when appealed to for help in such situations, occasionally took the part of the accused. In conclusion, Hamilton urged all women in Manhattan to lend their assistance in the battle against mashers, "for the sake of their own daughters and other women's daughters."[85]

That masher squad had been reorganized by Hamilton and was comprised of five policewomen: Ellen Newman, Margaret Solan, Anne Murphy, Mary Foley, and Catherine Brennan. Five male detectives were assigned to escort the policewomen. All of those men had the first name of William: Smith, Purcell, Norton, Jones, and Van Gostien. The masher squad would patrol its beats in couples during the morning and evening rush hours, and after the theater let out. They were to be on duty until 1:30 a.m. The women were to shadow men suspected of annoying women and, if complaints were justified, to arrest them. Those five policewomen were also slated to learn jiu jitsu.[86]

In October 1926 it was revealed that Miss Alice S. Scarberry was the Pittsburgh policewoman who almost single-handedly, it was said, had rid the north side of that city of nearly a score of "auto sheiks." In just a single night of walking the streets of the north side she had caused 16 would-be mashers to be arrested. All either posted the $30 bail or remained in jail to await hearings in court later the next morning. Scarberry explained that she gave the "gas hawks" two or three chances to "get off," but if they insisted then she got tough. The persistent ones, when rebuked, would simply drive the car up close to her again, open the car door and issue an invitation to go for a ride. After about the third such harassment Scarberry called in one or both of the two patrolmen who were stationed nearby, and had the masher arrested. Two of that group of men tried to escape by stepping on the gas, and Scarberry's police companions had to draw their revolvers to subdue them.[87]

Conclusion

One of the things that remained constant about sexual harassment in this period was the idea that the women accosted were attractive or pretty. Of all the articles that dealt with the issue, only one or two from this time period remarked that all women were at risk from mashers, no matter what the woman's age or the state of her attractiveness. That is, only one or two commentators of the era understood, at least at some level, that the sexual harassment of women was about power and the hatred of women; it had nothing to do with sexuality. A constant reference to pretty women being harassed brought up, albeit indirectly, the idea that men were somehow not to blame, or not completely to blame. They were victims of their hormones or some such nonsense.

Another constant was the idea that women were reluctant to do very much about the harassment. That is, women were not inclined to make any kind of scene on the street by way of confronting the harasser, and perhaps screaming at him or yelling for a police officer, for example. And that women were not inclined to formally prosecute the masher because they did not want to have to appear in court or have their name published in the newspaper. There certainly was some truth to those ideas. Perhaps by constantly publishing such ideas and opinions in the media the stereotype of the shy, retiring woman who would not say boo was reinforced. If something is repeated often enough and for a long enough period of time, it takes on the mantle of truth. Such images also perhaps made it more likely for a harasser to operate; it made him feel that he would likely get away with his behavior.

The legal system was never very amenable to efficiently dealing with mashers. No specific law ever existed to cope with the problem. While laws were apparently passed in a few jurisdictions, they don't appear to ever have been used. All incidents of sexual harassment were brought under one of three charges, all of them misdemeanors. The first fell under vagrancy/loitering statutes. This was used only a few times before being discarded, shot down by higher levels of the court system. Almost all charges of mashing were brought under either a disorderly conduct charge or one of disturbing the peace. Both had problems attached to their use. Causing even more trouble in the court system's handling of sexual harassment cases was the problem of fictitious identities. During the period covered by this book, nobody carried any identity cards (this began to change late in the period when the driving license began to make its appearance). It meant that somebody arrested by the police could give any name he chose to the authorities. It is likely that most of the names in this book of people charged and/or convicted of mashing were fictitious names given to the police and the courts by those accused. Courts did have the power to order the accused held while an investigation into his background was made. However, in the case of mashing complaints, always a misdemeanor charge, that was almost never done. It meant that serial harassers were not likely to be discovered by the system. Fingerprinting did not arrive in the legal system until about 1906. It took years before it became routine, and it took further time before it spread downward from felony cases to misdemeanors.

Police forces around the nation regularly declared war on the mashing evil, sometimes several times in the same calendar year. But they never managed to bring the problem under control. Sometimes an officer with a good memory and/or many years of service was able to recognize a serial harasser, or knew from his own local knowledge that somebody just arrested was not really named Tom Green. Mostly, though, the police were hobbled by the fictitious name problem. Feminists sometimes criticized the police, arguing they worked more efficiently and more vigorously when they went after women. That is, if women were reported to be soliciting men (prostitutes at work), then the police were more vigorous in putting an end to such behavior, or at least moving it to a place where complaints were less likely to be generated. It was also argued by some feminists that the police were more likely to believe a man when he reported he had been solicited by a prostitute, and arrest that woman solely on the man's word, than they were a woman wanting them to arrest a masher.

In the period covered by the book, a woman was as likely to be harassed in the daytime as she was at night. She was more likely to be harassed in a crowded place than in a quiet area. The main reason for that was the tendency of males in this period to congregate and gather together with no apparent reason behind the behavior except to loiter in groups. Nothing in North American society since the end of World War II is comparable to the huge amount of loitering behavior that took place in the 1880s through the 1920s. Today if we think of "hanging out" behavior at all, it is usually with respect to teenagers and malls. But back then it was all male groups, and all ages were involved. Some of it was specifically for the purpose of ogling and mashing females. When the first all-girls high school opened in New York City at the start of the 1900s, it drew huge crowds of loitering males, especially at the time classes let out, who gathered for no reason except to harass young female students. Crowds became so dense that area shopkeepers complained to police about the disruption to their businesses. Washington, D.C., was a magnet for young women in this period because of the job opportunities available to them in civil service employment that were not as readily available in the private sector. Thus, the nation's capital had a disproportionate number of working women. Crowds of loitering men used to assemble there around some of the buildings that contained those female government workers. The favorite time for those crowds of harassing males was, of course, around quitting time for the women.

If the police could not or would not effectively break up such groups, then changes in society accomplished the job. The arrival of the car culture, which took hold in serious fashion in the 1920s, saw men of all stripes give up loitering to hang out in and around their cars, or somebody else's car if they had none of their own. And the loitering herd faded away, as did all things pedestrian. At that point the woman was harassed by the "auto sheik," who pulled up to the curb with an invitation to go riding. The benefit of anonymity, along with speed, conferred on the earliest auto sheiks came to a quick end, however, with the arrival of license plates. Suddenly, anonymity was gone.

By 1930 the social norm that a man did not speak to a woman he did not know was on the way out. For decades women had been going out and about in a wider and wider sphere as they sought equality. In many such places they ran into men they did not know, such as at dances hosted by civic officials, at lectures held in various venues, and at public entertainments of different sorts. It seemed to make no sense to refuse to discuss, say, a lecture with the person who sat beside you just because he was of the opposite sex and you did not know him (in the sense of being formally introduced by a trusted third party). This social norm disappeared more quickly in the larger urban areas than it did in the smaller and more rural communities, but it was on its way out every-where. A man standing in the heart of State Street in Chicago in 1900 (the city's commercial district) on a busy afternoon, tipping his hat to passing females and saying "hello, there," was moved on by the police for such behavior. If he refused to heed police warnings he would have been arrested. In 1930 he most likely would have simply been ignored.

Throughout this period a woman was more likely to be sexually harassed during daylight hours in the busiest parts of town, by men who were part of a crowd of loiterers. She was still at risk, of course, for being harassed at other times of the day and in other parts of the city as well. By the end of the period much of the daylight harassing in busy parts of town was disappearing. The loitering crowds of men had dissipated due to the rising car culture, and women were more inclined to accept the idea of exchanging a few words with strange males on the street during daylight hours when it was obviously done with innocent intent. Sexual harassment became more and more what it is today, an activity that takes places mostly in the dark and mostly in quiet areas of the city. Also, it is perhaps more likely today to occur where she works and/or in interactions with coworkers outside of the work environment.

Notes

Chapter 1

1. "A new invention of the enemy." *The Pulaski Citizen* [TN], March 4, 1875.
2. "Hands off." *Nashville Union and American* [TN], June 4, 1875.
3. "May young women walk about alone." *The State Journal* [Jefferson City, MO], May 19, 1876.
4. Harriet Hubbard Ayer. "Practical lessons in the art of winning a wife." *Evening World* [NY], April 6, 1903.
5. "Good advice for girls." *The Intermountain Catholic* [Salt Lake City], January 30, 1904.
6. "Chased away the mashers." *The Columbus Journal* [NE], November 11, 1908.
7. "Girls warned against dances in Milwaukee." *Washington Times*, December 12, 1910.
8. Betty Vincent. "Betty Vincent's advice to lovers." *Evening World* [NY], June 19, 1914.
9. "A few words to the girls." *Tacoma Times*, June 20, 1916.
10. "London street etiquette." *New York Times*, November 27, 1927.
11. "Concerning mashers." *Daily Globe* [St Paul], December 29, 1882.
12. "Origin of masher." *Los Angeles Herald*, June 21, 1883
13. "General news." *McCook Weekly Tribune* [McCook, NE], November 1, 1883.
14. "The masher." *Salt Lake Daily Herald*, November 11, 1883.
15. No title. *The Anderson Intelligencer* [SC], September 7, 1904.

Chapter 2

1. "A masher's mash." *St. Paul Daily Globe*, August 3, 1880.
2. "Good times in Great Britain." *The Highland Weekly News* [Hillsborough, OH], April 25, 1883.
3. "Fable of the masher." *Daily Globe* [St Paul, MN], May 26, 1883.
4. "Life in New York City." *Brooklyn Eagle*, October 12, 1884.
5. "Another masher." *Los Angeles Daily Herald*, January 12, 1889; "The masher." *Los Angeles Daily Herald*, January 24, 1889.
6. "Giddy male mashers." *St. Paul Daily Globe*, January 27, 1889.
7. "Phases of life." *St Paul Daily Globe*, December 29, 1889.
8. "Show this hog no mercy." *The Sun* [NY], June 2, 1890.
9. "Marking a masher." *Pittsburg Dispatch*, April 18, 1891.
10. "The masher nuisance." *The Sunday Herald* [Washington, D.C.], October 11, 1891.
11. "Mashers out in force." *Los Angeles Herald*, January 22, 1893.
12. "Lottie Collins talks." *The Sun* [NY], April 16, 1893.
13. "Not yet abashed." *San Francisco Call*, May 1, 1893.
14. "After-dark mashers." *Evening Star* [Washington, D.C], May 6, 1893.
15. "Let the mashers go with the signs." *Washington Post*, January 20, 1895.
16. "Gay on top, but sad underneath—

Gotham's tenderloin." *The Morning Times* [Washington, D.C.], March 1, 1896.

17. "Bicycle mashers." *The Sun* [NY], May 28, 1896.

18. "Vermin on the cycle path." *Brooklyn Eagle*, May 13, 1897.

19. "The bicycle masher." *The Sun* [NY], August 2, 1899.

20. "A woman's essay on mashers." *The Sun* [NY], August 11, 1899.

21. Edna May. "Chorus girl to star." *Evening World* [NY], February 9, 1900.

22. Clara Morris. "Trials of a young actress." *Salt Lake Herald*, August 18, 1901.

23. Clara Morris. "What a masher really is." *Salt Lake Herald*, September 22, 1901.

24. "Annoyed girls on a car." *Washington Times* [Washington, D.C.], August 29, 1901.

25. "The masher." *Sunday Morning Globe* [Washington, D.C.], October 6, 1901.

26. "Broad St. masher a great nuisance." *The Times* [Richmond, VA], January 19, 1902.

27. "A masher again at work." *Evening World* [NY], October 28, 1902.

28. "The L masher." *Evening World* [NY], October 19, 1902.

29. "How mashers infest the L." *Evening World* [NY], October 29, 1902.

30. "Some things that might be done to an L masher." *Evening World* [NY], October 30, 1902; "Bad masher's victims weep." *Evening World* [NY, NY], October 30, 1902.

31. "Women and the mashers." *The Sun* [NY], November 9, 1902.

32. "Mashers insult high school girls." *Evening World* [NY], September 26, 1903.

33. "Mashers rouse ire of shoppers." *Evening World* [NY], November 16, 1904.

34. "Caruso jailed as park masher." *San Francisco Call*, November 17, 1906.

35. Ibid.

36. "Rich New Yorkers may be arraigned." *New Ulm Review* [New Ulm, MN], November 28, 1906.

37. "Caruso's fine paid." *Waterloo Daily Courier* [IA], May 15, 1907.

38. "Mashers here and abroad." *The Sun* [NY], December 2, 1906.

39. "Mashers insult women." *Salt Lake Herald*, March 5, 1908.

40. "Paradise for masher." *Washington Post*, March 23, 1908.

41. "A young girl's protest." *New York Times*, November 30, 1909; "Women's blank expression." *New York Times*, December 4, 1909.

42. "War on river masher." *Washington Post*, July 14, 1912.

43. "Auto-masher now police problem." *The Times Dispatch* [Richmond, VA], August 12, 1912.

44. "Mashers and insulting toughs annoy girls here." *Honolulu Star-Bulletin*, August 13, 1912.

45. "Rowboat masher is newest summer pest." *San Francisco Call*, September 7, 1912.

46. "Masher menace hit by working girl who tells experiences." *Evening Public Ledger* [Philadelphia], April 21, 1915.

47. "Porter blames city magistrates and politics for masher evil." *Evening Public Ledger* [Philadelphia], April 22, 1915.

48. "Get first phone masher." *Washington Times*, March 16, 1916.

49. "Mashers keep step with the times." *Burlington Hawk Eye* [IA], October 4, 1925.

50. "Decatur downtown streets good hunting grounds for mashers after nightfall." *Decatur Evening Herald* [IL], September 3, 1928.

Chapter 3

1. "A masher in merited mystery." *Brooklyn Eagle*, March 11, 1881.

2. "The masher." *Saguache Chronicle* [Saguache, CO], September 15, 1882.

3. "The masher." *Sedalia Weekly Bazoo* [MO], September 19, 1882.

4. "A few words about mashers." *San Antonio Light*, August 17, 1883.

5. No title. *New York Times*, July 21, 1884.

6. "Mash the mashers." *Evening World* [NY], January 4, 1888.

7. No title. *Sacramento Daily Record-Union*, July 30, 1899.

8. "Thoughts of a masher." *Aspen Tribune* [CO], October 6, 1898.

9. "The despicable masher." *Evening Star* [Washington, D.C.], July 3, 1900.

10. "An abominable evil." *The Evening Times* [Washington, D.C.], November 21, 1901; "The masher again." *The Evening Times* [Washington, D.C.], November 26, 1901.

11. "Decaying institutions." *The St. Louis Republic*, April 12, 1903.

12. "Punishment for mashers." *Evening World* [NY], July 25, 1903.

13. "A masher who needs mashing." Ocala Evening Star fl, September 24, 1903.

14. "Mashers on the streets." *San Francisco Call*, December 10, 1903.

15. "Arrest the mashers." *Salt Lake Herald*, February 2, 1904.

16. "What to do with mashers." *The Tacoma Times*, April 8, 1904.

17. "A source of revenue." *The Washington Times*, September 2, 1904.

18. "Methods of the masher." *Salt Lake Tribune*, October 2, 1904.

19. "The curse of the loafer." *The Seattle Star*, December 2, 1904.

20. "Men's meeting." *Deseret Evening News* [Salt Lake City], April 16, 1906.

21. "The mashers." *Salt Lake Herald*, August 27, 1906.

22. "Watch out for the goo goo man." *Washington Post*, December 23, 1906.

23. "Good thrashing cure for mashers." *Washington Times*, January 14, 1907.

24. "Street loafing." *Daily Press* [Newport News, VA], April 5, 1907.

25. "Lashes for mashers advocated by pastor." *Washington Herald*, November 10, 1913.

26. "Mashing in Cape Girardeau." *The Weekly Tribune and the Cape County Herald* [Cape Girardeau, MO], March 15, 1917.

27. Sophie Irene Loeb. "The molesting masher." *Evening World* [NY], April 14, 1917.

28. "Swat the masher." *The St. Joseph Observer* [MO], April 21, 1917.

29. "Cheap mashers must make themselves scarce." *The Bemidji Daily Pioneer* [MN], June 15, 1918.

30. "The motor masher." *Washington Herald*, August 29, 1921.

31. Sophie Irene Loeb. "Managing the masher." *Evening World* [NY], August 24, 1922.

32. "Would be sheiks annoy the ladies." *Carroll Times* [IA], June 25, 1925.

33. "Pretty police girls to lure petty mashers." *New Castle News* [PA], September 24, 1926.

34. "N.Y. subway is moving hell, says Aimee." *San Antonio Light*, March 2, 1927.

35. "Let's mash the curbing mashers." *Oshkosh Daily Northwestern* [WI], June 24, 1927.

Chapter 4

1. "Street flirtation." *Ouachita Sentinel* [Monroe, LA], April 21, 1883.

2. "Mashing the masher." *St. Paul Daily Globe*, September 6, 1887.

3. Clara Belle. "Clara Belle." *Fort Worth Gazette*, March 2, 1890.

4. Jennie Dean. "Street mashing in Gotham." *Thomas County Cat* [Colby, KS], April 17, 1890.

5. "They ride wooden horses." *Brooklyn Eagle*, January 26, 1892.

6. "Not always the men." *Los Angeles Herald*, November 20, 1892.

7. "Policemen too zealous." *Washington Post*, September 6, 1899.

8. "Good advice for girls." *The Intermountain Catholic* [Salt Lake City], January 30, 1904.

9. "Victims of the mashers." *Salt Lake Tribune*, September 25, 1904.

10. "A masher is a totally unnecessary nuisance unless he is encouraged." *The Washington Times*, January 12, 1905.

11. "Women consider mashing." *The Sun* [NY], November 5, 1905.

12. "Girls encourage mashers." *The Washington Times*, November 11, 1905.

13. "Old sinner talks." *The Tucumcari News* [NM], November 25, 1905.

14. Winifred Black. "How to avoid mashers." *Washington Post*, January 28, 1906.

15. "Women in hobble or harem skirts can't blame mashers." *The Tacoma Times*, May 31, 1911.

16. Clarence Cullen. "The judge and the mashers." *The Hawaiian Star* [Honolulu], July 8, 1911.

17. "Dress cause of evil." *Washington Post*, August 4, 1912.

18. "Mashers persist when girls dress to draw glances." *Washington Times*, August 7, 1912.

19. "Tight dress cause mashers." *San Francisco Call*, September 17, 1912.

20. "They are blaming low waists, short sleeves, clinging skirts for the bad morals of men even in Des Moines." *Des Moines Daily News*, September 22, 1912.

21. Dorothy Dix. "Dorothy Dix." *Omaha Daily Bee*, May 7, 1913.

22. Dorothy Dix. "Dorothy Dix talks." *Ogden Standard Examiner*, June 2, 1924.

23. "Judge blames girls." *Washington Post*, October 15, 1915.

24. "Invitation to evil-minded men, says magistrate of present styles." *Washington Post*, February 13, 1916.

Chapter 5

1. "Husband owns it." *Lancaster Daily Intelligencer* [PA], November 25, 1882.

2. "She accepted." *The Weekly Messenger* [St. Martinsville, LA], December 11, 1886.

3. "He was a masher." *St. Paul Daily Globe*, April 15, 1889.

4. No title. *Capital City Courier* [Lincoln, NE], November 9, 1889.

5. "He gave it up." *Omaha Daily Bee*, January 27, 1890.

6. "He went to the smoker." *The Princeton Union* [Princeton, MN], May 19, 1892.

7. "Outwitted a masher." *St. Paul Daily Globe*, January 22, 1893.

8. "Crushed the masher flat." *Princeton Union* [Princeton, MN], March 7, 1895.

9. "He was cured." *Los Angeles Herald*, May 30, 1895.

10. "A question of physics." *The Roanoke Daily Times* [VA], March 31, 1896.

11. "Now he will flirt no more." *The Morning Times* [Washington, D.C.], July 19, 1896.

12. "The downfall of a masher." *The Appeal* [St. Paul], February 10, 1900.

13. "One-cent cure for a masher." *Evening Star* [Washington, D.C.], July 28, 1900.

14. "Masher caught." *The Guthrie Daily Leader* [OK], October 5, 1904.

15. "Caught by foxy girls." *Los Angeles Herald*, September 23, 1906.

16. "Pretty girl has a new cure for mashers." *Albuquerque Evening Citizen*, November 9, 1906.

17. "American woman crushes Paris masher." *Los Angeles Herald*, June 9, 1907.

18. "Masher handed lemon by charming Virginian." *Washington Times*, August 7, 1907.

19. "Two mashers erred; jailed." *Chester Times* [PA], November 10, 1930.

Chapter 6

1. "State notes." *The Elk County Advocate* [Ridgway, PA], August 9, 1877.

2. "She was a smasher." *St. Paul Daily Globe*, September 19, 1892.

3. "Boxed his ears." *The Morning Times* [Washington, D.C.], November 17, 1895.

4. "Masher pummeled by girls." *Alexandria Gazette* [VA], October 22, 1896.

5. "Slapped the masher's face." *The Sun* [NY], December 19, 1897.

6. "Girls whip masher." *The Evening World* [NY], July 3, 1900.

7. "Actress sends him sprawling." *San Francisco Call*, April 23, 1901.

8. "Girl slapped a bold masher." *The Evening World* [NY], October 12, 1901.

9. "Used her fist on a masher." *The St. Louis Republic*, April 4, 1902.

10. "Minneapolis woman knocks masher down." *The St. Paul Globe*, August 18, 1902.

11. "Slapped a masher, she says." *The Sun* [NY], May 15, 1903.

12. "Masher knocked out." *The Minneapolis Journal*, September 7, 1903.

13. "Woman's fists land on masher." *The Evening World* [NY], December 3, 1903.

14. "The masher." *The Evening World* [NY], December 5, 1903.

15. "Two months for Davis." *The Evening World* [NY], December 11, 1903.

16. "Alleged masher arrested." *The St. Louis Republic*, May 8, 1904.

17. "Slapped masher's face." *The Sun* [NY], July 22, 1904.

18. "Masher whipped by woman." *The Evening World* [NY], August 18, 1904.

19. "Girl slugs bold masher." *Richmond Planet* [VA], August 27, 1904.

20. "Gave him a poke." *The Minneapolis Journal*, October 22, 1904.

21. "Jiu Jitsu vanquishes a masher." *San Francisco Call*, December 30, 1904.

22. Nixola Greeley-Smith. "Jiu-Jitsu for the masher." *The Evening World* [NY], January 2, 1905.

23. Nixola Greeley-Smith. "How a girl can repel a masher's attack." *The Evening World* [NY], January 3, 1905.

24. James C. Crawford. "Stalwart maiden throws masher through window." *San Francisco Call*, August 12, 1905.

25. "Masher hit by society beauty." *The Minneapolis Journal*, August 25, 1905.

26. "Needed no protector." *Mount Vernon Signal* [Mt. Vernon, KY], May 4, 1906.

27. "Woman slugs masher." *The Minneapolis Journal*, July 25, 1906.

28. "A masher well served." *The Evening World* [NY], July 27, 1906.

29. "Handsome girl hammers a masher." *The Spokane Press*, August 25, 1906.

30. "Girl stenographer uses glove on masher." *Spanish Fork Press* [Spanish Fork, UT], January 30, 1908.

31. "Masher chastised by plucky woman." *Washington Times*, May 14, 1908.

32. "Young woman sends a masher sprawling in a car." *The Evening World* [NY], March 31, 1909.

33. "Athletic woman thrashes masher." *San Francisco Call*, September 9, 1909.

34. "Actress punches a tipsy masher." *Washington Times*, January 11, 1911; "Margaret Illington lands rights and lefts on masher." *Tacoma Times*, January 11, 1911.

35. "Athletic college woman whips and

arrests masher." *San Francisco Call,* August 17, 1911.
36. "Little woman chokes a 200-pound masher." *The Evening World* [NY], December 13, 1911.
37. "Girl fights a masher." *The Day Book* [Chicago], June 15, 1912.
38. "Girl slugs masher on elevated car." *The Madison Journal* [Tallulah, LA], May 17, 1913.
39. "Girl in subway collars masher." *New York Tribune,* March 24, 1914.
40. "Wife helps free masher." *The Sun* [NY], March 26, 1914.
41. "No one interfered." *Evening World* [NY], March 25, 1914.
42. "Headlock recommended for subduing mashers." *Thomasville Times Enterprise* (GA) July 31, 1929.

Chapter 7

1. "A masher routed." *New Ulm Weekly Review* [New Ulm, MN], August 27, 1884.
2. "Thrashed by a girl." *Fort Worth Daily Gazette,* January 14, 1886.
3. "The brave Western girl." *St. Paul Daily Globe,* February 24, 1886.
4. "Show this hog no mercy." *The Sun* [NY], June 2, 1890.
5. "One masher who gets his deserts," *The McCook Tribune* [NE], October 10, 1890.
6. "She will send for him." *Pittsburg Dispatch,* April 18, 1891.
7. "Horsewhipped a masher." *Aspen Weekly Times* [CO], January 30, 1892.
8. "She beat the masher." *The Evening World* [NY], June 20, 1894.
9. "Lashed him." *Alexandria Gazette* [VA], September 24, 1895.
10. "She defended her honor." *Washington Post,* January 12, 1896.
11. "Were almost acquitted." *The Morning Times* [Washington, D.C.], April 3, 1896.
12. "Ferryboat masher held in $500." *The Sun* [NY], June 19, 1896.
13. "Masher comes to grief." *Kansas City Journal* [MO], December 6, 1897.
14. "Lashed her tormentor." *The Evening World* [NY, NY], July 21, 1900.
15. "The crowd cheered." *The Columbian* [Bloomsburg, PA], May 23, 1901.
16. "Girls pound a masher." *The Sun* [NY], August 5, 1901.
17. "Slashed masher's ear, she says." *The Sun* [NY], January 1, 1903.

18. "Catch a masher and drill his ears." *The Evening World* [NY], January 2, 1903.
19. "Young woman uses hatpin on an offensive masher." *The St. Louis Republic,* April 20, 1903.
20. "Actress threshes masher on street." *The Spokane Press,* May 12, 1903.
21. "Stuck hatpin into a masher." *The Evening World* [NY], May 27, 1903.
22. "Draws on a masher." *Saint Paul Globe,* December 10, 1903.
23. "Masher mashed." *The Stark County Democrat* [Canton, OH], August 15, 1905.
24. "Masher cowhided by pretty widow." *The Minneapolis Journal,* November 26, 1905.
25. "Mashed a masher." *Valentine Democrat* [NE], September 13, 1906.
26. "Girl fells two mashers." *Washington Post,* September 15, 1906.
27. "Routs mashers with revolver." *San Francisco Call,* January 24, 1908.
28. "Stabbed masher with hatpin." *New York Tribune,* October 18, 1909.
29. "Masher squelched by small whistle." *Los Angeles Herald,* November 10, 1909.
30. "Man routed by hatpin held in city jail." *Los Angeles Herald,* January 16, 1910; "Masher who annoyed young woman is fined." *Los Angeles Herald,* January 18, 1910.
31. "Parasol bombardment fails to stop masher." *New York Tribune,* August 9, 1916.
32. "Her face powder bomb routs ardent masher." *New York Tribune,* November 12, 1916.
33. "Beats up mashers." *Danville Bee* (VA), March 26, 1929.

Chapter 8

1. "The masher mashed." *Los Angeles Herald,* July 22, 1884.
2. "Jealousy." *The Tombstone* [AZ], March 21, 1885.
3. "A masher mashed." *Wichita Daily Eagle,* February 16, 1886.
4. "Saintly city doings." *St. Paul Globe,* December 31, 1887.
5. "Killen punched him." *St. Paul Daily Globe,* August 7, 1888.
6. "Damaged his nose." *St. Paul Daily Globe,* October 31, 1888.
7. "A masher punished." *San Francisco Call,* May 3, 1892.
8. "A masher killed." *The Wichita Daily Eagle,* May 17, 1892.

9. "Served them right." *The Hazel Green Herald* [Hazel Green, KY], June 10, 1892.
10. "A rare bird." *The Weekly Republican* [Phoenix], July 28, 1892.
11. "Served 'em right." *The Evening Bulletin* [Maysville, KY], October 27, 1892.
12. "A masher punished." *San Francisco Call*, March 28, 1893.
13. "An angry father." *San Francisco Call*, April 20, 1893.
14. "A masher fined." *San Francisco Call*, September 6, 1893.
15. "A masher well thrasher." *The Sun* [NY], September 21, 1893.
16. "A masher caned." *San Francisco Call*, October 27, 1895.
17. "A masher trapped." *Alexandria Gazette* [VA], July 9, 1897.
18. "She fixed the masher." *Los Angeles Herald*, December 6, 1898.
19. "Mashers get deserts from angry fathers." *San Francisco Call*, November 22, 1899.
20. "Masher punched in open court." *The Evening World* [NY], April 14, 1900.
21. "Smashed a masher." *The St. Louis Republic*, April 20, 1900.
22. "Smashed the Masher." *The Richmond Planet* [VA], March 9, 1901.
23. "Not the first time she has had mashers beaten." *St. Louis Republic*, March 10, 1901.
24. "Husband stabbed by Chicago masher." *The Guthrie Daily Leader* [OK], January 20, 1902.
25. "Fate of a masher." *The Salt Lake Herald*, July 5, 1903.
26. "Mashers stab escort." *The Sun* [NY], August 1, 1903.
27. "Woman lashes a masher." *New York Times*, January 25, 1904.
28. "Masher badly beaten." *Salt Lake Tribune*, September 15, 1904.
29. "Congressman's fist punishes a masher." *The Minneapolis Journal*, November 11, 1904.
30. "Horsewhip sets fire to masher." *San Francisco Call*, February 28, 1905.
31. "Christie mashes masher." *Salt Lake Herald*, December 30, 1905.
32. "Slugs masher; fined $5." *The Minneapolis Journal*, August 3, 1906.
33. "Masher stabs girl's escort on late car." *The Seattle Star*, March 9, 1910.
34. "Masher thrashed, thrasher acquitted." *Oak Creek Times* [CO], May 12, 1910.
35. "Angry husbands pounce on avenue mashers." *Washington Times*, June 23, 1911.
36. "Detective gives masher a beating." *El Paso Herald*, August 1, 1914.

Chapter 9

1. "A whip for scoundrels' backs." *New York Times*, January 17, 1883.
2. "Whipped a masher." *San Francisco Call*, October 9, 1897.
3. "Make football of masher." *New York Tribune*, July 13, 1900.
4. "Masher pleaded guilty." *The Evening World* [NY], November 13, 1900.
5. "Whip the masher." *The Minneapolis Journal*, April 15, 1901.
6. "Athlete won a bride by vanquishing a masher." *St. Louis Republic*, December 4, 1901.
7. "Praised by court for felling a man." *The Evening World* [NY], August 4, 1902.
8. "Jack the hugger in law's embrace." *The Evening World* [NY], January 27, 1903.
9. "Woman gives alleged masher big black eye for flirting." *St. Louis Republic*, April 9, 1903.
10. "Women beat masher into unconsciousness." *St. Louis Republic*, September 5, 1903.
11. "Reserves save masher from crowd." *The Evening World* [NY], September 2, 1905.
12. "This trolley car masher got an awful drubbing." *The Evening World* [NY], December 18, 1906.
13. "Mashed the masher." *Daily Capital Journal* [Salem, OR], September 7, 1907.
14. "Masher is thrashed and sent to jail." *Washington Times*, September 18, 1907.
15. "Woman punched on street fails to press charge." *The Evening World* [NY], January 13, 1909.
16. "Colonel Thompson smashes a masher." *Daily Capital Journal* [Salem, OR], May 27, 1909.
17. "Slapped masher's face." *The Spanish Fork Press* [Spanish Fork, UT], November 11, 1909.
18. "Mashers are chastised." *Salt Lake Herald*, December 4, 1909.
19. "L train masher held in night court." *The Evening World* [NY], December 14, 1910.
20. "Subway squeezer squeezed into cell." *New York Tribune*, June 24, 1915.
21. "Masher mobbed for kiss theft." *New York Tribune*, October 14, 1916.
22. "Houston masher whipped." *Durant Weekly News* [Durant, Indian Territory, OK], June 17, 1921.
23. "Subway masher gets 10 days." *New York Times*, March 13, 1928.
24. "Subway masher jailed." *New York Times*, April 16, 1930.

Chapter 10

1. "Under advisement." *San Francisco Call*, July 17, 1891.
2. "Miller sentenced." *San Francisco Call*, July 19, 1891.
3. "The case of the masher." *The Record-Union* [Sacramento], July 20, 1891.
4. "For annoying ladies." *Herald Democrat* [Leadville, CO], August 21, 1891.
5. "The masher bill." *Aspen Daily Chronicle* [CO], April 8, 1893.
6. "Mustn't look at the girls." *The Sun* [NY], October 12, 1894.
7. "Virginia's anti-flirting bill. *The Anderson Intelligencer* [SC], January 19, 1898.
8. "The lawful use of fists." *The Wichita Daily Eagle*, February 15, 1899.
9. "No law for the masher." *Brooklyn Eagle*, January 10, 1900.
10. Ibid.
11. "Heavy fines for mashers." *The Evening World* [NY], October 1, 1903.
12. "Houston makes goo-goo eyes a misdemeanor." *The St. Louis Republic*, September 9, 1905.
13. "Kansas town after mashers." *The Red Cloud Chief* [Red Cloud, NE], October 20, 1905.
14. "Flirting is a game." *Washington Post*, December 30, 1905.
15. "Aldermen favor masher service." *Racine Journal News* [WI], November 27, 1912.
16. "Flirting may be tabooed in Phoenix." *Bisbee Daily Review*, March 8, 1914.
17. "Bill to punish mashers advanced." *New York Times*, June 24, 1914.
18. "Texas chooses prettiest girl." *San Antonio Light*, April 7, 1929.

Chapter 11

1. "A good lesson to young loafers." *Brooklyn Eagle*, August 28, 1880.
2. "Metropolitan mashers." *Brooklyn Eagle*, July 21, 1884.
3. "The deceive deceived." *Daily Globe* [St. Paul, MN], October 15, 1884.
4. "Crushing a masher." *Brooklyn Eagle*, April 18, 1886.
5. No title. *Fort Worth Daily Gazette*, June 21, 1886, June 21, 1886.
6. "Dodged a fine." *Brooklyn Eagle*, October 31, 1887.
7. "A middle-aged masher." *The Evening World* [NY], September 11, 1888.

8. "Ogling is expensive." *St. Paul Daily Globe*, March 10, 1889.
9. "Street mashing." *St. Paul Daily Globe*, March 10, 1889.
10. "A masher in the toils." *Brooklyn Eagle*, May 26, 1889.
11. "Guilty of mashing." *Los Angeles Herald*, July 15, 1892.
12. "Ninety days and a fine." *Los Angeles Herald*, July 16, 1892.
13. "Blow to Broadway mashing." *The Evening World* [NY], September 24, 1892.
14. "Market-street mashers." *San Francisco Call*, June 17, 1893.
15. "Served the masher right." *The Evening World* [NY], August 10, 1894.
16. "Insulted white women." *Graham Guardian* [Stafford, AZ], June 15, 1895.
17. "A masher punished." *Washington Post*, September 15, 1895.
18. "Market-street masher." *San Francisco Call*, January 27, 1897; "Market-street masher." *San Francisco Call*, January 28, 1897.
19. "Brimful of nerve." *Kansas City Journal* [MO], November 18, 1897.
20. "Arrested for mashing." *Kansas City Journal* [MO], June 10, 1898; "Fate of the masher." *Kansas City Journal* [MO], June 11, 1898.
21. "She punched the masher." *The Sun* [NY], December 8, 1898.
22. "Rebuffed masher fined." *Kansas City Journal* [MO], August 3, 1899.
23. "He insulted army lassie." *The Evening World* [NY], January 6, 1900.
24. "Short news stories." *The Bourbon News* [Paris, KY], June 22, 1900.
25. "A masher mulcted." *The Bourbon News* [Paris, KY], August 3, 1900.
26. "Insulter was fined." *Brooklyn Eagle*, September 6, 1900.
27. "May mash less now." *The Minneapolis Journal*, July 2, 1901.
28. "Refused to prosecute." *The Washington Times*, September 6, 1901.
29. "Masher fined $1,000." *St. Paul Globe*, January 16, 1902.
30. "Masher gets long sentence." *The Minneapolis Journal*, October 10, 1903.
31. "Alleged masher arrested." *St. Louis Republic*, April 6, 1904.
32. "Sad ending of a masher." *The Bourbon News* [Paris, KY], July 19, 1904.
33. "Proper thing to hit masher." *San Francisco Call*, September 3, 1904.
34. "Preferred Chicago." *Minneapolis Journal*, October 12, 1904.

35. "Woman's modesty saves a masher." *Salt Lake Tribune*, February 2, 1905.

36. "Masher gets six months." *New York Times*, July 16, 1905.

37. "Punish the masher." *Salt Lake Herald*, July 21, 1905.

38. "The chain-gang cure." *Los Angeles Herald*, July 22, 1905.

39. "Judge fines a St. Louis masher $300." *San Francisco Call*, September 14, 1905.

40. "Masher sent to jail." *Washington Post*, December 29, 1905.

41. "Gallant and robust judge." *The Sun* [NY], August 2, 1906.

42. "Court convicts four mashers." *San Francisco Call*, August 28, 1906.

43. "Mashers will be well punished." *San Francisco Call*, February 1, 1907; "Masher is given nine months." *San Francisco Call*, February 3, 1907.

44. "Aged masher must serve sixty days." *San Francisco Call*, July 28, 1907.

45. "The masher mashed." *Deseret Evening News* [Salt Lake City], May 12, 1908.

46. "Skating masher fails to appear." *San Francisco Call*, July 19, 1908.

47. "Mashers to get limit sentences." *Salt Lake Herald*, October 28, 1909.

48. "One Phoenix masher who will mash no more." *Arizona Republican*, December 23, 1909.

49. "Masher gets two hard jolts." *The Tacoma Times*, June 8, 1910.

50. "The news minutely told." *Edgefield Advertiser* [SC], August 3, 1910.

51. "Masher gets 30 days for following woman." *The Evening World* [NY], February 1, 1911.

52. "Pullman masher broke no law." *Pullman Herald* [WA], October 13, 1911.

53. "Does a smile and a wink make a masher." *San Francisco Call*, November 11, 1911.

54. "Ban on 'Oh, you kid,' in Chicago." *San Francisco Call*, July 18, 1912.

55. "Kiss, $100; wink, $40; 'Good afternoon,' $50; fines for mashers." *Washington Herald*, July 27, 1912

56. "Masher gets 10 days for annoying young woman in street." *The Evening World* [NY], August 8, 1912.

57. "Masher pays $10 each word." *The Evening Herald* [Klamath Falls, OR], August 30, 1912.

58. "Buffalo lawyer gets 30 days as a Broadway masher." *The Evening World* [NY], October 3, 1912.

59. "Prison in store for masher girl says struck her." *Evening World* [NY], October 3,

1912; "Not a Heroine after all." *The Sun* [NY], October 5, 1912.

60. "Masher poses as policeman gets 30 days." *The Evening World* [NY], November 13, 1912.

61. "Dictionary frees masher." *New York Tribune*, January 19, 1913.

62. "Tries to flirt but lands in jail." *Weekly Journal-Miner* [Prescott, AZ], February 12, 1913.

63. "Omaha judge smashes the mashers." *The Day Book* [Chicago], May 13, 1913.

64. "Six months for masher." *The Maui News* [Wailuku, Maui], August 16, 1913.

65. "'She's too pretty to walk alone,' says the judge." *Day Book* [Chicago], January 26, 1914.

66. "Too beautiful to remain in city, so judge makes her go home." *Day Book* [Chicago], March 10, 1914.

67. "Masher gets 10 days to pine over his love for a strange girl." *Evening World* [NY], July 23, 1914.

68. "Girl forced to flee to escape from masher." *The Evening Herald* [Albuquerque], February 26, 1915.

69. "Ex-sleuth, masher, fined." *The Day Book* [Chicago], May 29, 1915.

70. "Woman had right to whip the masher." *Evening World* [NY], March 7, 1916.

71. "Finger prints for the masher." *The Ogden Standard*, August 12, 1916.

72. "Masher, ex-convict sent to workhouse." *New York Tribune*, October 7, 1916.

73. "Girl sentences masher to jail with court's O.K." *Evening World* [NY], August 22, 1917.

74. "Masher in movies fined by court." *Washington Times*, October 3, 1919.

75. "Tip in headline cost a masher in subway $50." *Evening World* [NY], February 15, 1921.

76. "Taxicab masher gets 5 days in workhouse." *New York Times*, August 7, 1921.

77. "Masher to work 6 days, spend seventh in jail." *New York Tribune*, January 17, 1922.

78. "Law too lenient with mashers, jurist says." *The Morning Tulsa World*, June 29, 1922.

79. "Slapped as masher then gets $100 fine." *Washington Post*, September 28, 1923.

80. "Girl fixes masher's term." *New York Times*, March 25, 1928.

81. "Mashers jolted in police court." *Ames Daily Tribune* [IA], May 21, 1928.

82. "Mashers arrested; one gets fine of $25." *Berkeley Daily Gazette*, October 1, 1928.

83. "Movie masher is jailed." *New York Times*, January 24, 1929.

84. "Mashers fined $25 in court today." *Hamilton Evening Journal* [OH], April 20, 1929.

85. "Auto masher is fined twice, in two courts." *Washington Post*, June 30, 1929.

86. "Mashers liable to 90 days and $100." *Bismarck Tribune* [ND], August 26, 1929.

Chapter 12

1. "How to paralyze a masher." *Cheyenne Transporter* [Darlington, WY], January 25, 1882.

2. "How to treat mashers." *The Evening Times* [Washington, D.C.], March 28, 1898.

3. J. J. O'Brien. "How a frail woman can resist bold masher without weapons," *Evening World* [NY], January 8, 1901.

4. "Society women and revolvers." *The Times Dispatch* [Richmond, VA], April 22, 1903.

5. "Mashers and thugs beware. Girls plan Jiu-Jitsu club." *Los Angeles Herald*, April 29, 1906.

6. "Hello girls practice punching bags in telephone gymnasium." *The Paducah Evening Sun* [KY], June 13, 1906.

7. "Women who fence are terrors to mashers." *Spokane Press*, August 28, 1906.

8. "You won't fear mashers if you learn to skate." *The Tacoma Times*, January 28, 1910.

9. "Advises women to use hatpins when attacked." *Los Angeles Herald*, March 23, 1910.

10. "Is hatpin man's menace? Police chief's opinions." *Salt Lake Herald*, March 27, 1910.

11. "How about the hatpin as a teacher for mashers?" *The Marion Daily Mirror* [OH], August 16, 1910.

12. "New way to rebuff mashers." *New York Tribune*, September 3, 1910.

13. "Mashing the mashers." *The Tacoma Times*, July 7, 1911.

14. "Boston woman wants gallery of mashers." *Washington Times*, July 29, 1912.

15. "Minister would boom marriage and beat mashers." *Washington Herald*, August 13, 1912.

16. Ethel Intrapodi. "Smashing cures mashing—get busy girls!" *The Day Book* [Chicago], August 26, 1912.

17. "Menace of flirts." *Washington Post*, September 23, 1912.

18. "Taming the masher." *San Francisco Call*, April 28, 1913.

19. Marguerite Mooers Marshall. "Use hatpin or fists on mashers, says Mrs. Brophy." *Evening World* [NY], August 9, 1913.

20. Caroline Josefson. "Iceland shows the American girl how to repel the masher." *Omaha Daily Bee*, April 12, 1914, pt. 2.

21. "Fences to eliminate mashing at movies." *Aspen Democrat-Times* [CO], August 24, 1914.

22. "Girls training to rout mashers." *The Bemidji Daily Pioneer* [MN], December 6, 1914.

23. "Invents spurs to stop mashers." *Washington Herald*, March 14, 1915.

24. "Periscope in hats, girls watch flirts." *Washington Times*, December 3, 1915.

25. "Teaching girls how to deal with mashers." *Washington Times*, February 15, 1918.

26. "Don't be afraid of mashers, girls; learn jiu-jitsu." *Washington Times*, July 8, 1918.

27. "Jury in Baltimore Indicts 4 in holdup of bank collector." *Washington Post*, March 24, 1925.

28. "Gives mashers a shock." *New York Times*, August 15, 1926.

Chapter 13

1. "Mashers in New York." *Chaffee County Republican* [Buena Vista, CO], January 8, 1896.

2. "Park mashers, beware." *Los Angeles Herald*, May 25, 1896.

3. "Gloucester girls will whip mashers." *The Times* [Richmond, VA], October 3, 1902.

4. "They'll put an end to mashers." *The Evening World* [NY], April 4, 1903.

5. "Mashers beg for mercy." *New York Tribune*, August 17, 1903.

6. "Suppressing the masher." *The Daily Journal* [Salem, OR], October 6, 1903.

7. "Mashers to be arrested." *Aspen Democrat* [CO], October 15, 1903.

8. "Detectives to capture flirting men." *The Paducah Sun* [KY], November 4, 1903.

9. "Will wage war on the masher." *San Francisco Call*, November 9, 1903.

10. "Pretty Denver girls to wage war on mashers." *St. Paul Globe*, November 9, 1903.

11. "War on masher." *The Hartford Republic* [KY], December 25, 1903.

12. "Against mashers." *The Spokane Press*, November 14, 1903.

13. "War on masher in big Chicago stores." *Minneapolis Journal*, October 26, 1904.

14. "Missouri girls decide to carry revolvers." *The Paducah Sun* [KY], March 15, 1905.

15. "Organize to smash mashers." *San Francisco Call*, August 8, 1905.

16. "War on park mashers." *The Minneapolis Journal*, June 19, 1906.

17. "Police asked to arrest mashers." *The Seattle Star*, April 16, 1908.

18. "To beat up mashers is object of club." *Washington Times*, August 7, 1908.

19. "Vigilance committee formed." *Gainesville Daily Sun*, September 19, 1908.

20. "After the mashers." *Washington Times*, May 21, 1909.

21. "Youngstown women look for a masher." *The Marion Daily Mirror* [OH], May 28, 1909.

22. "Public calls on police board to protect women." *The Times Dispatch* [Richmond, VA], February 13, 1911.

23. "Boston women will cane all mashers." *San Francisco Call*, July 24, 1913.

24. "Women police to rid Boston of mashers." *Washington Herald*, August 11, 1913.

25. "Mrs. Howe's masher now mashing spuds in jail." *Washington Herald*, October 21, 1914.

26. "Flirting M.D. now cook." *New York Tribune*, October 21, 1914.

27. Marguerite Mooers Marshall. "Girls with r.s.v.p. eyes invite mashers." *Evening World* [NY], October 21, 1914.

28. "Mashers here? Not many." *Washington Herald*, October 25, 1914.

29. "Militant woman organizes army to rout mashers." *Evening World* [NY], January 26, 1914.

30. Nixola Greeley-Smith. "Flirtation squad of girl detectives will clear all the Peacock Alleys of the hotel mashers of both sexes." *Evening World* [NY], January 2, 1917.

31. "District clubwomen start crusade to eradicate 'movie lizards' and mashers from Capital theaters." *Washington Post*, September 26, 1920.

32. "Woman has scalps of nine mashers." *New York Times*, August 14, 1921.

33. "She's masher's nemesis." *Evening Public Ledger* [Philadelphia], August 15, 1921.

34. Fay Stevenson. "Using jiu-jitsu on time and mashers." *Evening World* [NY], August 17, 1921.

35. No title. *New York Times*, November 21, 1922.

36. "Anti-flirts to wear pierced lizard badge." *Evening World* [NY], November 23, 1922.

37. "Flirting?" *Bemidji Daily Pioneer* [MN], December 4, 1922.

38. "Jail the flirt." *The Watchman and Southron* [Sumter, SC], December 9, 1922.

39. "Anti-flirt club being organized in Washington." *Danville Bee* [VA], March 1, 1923.

40. "Antiflirts warned of evil by Herrick." *Washington Post*, March 6, 1923.

41. "Herrick talks at anti-flirt club meeting." *Sandusky Register* [OH], March 9, 1923.

42. "Washington observer." Berkeley Daily Gazette, March 12, 1923.

Chapter 14

1. "He hates dudes." *San Francisco Call*, February 9, 1893.

2. Ibid.

3. "Two mashers punished." *The Sun* [NY], August 1, 1897.

4. "Policeman thrashes a masher." *The Sun* [NY], December 21, 1897.

5. "Mashers at Troost Park." *Kansas City Journal* [MO], June 30, 1899.

6. No title. *The Star* [Reynoldsville, PA], August 23, 1899.

7. "Orders to smash the mashers." *The Guthrie Daily Leader* [OK], July 3, 1901.

8. "The war on mashers." *The Watchman and Southron* [Sumter, SC], January 1, 1902.

9. "The season of flirting is now at its dizziest height." *Washington Times*, July 13, 1902.

10. "Police Capt. Dillon opens war on mashers." *Evening World* [NY], March 21, 1903.

11. "Chicago women war on street mashers." *The Spokane Press*, June 26, 1903.

12. "City of mashers." *The Wichita Daily Eagle*, September 6, 1903.

13. "Bible teacher acts a decoy." *Evening World* [NY], April 25, 1904.

14. "Warm weather brings out mashers." *Salt Lake Herald*, May 14, 1904.

15. "Hustled the oglers." *Washington Post*, September 17, 1905.

16. "Street mashers." *The Washington Times*, September 18, 1905.

17. "No fault of mashers, declares Major Sylvester." *Washington Times*, September 26, 1905.

18. "Tried to be a masher; it cost him fifteen." *The Minneapolis Journal*, September 28, 1905.

19. "To mashers; keep off of 14th Street." *Evening World* [NY], September 30, 1905.

20. "Police chasing street loafers." *Salt Lake Herald*, October 2, 1905.

21. "Masher is punched." *Los Angeles Herald*, December 11, 1905.

22. "Punishes mashers." *San Francisco Call*, April 21, 1906.

23. "Crusade against mashers." *Minneapolis*

Journal, June 26, 1906; "Mankato masher fined." *Minneapolis Journal,* June 29, 1906.

24. "No goo-goo eyes allowed in Alton," *Bisbee Daily Review* [AZ], January 2, 1907.

25. "Arrest theater mashers." *Washington Post,* October 6, 1907.

26. "Mashers are arrested." *The Spokane Press,* November 19, 1907.

27. "Mashers must go is order of police board." *San Francisco Call,* November 14, 1907.

28. "Loiterers in police net." *Washington Post,* September 22, 1908.

29. "Crusade against Berkeley mashers." *San Francisco Call,* May 21, 1909.

30. "Police arrest five mashers." *Los Angeles Herald,* September 27, 1909.

31. "Patrolman gives masher a lesson." *Salt Lake Herald,* November 26, 1909.

32. "Weeks news from all over Colorado." *Eagle County Blade* [Red Cliff, CO], March 24, 1910.

33. "Chic girls come when flirting barred? Never." *Los Angeles Herald,* May 14, 1910.

34. "Smashing the mashers newest aim of police." *Washington Times,* July 10, 1910.

35. "Public spanking for Minneapolis mashers." *Medford Mail Tribune* [OR], July 27, 1910.

36. "Avenue made safe for young women." *Washington Times,* September 2, 1910.

37. "Hibbing mashers due for downfall." *Bemidji Daily Pioneer* [MN], September 23, 1910.

38. "Moving on mashers." *The Washington Herald,* September 27, 1910.

39. "Mayor after the mashers." *The Marion Daily Mirror* [OH], October 3, 1910.

40. "First masher to draw fire." *The Marion Daily Mirror* [OH], October 6, 1910.

41. "War upon the mashers." *Salt Lake Herald-Republican,* November 18, 1910.

42. "Crusade started against mashers." *Washington Herald,* July 19, 1911.

43. "Mashers face arrest." *Washington Post,* July 19, 1912.

44. "Jail for all mashers." *Washington Post,* July 20, 1912.

45. "Mashers' foes unite." *Washington Post,* July 21, 1915.

46. "Smashers of mashers to escape punishment." *Washington Herald,* May 27, 1913.

47. "Fight on dept store flirts is thrown in ash heap." *Day Book* [Chicago], September 11, 1916.

48. "The anti-flirt squad is going to be on the job." *Day Book* [Chicago], September 15, 1916.

49. "Dancer spanks a masher while cop holds him." *Washington Herald,* February 23, 1917.

50. "Open war on mashers here." *The Ogden Standard-Examiner,* July 5, 1920.

51. "Motor masher has to dodge." *Washington Herald,* July 27, 1920.

52. "Workhouse sentences to curb Broadway mashers." *New York Tribune,* August 5, 1920.

53. "Mashers war in full swing." *Washington Times,* October 16, 1920.

54. "4 mashers nabbed after they picked up leader of copettes." *Washington Times,* October 19, 1920.

55. "After motor mashers." *Evening Public Ledger* [Philadelphia], October 26, 1920.

56. "Masher drive begins on drug store cowboys." *Washington Post,* March 30, 1924.

57. "Fined for annoying girls." *New York Times,* September 12, 1924.

58. "Police ask girls to help curb activity of mashers." *Emporia Gazette* [KS], March 2, 1926.

59. "Armed squad to fight mashers." *Athens Messenger* [GA], September 19, 1926.

60. "Jail for mashers, decreed at Fresno." *Bakersfield Californian,* September 29, 1927.

61. "Gives warning to mashers." *Portsmouth Herald* [NH], January 8, 1929.

62. "Mashers weep in explaining being in jail." *Albuquerque Journal,* March 17, 1929.

63. "Police plan to rid city of mashers." *Berkeley Daily Gazette,* April 24, 1929.

64. "Mashers are sent home." *Greeley Daily Tribune* [CO], August 24, 1929.

65. "Lynn mayor orders anti-flirting drive." *New York Times,* October 3, 1929.

66. "Police chief wars on mashers after his own wife is annoyed." *New York Times,* October 24, 1930.

67. "Declares war on auto Lotharios." *Ogden Standard Examiner,* November 11, 1930.

68. "Women as decoys in masher crusade." *Washington Times,* June 3, 1908.

69. "Clothes cause flirt cop to lose job." *Washington Times,* August 31, 1911.

70. "Lures on male mashers." *The Mahoning Dispatch* [Canfield, OH], September 1, 1911.

71. "No mashers in Chicago." *The Evening Standard* [Ogden City, UT], September 1, 1911.

72. "Official flirts rush to squelch mashers." *Omaha Daily Bee,* September 7, 1911.

73. "Man who refuses to wink inhuman." *Washington Herald,* September 10, 1911.

74. "El Paso in need of female police." *El Paso Herald,* September 19, 1911.

75. Nixola Greeley-Smith. "Let the masher beware." *Evening World* [NY], January 3, 1912.

76. "Letter masher caught." *Day Book* [Chicago], October 7, 1912.

77. "Police matron arrests mashers." *San Francisco Call*, June 6, 1913.

78. "Cold stare to put masher to route." *Omaha Daily Bee*, August 5, 1913.

79. "Policewoman chases masher." *San Francisco Call*, August 7, 1913.

80. "Death to mashers." *Washington Times*, August 26, 1913.

81. Nixola Greeley-Smith. "Says more policewomen will rid streets of mashers who pester young girls." *Day Book* [Chicago], February 10, 1914.

82. "You'd better make your eyes behave." *The Ogden Standard*, October 23, 1915, mag. sec.

83. "Fined $10 as escort of policewoman in park." *New York Tribune*, May 31, 1920.

84. "Blond man-traps capture 5 as mashers in 3 hours." *New York Tribune*, June 1, 1920.

85. "Women police grapple with the masher evil." *New York Times*, March 23, 1924.

86. "War on subway mashers begun by lady dicks." *Naugatuck Daily News* [CT], March 15, 1924.

87. "16 would-be mashers caught single handed by Pittsburgh decoy." *Clearfield Progress* [PA], October 8, 1926.

Bibliography

"An Abominable Evil." *The Evening Times* [Washington, DC], November 21, 1901.

"Actress punches a tipsy masher." *Washington Times*, January 11, 1911.

"Actress sends him sprawling." *San Francisco Call*, April 23, 1901.

"Actress threshes masher on street." *The Spokane Press*, May 12, 1903.

"Advises women to use hatpins when attacked." *Los Angeles Herald*, March 23, 1910.

"After-dark mashers." *Evening Star* [Washington, DC], May 6, 1893.

"After motor mashers." *Evening Public Ledger* [Philadelphia], October 26, 1920.

"After the mashers." *Washington Times*, May 21, 1909.

"Against mashers." *The Spokane Press*, November 14, 1903.

"Aged masher must serve sixty days." *San Francisco Call*, July 28, 1907.

"Aldermen favor masher service." *Racine Journal News* [WI], November 27, 1912.

"Alleged masher arrested." *The St. Louis Republic*, April 6, 1904.

"American woman crushes Paris masher." *Los Angeles Herald*, June 9, 1907.

"An Angry father." *San Francisco Call*, April 20, 1893.

"Angry husbands pounce on avenue mashers." *Washington Times*, June 23, 1911.

"Annoyed girls on a car." *The Washington Times*, August 29, 1901.

"Another masher." *Los Angeles Daily Herald*, January 12, 1889.

"Anti-flirt club being organized in Washington." *Danville Bee* [VA], March 1, 1923.

"Anti-flirt squad is going to be on the job." *Day Book* [Chicago], September 15, 1916.

"Anti-flirts to wear pierced lizard badge." *Evening World* [NY], November 23, 1922.

"Anti flirts warned of evil by Herrick." *Washington Post*, March 6, 1923.

"Armed squad to fight mashers." *Athens Messenger* [GA], September 19, 1926.

"Arrest the mashers." *The Salt Lake Herald*, February 2, 1904.

"Arrest theater mashers." *Washington Post*, October 6, 1907.

"Arrested for mashing." *Kansas City Journal* [MO], June 10, 1898.

"Athlete won a bride by vanquishing a masher." *St. Louis Republic*, December 4, 1901.

"Athletic college woman whips and arrests masher." *San Francisco Call*, August 17, 1911.

"Athletic woman thrashes masher." *San Francisco Call*, September 9, 1909.

"Auto masher is fined twice, in two courts." *Washington Post*, June 30, 1929.

"Auto-mashing now police problem." *The Times Dispatch* [Richmond, VA], August 12, 1912.

"Avenue made safe for young women." *Washington Times*, September 2, 1910.

Ayer, Harriet Hubbard. "Practical lessons in the art of winning a wife." *Evening World* [NY], April 6, 1903.

"Bad masher's victims weep." *Evening World* [NY], October 30, 1902.

"Ban on 'Oh, you kid,' in Chicago." *San Francisco Call*, July 18, 1912.

"Beats up mashers." *Danville Bee* [VA], March 26, 1929.

Belle, Clara. "Clara Belle." *Fort Worth Daily Gazette*, March 2, 1890.

"Bible teacher acts as decoy." *Evening World* [NY], April 25, 1904.

"The Bicycle masher." *The Sun* [NY], August 2, 1899.

"Bicycle mashers." *The Sun* [NY], May 28, 1896.

"Bill to punish mashers advanced." *New York Times*, June 24, 1914.

"Black hand is after Brooklyn girl." *Salt Lake Tribune*, September 19, 1905.

Black, Winifred. "How to avoid mashers." *Washington Post*, January 28, 1906.

"Blond man-traps capture 5 as mashers in 3 hours." *New York Tribune*, June 1, 1920.

"Blow to Broadway mashing." *Evening World* [NY], September 24, 1892.

"Boston woman wants gallery of mashers." *Washington Times*, July 29, 1912.

"Boston women will cane all mashers." *San Francisco Call,* July 24, 1913.

"Boxed his ears." *The Morning Times* [Washington, DC], November 17, 1895.

"The Brave Western girl." *St. Paul Daily Globe* [MN], February 24, 1886.

"Brimful of nerve." *San Francisco Call*, October 9, 1897.

"Broad St. masher a great nuisance." *The Times* [Richmond, VA], January 19, 1902.

"Buffalo lawyer gets 30 days as a Broadway masher." *Evening World* [NY], October 3, 1912.

"Caruso arrested as masher." *Washington Herald*, November 17, 1906.

"Caruso jailed as park masher." *San Francisco Call*, November 17, 1906.

"Caruso's fine paid." *Waterloo Daily Courier* [IA], May 15, 1907.

"The Case of the masher." *The Record-Union* [Sacramento], July 20, 1891.

"Catch a masher and drill his ears." *Evening World* [NY], January 2, 1903.

"Caught by foxy girls." *Los Angeles Herald*, September 23, 1906.

"The Chain-gang cure." *Los Angeles Herald*, July 22, 1905.

"Chased away the mashers." *The Columbus Journal* [NE], November 11, 1908.

"Cheap mashers must make themselves scarce." *The Bemidji Daily Pioneer* [MN], June 15, 1918.

"Chic girls come when flirting barred? Never." *Los Angeles Herald*, May 14, 1910.

"Chicago women war on street mashers." *The Spokane Press*, June 26, 1903.

"Christie mashes masher." *Salt Lake Herald*, December 30, 1905.

"City of mashers." *The Wichita Daily Eagle*, September 6, 1903.

"Clothes cause flirt cop to lose job." *Washington Times*, August 31, 1911.

"Cold stare to put masher to route." *Omaha Daily Bee*, August 5, 1913.

"Colonel Thompson smashes a masher." *Daily Capital Journal* [Salem, OR], May 27, 1909.

"Concerning mashers." *Daily Globe* [St. Paul], December 29, 1882.

"Congressman's fist punishes a masher." *The Minneapolis Journal*, November 11, 1904.

"Court convicts four mashers." *San Francisco Call*, August 28, 1906.

Crawford, James C. "Stalwart maiden throws masher through window." *San Francisco Call*, August 12, 1905.

"The Crowd cheered." *The Columbian* [Bloomsburg, PA], May 23, 1901.

"Crusade against Berkeley mashers." *San Francisco Call, May 21, 1909.*

"Crusade against mashers." *Minneapolis Journal*, June 26, 1906.

"Crusade started against mashers." *Washington Herald*, July 19, 1911.

"Crushed the masher flat." *Princeton Union* [Princeton, MN], March 7, 1895.

"Crushing a masher." *Brooklyn Eagle*, April 28, 1886.

Cullen, Clarence. "The judge and the mashers." *The Hawaiian Star* [Honolulu], July 8, 1911.

"The Curse of the loafer." *The Seattle Star*, December 2, 1904.

"Damaged his nose." *St. Paul Daily Globe*, October 31, 1888.

"Dancer spanks a masher while cop holds him." *Washington Herald*, February 23, 1917.

Dean, Jennie. "Street mashing in Gotham." *Thomas County Cat* [Colby, KS], April 17, 1890.

"Death to mashers." *Washington Times*, August 26, 1913.

"Decatur downtown streets good hunting grounds for mashers after nightfall." *Decatur Evening Herald* [IL], September 3, 1928.

"Decaying institutions." *The St. Louis Republic*, April 12, 1903.

"The Deceiver deceived." *Daily Globe* [St. Paul], October 15, 1884.

"Declares war on auto Lotharios." *Ogden Standard Examiner.*" November 11, 1930.

"The Despicable masher." *Evening Star* [Washington, DC], July 3, 1900.

"Detective gives masher a beating." *El Paso Herald*, August 1, 1914.

"Detectives to capture flirting men." *The Paducah Sun* [KY], November 4, 1903.

"Dictionary frees masher." *New York Tribune*, January 19, 1913.

"District clubwomen start crusade to eradicate 'movie lizards' and mashers from capital theaters." *Washington Post*, September 26, 1920.

Dix, Dorothy. "Dorothy Dix." *Omaha Daily Bee*, May 7, 1913.

Dix, Dorothy. "Dorothy Dix talks." *Ogden Standard Examiner*, June 2, 1924.

"Dodged a fine." *Brooklyn Eagle*, October 31, 1887.

"Does a smile and a wink make a masher." *San Francisco Call*, November 11, 1911.

"Don't be afraid of mashers, girls; learn jiu jitsu." *Washington Times*, July 8, 1918.

"The Downfall of a masher." *The Appeal* [St. Paul], February 10, 1900.

"Draws on a masher." *St. Paul Globe*, December 10, 1903.

"Dress cause of evil." *Washington Post*, August 4, 1912.

"El Paso in need of female police." *El Paso Herald*, September 19, 1911.

"Ex-sleuth, masher, fined." *Day Book* [Chicago], May 29, 1915.

"Fable of the masher." *Daily Globe* [St. Paul], May 26, 1883.

"Fate of a masher." *The Salt Lake Herald*, July 5, 1903.

"Fate of the masher." *Kansas City Journal* [MO], June 11, 1898.

"Fences to eliminate mashing at movies." *Aspen Democrat-Times* [CO], August 24, 1914.

"Ferryboat masher held in $500." *The Sun* [NY], June 19, 1896.

"A few words about mashers." *San Antonio Light*, August 17, 1883.

"A few words to the girls." *Tacoma Times*, June 20, 1916.

"Fight on Dep't store flirts is thrown in ash heap." *Day Book* [Chicago], September 11, 1916.

"Fined for annoying girls." *New York Times*, September 12, 1924.

"Fined $10 as escort of policewoman in park." *New York Tribune*, May 31. 1920.

"Finger prints for the masher." *The Ogden Standard*, August 12, 1916.

"First masher to draw fire." *The Marion Daily Mirror* [OH], October 6, 1910.

"Flirting." *Bemidji Daily Pioneer* [MN], December 4, 1922.

"Flirting is a game." *Washington Post*, December 30, 1905.

"Flirting may be tabooed in Phoenix." *Bisbee Daily Review*, March 8, 1914.

"Flirting M.D. now cook." *New York Tribune*, October 21, 1914.

"For annoying ladies." *Herald Democrat* [Leadville, CO], August 21, 1891.

"4 mashers nabbed after they picked up leader of copettes." *Washington Times*, October 19, 1920.

"Gallant and robust judge." *The Sun* [NY], August 2, 1906.

"Gave him a poke." *Minneapolis Journal*, October 22, 1904.

"Gay on top, but sad underneath—Gotham's tenderloin." *The Morning Times* [Washington, DC], March 1, 1896.

"General news." *McCook Weekly Tribune* [McCook, NE], November 1, 1883.

"Get first phone masher." *Washington Times*, March 16, 1916.

"Giddy male mashers." *St. Paul Daily Globe*, January 27, 1889.

"Girl fells two mashers." *Washington Post*, September 15, 1906.

"Girl fights a masher." *Day Book* [Chicago], June 15, 1912.

"Girl fixes masher's term." *New York Times*, March 25, 1928.

"Girl forced to flee to escape from masher." *The Evening Herald* [Albuquerque], February 26, 1915.

"Girl in subway collars masher." *New York Tribune*, March 24, 1914.

"Girl sentences masher to jail with court's O.K." *Evening World* [NY], August 22, 1917.

"Girl slapped a bold masher." *Evening World* [NY], October 12, 1901.

"Girl slugs bold masher." *Richmond Planet* [VA], August 27, 1904.

"Girl slugs masher on elevated car." *The Madison Journal* [Tallulah, LA], May 17, 1913.

"Girl stenographer uses glove on masher." *Spanish Fork Press* [Spanish Fork, UT], January 30, 1908.

"Girl's life is threatened by mashers." *Evening World* [NY, NY], September 15, 1905.

"Girls encourage mashers." *The Washington Times*, November 11, 1905.

"Girls pound a masher." *The Sun* [NY], August 5, 1901.

"Girls training to rout mashers." *The Bemidji Daily Pioneer* [MN], December 16, 1914.

"Girls warned against dances in Milwaukee." *Washington Times*, December 12, 1910.

"Girls whip masher." *Evening World* [NY], July 3, 1900.

"Gives mashers a shock." *New York Times*, August 15, 1926.

"Gives warning to mashers." *Portsmouth Herald* [NH], January 8, 1929.

"Gloucester girls will whip mashers." *The Times* [Richmond, VA], October 3, 1902.

"Good advice for girls." *The Intermountain Catholic* [Salt Lake City], January 30, 1904.

"A Good lesson to young loafers." *Brooklyn Eagle*, August 28, 1880.

"Good thrashing cure for mashers." *Washington Times*, January 14, 1907.

"Good times in Great Britain." *The Highland Weekly News* [Hillsborough, OH], April 25, 1883.

Greeley-Smith, Nixola. "Flirtation squad of girl detectives will clear all the Peacock Alleys of the hotel mashers of both sexes." *Evening World* [NY], January 2, 1917.

Greeley-Smith, Nixola. "How a girl can repel a masher's attack." *Evening World* [NY], January 3, 1905.

Greeley-Smith, Nixola. "Jiu Jitsu for the masher." *Evening World* [NY], January 2, 1905.

Greeley-Smith, Nixola. "Let the masher beware." *Evening World* [NY], January 3, 1912.

Greeley-Smith, Nixola. "Says more police-women will rid streets of mashers who pester young girls." Day Book [Chicago], February 10, 1914.

"Guilty of mashing." *Los Angeles Herald*, July 15, 1892.

"Hands off." *Nashville Union and American* [TN], June 4, 1875.

"Handsome girl hammers a masher." *The Spokane Press*, August 25, 1906.

"He gave it up." *Omaha Daily Bee*, January 27, 1890.

"He hates dudes." *San Francisco Call*, February 9, 1893.

"He insulted army lassie." *Evening World* [NY], January 6, 1900.

"He was a masher." *St. Paul Daily Globe*, April 15, 1889.

"He was cured." *The Sun* [NY], June 28, 1895.

"He went to the smoker." *The Princeton Union* [Princeton, MN], May 19, 1892.

"Headlock recommended for subduing mashers." *Thomasville Times Enterprise* [GA], July 31, 1929.

"Heavy fines for mashers." *Evening World* [NY], October 1, 1903.

"Hello girls practice punching bags in telephone gymnasium." *The Paducah Evening Sun* [KY], June 13, 1906.

"Her face powder bomb routs ardent masher." *New York Tribune*, November 12, 1916.

"Herrick talks at anti-flirt club meeting." *Sandusky Register* [OH], March 9, 1923.

"Hibbing mashers due for downfall." *Bemidji Daily Pioneer* [MN], September 23, 1910.

"Horsewhip sets fire to masher." *San Francisco Call*, February 28, 1905.

"Horsewhipped a masher." *Aspen Weekly Times* [CO], January 30, 1892.

"Houston makes goo-goo eyes a misdemeanor." *The St. Louis Republic*, September 9, 1905.

"Houston masher whipped." *Durant Weekly News* [Durant, Indian Territory, OK], June 17, 1921.

"How about the hatpin as a teacher for mashers? *The Marion Daily Mirror* [OH], August 16, 1910.

"How mashers infest the L." *Evening World* [NY], October 29, 1902.

"How to paralyze a masher." *Cheyenne Transporter* [Darlington, Indian Territory, OK], January 25, 1882.

"How to treat mashers." *The Evening Times* [Washington, DC], March 28, 1898.

"Husband owns it." *Lancaster Daily Intelligencer* [PA], November 25, 1882.

"Husband stabbed by Chicago masher." *The Guthrie Daily Leader* [OK], January 20, 1902.

"Hustled the oglers." *Washington Post*, September 17, 1905.

"Insulted white women." *Graham Guardian* [Safford, AZ], June 15, 1895.

"Insulter was fined." *Brooklyn Eagle*, September 6, 1900.

Intrapodi, Ethel. "Smashing cures mashing—get busy girls!" *Day Book* [Chicago], August 26, 1912.

"Invents spurs to stop mashers." *Washington Herald*, March 14, 1915.

"Invitation to evil-minded men, says magistrate of present styles." *Washington Post*, February 13, 1916.

"Is hatpin man's menace? Police chiefs' opinions." *Salt Lake Herald*, March 27, 1910.

"Jack the hugger in law's embrace." *Evening World* [NY], January 27, 1903.

"Jail for all mashers." *Washington Post*, July 20, 1912.

"Jail for mashers, decreed at Fresno." *Bakersfield Californian*, September 29, 1927.

"Jail the flirt." *The Watchman and Southron* [Sumter, SC], December 9, 1922.

"Jealousy." *The Tombstone* [AZ], March 21, 1885.

"Jiu Jitsu vanquishes a masher." *San Francisco Call*, December 30, 1904.

Josefson, Caroline. "Iceland shows the American girl how to repel the masher." *Omaha Daily Bee*, April 12, 1914, pt. 2.

"Judge blames girls." *Washington Post*, October 15, 1915.

"Judge fines a St. Louis masher $300." *San Francisco Call*, September 14, 1905.

"Jury in Baltimore indicts 4 in holdup of bank collector." *Washington Post*, March 24, 1925.

"Kansas town after mashers." *The Red Cloud Chief* [Red Cloud, NE], October 20, 1905.

"Killen punched him." *St. Paul Daily Globe*, August 7, 1888.

"Kiss, $100; wink, $40; 'good afternoon,' $50; fines for mashers." *Washington Herald*, July 27, 1912.

"The L masher." *Evening World* [NY], October 29, 1902.

"L mashers again at work." *Evening World* [NY], October 28, 1902.

"L train masher held in night court." *Evening World* [NY], December 14, 1910.

"Lashed her tormentor." *Evening World* [NY], July 21, 1900.

"Lashed him." *Alexandria Gazette* [VA], September 24, 1895.

"Lashes for mashers advocated by pastor." *Washington Herald*, November 10, 1913.

"Law too lenient with mashers, jurist says." *The Morning Tulsa World*, June 29, 1922.

"The Lawful use of fists." *The Wichita Daily Eagle*, February 15, 1899.

"Let the mashers go with the signs." *Washington Post*, January 20, 1895.

"Let's mash the curbing mashers." *Oshkosh Daily Northwestern* [WI], June 24, 1927.

"Letter masher caught." *Day Book* [Chicago], October 7, 1912.

"Life in New York City." *Brooklyn Eagle*, October 12, 1884.

"Little woman chokes a 200-pound masher." *Evening World* [NY], December 13, 1911.

Loeb, Sophie Irene. "Managing the masher." *Evening World* [NY], August 24, 1922.

Loeb, Sophie Irene. "The molesting masher." *Evening World* [NY], April 14, 1917.

"Loiterers in police net." *Washington Post*, September 22, 1908.

"London street etiquette." *New York Times*, November 20, 1927.

"Lottie Collins talks." *The Sun* [NY], April 16, 1893.

"Lures on male mashers." *The Mahoning*

Dispatch [Canfield, OH], September 1, 1911.

"Lynn mayor orders anti-flirting drive." *New York Times*, October 3, 1929.

"Make football of masher." *New York Tribune*, July 13, 1900.

"Man routed by hatpin held in city jail." *Los Angeles Herald*, January 16, 1910.

"Man who refuses to wink inhuman." *Washington Herald*, September 10, 1911.

"Mankato masher fined." *Minneapolis Journal*, June 29, 1906.

"Margaret Illington lands rights and lefts on masher." *Tacoma Times*, January 11, 1911.

"Market-street masher." *San Francisco Call*, January 27, 1897.

"Market-street masher." *San Francisco Call*, January 28, 1897.

"Market-street mashers." *San Francisco Call*, June 17, 1893.

"Marking a masher." *Pittsburg Dispatch*, April 18, 1891.

Marshall, Marguerite Mooers. "Girls with r.s.v.p. eyes invite mashers." *Evening World* [NY], October 21, 1914.

Marshall, Marguerite Mooers. "Use hatpin or fists on mashers, says Mrs. Brophy." *Evening World* [NY], August 9, 1913.

"Mash the mashers." *Evening World* [NY], January 4, 1888.

"Mashed a masher." *Valentine Democrat* [NE], September 13, 1906.

"Mashed the masher." *Daily Capital Journal* [Salem, OR], September 7, 1907.

"The Masher." *Saguache Chronicle* [Saguache, CO], September 15, 1882.

"The Masher." *Sedalia Weekly Bazoo* [MO], September 19, 1882.

"The Masher." *Salt Lake Daily Herald*, November 11, 1883.

"The Masher." *Los Angeles Daily Herald*, January 24, 1889.

"The Masher." *Sunday Morning Globe* [Washington, DC], October 6, 1901.

"The Masher." *Evening World* [NY], December 5, 1903.

"The Masher again." *The Evening Times* [Washington, DC], November 26, 1901.

"Masher badly beaten." *Salt Lake Tribune*, September 15, 1904.

"The Masher bill." *Aspen Daily Chronicle* [CO], April 8, 1893.

"A Masher caned." *San Francisco Call*, October 27, 1895.

"Masher caught." *The Guthrie Daily Leader* [OK], October 5, 1904.

"Masher chastised by plucky woman." *Washington Times*, May 14, 1908.

"Masher comes to grief." *Kansas City Journal* [MO], December 6, 1897.

"Masher cowhided by pretty widow." *The Minneapolis Journal*, November 26, 1905.

"Masher drive begins on drugstore cowboys." *Washington Post*, March 30, 1924.

"Masher, ex-convict sent to workhouse." *New York Tribune*, October 7, 1916.

"A Masher fined." *San Francisco Call*, September 6, 1893.

"Masher fined $1,000." *St. Paul Globe*, January 16, 1902.

"Masher gets long sentence." *The Minneapolis Journal*, October 10, 1903.

"Masher gets six months." *New York Times*, July 16, 1905.

"Masher gets 10 days for annoying young woman in street." *Evening World* [NY], August 8, 1912.

"Masher gets 10 days to pine over his love for a strange girl." *Evening World* [NY], July 23, 1914.

"Masher gets 30 days for following woman." *Evening World* [NY], February 1, 1911.

"Masher gets two hard jolts." *The Tacoma Times*, June 8, 1910.

"Masher handed lemon by charming Virginian." *Washington Times*, August 7, 1907.

"Masher hit by society beauty." *The Minneapolis Journal*, August 25, 1905.

"A Masher in merited mystery." *Brooklyn Eagle*, March 11, 1881.

"Masher in movies fined by court." *Washington Times*, October 3, 1919.

"A Masher in the toils." *Brooklyn Eagle*, May 26, 1889.

"A Masher is a totally unnecessary nuisance unless he is encouraged." *The Washington Times,* January 12, 1905.

"Masher is given nine months." *San Francisco Call*, February 3, 1907.

"Masher is punched." *Los Angeles Herald*, December 11, 1905.

"Masher is thrashed and sent to jail." *Washington Times*, September 18, 1907.

"A Masher killed." *The Wichita Daily Eagle* [KS], May 17, 1892.

"Masher knocked out." *The Minneapolis Journal*, September 7, 1903.

"The Masher mashed." *Deseret Evening News* [Salt Lake City], May 12, 1908.

"The Masher mashed." *Los Angeles Herald*, July 22, 1884.

"Masher mashed." *The Stark County Democrat* [Canton, OH], August 15, 1905.

"A Masher mashed." *Wichita Daily Eagle* [Kansas], February 16, 1886.

"Masher menace hit by working girl who tells experiences." *Evening Public Ledger* [Philadelphia], April 21, 1915.

"Masher mobbed for kiss theft." *New York Tribune*, October 14, 1916.

"A Masher mulcted." *The Bourbon News* [Paris, KY], August 3, 1900.

"The Masher nuisance." *The Sunday Herald* [Washington, DC], October 11, 1891.

"Masher pays $10 each word." *The Evening Herald* [Klamath Falls, OR], August 30, 1912.

"Masher pleaded guilty." *Evening World* [NY], November 13, 1900.

"Masher poses as policeman gets 30 days." *Evening World* [NY], November 13, 1912.

"Masher pummeled by girls." *Alexandria Gazette* [VA], October 22, 1896.

"Masher punched in open court." *Evening World* [NY], April 14, 1900.

"A Masher punished." *San Francisco Call*, May 3, 1892.

"A Masher punished." *San Francisco Call*, March 28, 1893.

"A Masher punished." *Washington Post*, September 15, 1895.

"A Masher routed." *New Ulm Weekly Review* [New Ulm, MN], August 27, 1884.

"Masher sent to jail." Washington Post, December 29, 1905.

"Masher squelched by small whistle." *Los Angeles Herald*, November 10, 1909.

"Masher stabs girl's escort on late car." *The Seattle Star*, March 9, 1910.

"Masher thrashed; thrasher acquitted." *Oak Creek Times* [CO], May 12, 1910.

"Masher to work 6 days, spend seventh in jail." *New York Tribune*, January 17, 1922.

"A Masher trapped." *Alexandria Gazette* [VA], July 9, 1897.

"A Masher well served." *Evening World* [NY], July 27, 1906.

"A Masher well thrashed." *Los Angeles Herald*, November 28, 1893.

"Masher whipped by woman." *Evening World* [NY], August 18, 1904.

"Masher who annoyed young woman is fined." *Los Angeles Herald*, January 18, 1910.

"A Masher who needs mashing." *Ocala Evening Star* fl, September 24, 1903.

"A Masher's mash." *St. Paul Daily Globe*, August 3, 1880.

"The Mashers." *Salt Lake Herald*, August 27, 1906.

"Mashers and insulting toughs annoy girls here." *Honolulu Star-Bulletin*, August 13, 1912.

"Mashers and thugs beware! Girls plan jiu jitsu club." *Los Angeles Herald*, April 29, 1906.

"Mashers are arrested." *The Spokane Press*, November 19, 1907.

"Mashers are sent home." *Greeley Daily Tribune* [CO], August 24, 1929.

"Mashers arrested; one gets fine of $25." *Berkeley Daily Gazette*, October 1, 1928.

"Mashers at Troost Park." *Kansas City Journal* [MO], June 30, 1899.

"Mashers beg for mercy." *New York Tribune*, August 17, 1903.

"Mashers face arrest." *Washington Post*, July 19, 1912.

"Mashers fined $25 in court today." *Hamilton Evening Journal* [OH], April 20, 1929.

"Mashers' foes united." *Washington Post*, July 21, 1915.

"Mashers get deserts from angry fathers." *San Francisco Call*, November 22, 1899.

"Mashers here and abroad." *The Sun* [NY], December 2, 1906.

"Mashers here? Not many." *Washington Herald*, October 25, 1914.

"Mashers in New York." *Chaffee County Republican* [Buena Vista, CO], January 8, 1896.

"Mashers insult high school girls." *Evening World* [NY], September 26, 1903.

"Mashers insult women." *Salt Lake Herald*, March 5, 1908.

"Mashers jolted in police court." *Ames Daily Tribune* [IA], May 21, 1928.

"Mashers keep step with the times." *Burlington Hawk Eye* [IA], October 4, 1925.

"Mashers liable to 90 days and $100." *Bismarck Tribune* [ND], August 26, 1929.

"Mashers must go is order of police board." *San Francisco Call*, November 14, 1907.

"Mashers on the streets." *San Francisco Call*, December 10, 1903.

"Mashers out in force." *Los Angeles Herald*, January 22, 1893.

"Mashers persist when girls dress to draw glances." *Washington Times*, August 7, 1912.

"Mashers rouse ire of shoppers." *Evening World* [NY], November 16, 1904.

"Mashers stab escort." *The Sun* [NY], August 1, 1903.

"Mashers to be arrested." *Aspen Democrat* [CO], October 15, 1903.

"Mashers to get limited sentences." *Salt Lake Herald*, October 28, 1909.

"Mashers war in full swing." *Washington Times*, October 16, 1920.

"Mashers weep in explaining being in jail." *Albuquerque Journal*, March 17, 1929.

"Mashers will be well punished." *San Francisco Call*, February 1, 1907.

"Mashing in Cape Girardeau." *The Weekly Tribune* [Cape Girardeau, MO], March 15, 1917.

"Mashing the masher." *St. Paul Daily Globe* [MN], September 6, 1887.

"Mashing the mashers." *The Tacoma Times*, July 7, 1911.

May, Edna. "Chorus girl to star." *Evening World* [NY], February 9, 1900.

"May mash less now." *The Minneapolis Journal*, July 2, 1901.

"May young women walk about alone?" *The State Journal* [Jefferson City, MO], May 19, 1876.

"Mayor after the mashers." *The Marion Daily Mirror* [OH], October 3, 1910.

"Menace of flirts." *Washington Post*, September 23, 1912.

"Men's meeting." *Deseret Evening News* [Salt Lake City], April 16, 1906.

"Methods of the masher." *Salt Lake Tribune*, October 2, 1904.

"Metropolitan mashers." *Brooklyn Eagle*, July 21, 1884.

"A Middle-aged masher." *Evening World* [NY], September 11, 1888.

"Militant woman organizes army to rout mashers." *Evening World* [NY], January 26, 1916.

"Miller sentenced." *San Francisco Call*, July 19, 1891.

"Minister would boom marriage and beat mashers." *Washington Herald*, August 13, 1912.

"Minneapolis woman knocks masher down." *St. Paul Globe*, August 18, 1902.

"Missouri girls decide to carry revolvers." *The Paducah Sun* [NY], March 15, 1905.

Morris, Clara. "Trials of a young actress." *The Salt Lake Herald*, August 18, 1901.

Morris, Clara. "What a masher really is." *The Salt Lake Herald*, September 22, 1901.

"The Motor masher." *Washington Herald*, August 29, 1921.

"Motor masher has to dodge." *Washington Herald*, July 27, 1920.

"Movie masher is jailed." *New York Times*, January 24, 1929.

"Moving on mashers." *The Washington Herald*, September 27, 1910.

"Mrs. Howe's masher now mashing spuds in jail." *Washington Herald*, October 21, 1914.

"Mustn't look at the girls." *The Sun* [NY], October 12, 1894.

"Needed no protector." *Mount Vernon Signal* [KY], May 4, 1906.

"A New invention of the enemy." *The Pulaski Citizen* [TN], March 4, 1875.

"New way to rebuff mashers." *New York Tribune*, September 3, 1910.

"N.Y. subway is moving hell, says Aimee." *San Antonio Light*, March 2, 1927.

"The News minutely told." *Edgefield Advertiser* [SC], August 3, 1910.

"Ninety days and a fine." *Los Angeles Herald*, July 16, 1892.

"No fault of mashers, declares Major Sylvester." *Washington Times*, September 26, 1905.

"No goo-goo eyes allowed in Alton." *Bisbee Daily Review*, January 2, 1907.

"No law for the masher." *Brooklyn Eagle*, January 10, 1900.

"No mashers in Chicago." *The Evening Standard* [Ogden City, UT], September 1, 1911.

"No one interfered." *Evening World* [NY], March 25, 1914.

No title. *The Anderson Intelligencer* [SC], September 7, 1904.

No title. *Capital City Courier* [Lincoln, NE], November 9, 1889.

No title. *Fort Worth Daily Gazette*, June 21, 1886.

No title. *New York Times*, July 21, 1884.

No title. *New York Times*, November 21, 1922.

No title. *Sacramento Daily Record-Union*, July 30, 1889.

No title. *The Star* [Reynoldsville, PA], August 23, 1899.

"Not a heroine after all." *The Sun* [NY], October 5, 1912.

"Not always the men." *Los Angeles Herald*, November 20, 1892.

"Not the first time she has had mashers beaten." *St. Louis Republic*, March 10, 1901.

"Not yet abashed." *San Francisco Call*, May 1, 1893.

"Now he will flirt no more." *The Morning Times* [Washington, DC], July 19, 1896.

O'Brien, J. J. "How a frail woman can resist bold basher without weapons." *Evening World* [NY], January 8, 1901.

"Official flirts rush to squelch mashers." *Omaha Daily Bee*, September 7, 1911.

"Ogling is expensive." *St. Paul Daily Globe* [MN], March 10, 1889.

"Old sinner talks." *The Tucumcari News* [NM], November 25, 1905.

"Omaha judge smashes the mashers." *Day Book* [Chicago], May 13, 1913.

"One-cent cure for a masher." *Evening Star* [Washington, DC], July 28, 1900.

"One masher who gets his deserts." *The McCook Tribune* [NE], October 10, 1890.

"One Phoenix masher who will mash no more." *Arizona Republican*, December 23, 1909.

"Open war on mashers here." *The Ogden Standard-Examiner*, July 5, 1920.

"Orders to smash the mashers." *The Guthrie Daily Leader* [OK], July 3, 1901.

"Organize to smash mashers." *San Francisco Call*, August 8, 1905.

"Origin of masher." *Los Angeles Herald*, June 21, 1883.

"Outwitted a masher." *St. Paul Daily Globe*, January 22, 1893.

"Paradise for masher." *Washington Post*, March 23, 1908.

"Parasol bombardment fails to stop masher." *New York Tribune*, August 9, 1916.

"Park mashers beware." *Los Angeles Herald*, May 25, 1896.

"Patrolman gives masher a lesson." *Salt Lake Herald*, November 26, 1909.

"Periscope in hats, girls watch flirts." *Washington Times*, December 3, 1915.

"Phases of life." *St. Paul Daily Globe*, December 29, 1889.

"Pinched at Los Angeles." *San Francisco Call*, October 10, 1894.

"Police arrest five mashers." *Los Angeles Herald*, September 27, 1909.

"Police ask girls to help curb activity of mashers." *Emporia Gazette* [KS], March 2, 1926.

"Police asked to arrest mashers." *The Seattle Star*, April 16, 1908.

"Police Capt. Dillon opens war on mashers." *Evening World* [NY], March 21, 1903.

"Police chasing street loafers." *Salt Lake Herald*, October 2, 1905.

"Police chief wars on mashers after his own wife is annoyed." *New York Times*, October 24, 1930.

"Police matron arrests masher." *San Francisco Call*, June 6, 1913.

"Police plan to rid city of mashers." *Berkeley Daily Gazette*, April 24, 1929.

"Policeman thrashes a masher." *The Sun* [NY], December 21, 1897.

"Policemen too zealous." *Washington Post*, September 6, 1899.

"Policewoman chases masher." *San Francisco Call*, August 7, 1913.

"Porter blames city magistrates and politics for masher evil." *Evening Public Ledger* [Philadelphia], April 22, 1915.

"Praised by court for felling a man." *Evening World* [NY], August 4, 1902.

"Preferred Chicago." *Minneapolis Journal*, October 12, 1904.

"Pretty Denver girls to wage war on mashers." *St. Paul Globe*, November 9, 1903.

"Pretty girl has a new cure for mashers." *Albuquerque Evening Citizen*, November 9, 1906.

"Pretty police girls to lure petty mashers."

New Castle News [PA], September 24, 1926.

"Prison in store for masher girl says struck her." *Evening World* [NY], October 3, 1912.

"Proper thing to hit masher." *San Francisco Call*, September 3, 1904.

"Public calls on police board to protect women." *The Times Dispatch* [Richmond, VA], February 13, 1911.

"Public spankings for Minneapolis mashers." *Medford Mail Tribune* [OR], July 27, 1910.

"Pullman masher broke no law." *Pullman Herald* [WA], October 13, 1911.

"Punish the masher." *Salt Lake Herald*, July 21, 1905.

"Punishes mashers." *San Francisco Call*, April 21, 1906.

"Punishment for mashers." *Evening World* [NY], July 25, 1903.

"A Question of physics." *The Roanoke Daily Times* [VA], March 31, 1896.

"A Rare bird." *The Weekly Republican* [Phoenix], July 28, 1892.

"Rebuffed mashed fined." *Kansas City Journal* [MO], August 3, 1899.

"Refused to prosecute." *The Washington Times*, September 6, 1901.

"Reserves save masher from crowd." *Evening World* [NY], September 2, 1905.

"Rich New Yorkers may be arraigned." *New Ulm Review* [New Ulm, MN], November 28, 1906.

"Routs mashers with revolver." *San Francisco Call*, January 24, 1908.

"Rowboat masher is newest summer pest." *San Francisco Call*, September 7, 1912.

"Sad ending of a masher." *The Bourbon News* [Paris, KY], July 19, 1904.

"Saintly city doings." *St. Paul Globe*, December 31, 1887.

"The Season of flirting is now at its dizziest height." *Washington Times*, July 13, 1902.

"Served 'em right." *The Evening Bulletin* [Maysville, KY], October 27, 1892.

"Served the masher right." *Evening World* [NY], August 10, 1894.

"Served them right." *The Hazel Green Herald* [Hazel Green, KY], June 10, 1892.

"She accepted." *The Weekly Messenger* [St. Martinsville, LA], December 11, 1886.

"She beat the masher." *Evening World* [NY], June 20, 1894.

"She defended her honor." *Washington Post*, January 12, 1896.

"She fixed the masher." *Los Angeles Herald*, December 6, 1898.

"She punched the masher." *The Sun* [NY], December 8, 1898.

"She was a smasher." *St. Paul Daily Globe*, September 19, 1892.

"She will send for him." *Pittsburg Dispatch*, April 18, 1891.

"She's masher's nemesis." *Evening Public Ledger* [Philadelphia], August 15, 1921.

"She's too pretty to walk alone, says the judge." *Day Book* [Chicago], January 26, 1914.

"Short news stories." *The Bourbon News* [Paris, KY], June 22, 1900.

"Show this hog no mercy." *The Sun* [NY], June 2, 1890.

"Six months for masher." *The Maui News* [Wailuku, Maui], August 16, 1913.

"16 would-be mashers caught single handed by Pittsburgh decoy." *Clearfield Progress* [PA], October 8, 1926.

"Skating masher fails to appear." *San Francisco Call*, July 19, 1908.

"Slapped a masher, she says." *The Sun* [NY], May 15, 1903.

"Slapped as masher then gets $100 fine." *Washington Post*, September 28, 1923.

"Slapped masher's face." *The Spanish Fork Press* [Spanish Fork, UT], November 11, 1909.

"Slapped masher's face." *The Sun* [NY], July 22, 1904.

"Slapped the masher's face." *The Sun* [NY], December 19, 1897.

"Slashed masher's ear, she says." *The Sun* [NY], January 1, 1903.

"Slugs masher; fined $5." *The Minneapolis Journal*, August 3, 1906.

"Smashed a masher." *The St. Louis Republic*, April 20, 1900.

"Smashed the masher." *The Richmond Planet* [VA], March 9, 1901.

"Smashers of mashers to escape punishment." *Washington Herald*, May 27, 1913.

"Smashing the mashers newest aim of police." *Washington Times*, July 10, 1910.

"Society women and revolvers." *The Times Dispatch* [Richmond, VA], April 22, 1903.

"Some things that might be done to an L masher." *Evening World* [NY], October 30, 1902.

"A Source of revenue." *The Washington Times*, September 2, 1904.

"Stabbed masher with hatpin." *New York Tribune*, October 18, 1909.

"State Notes." *The Elk County Advocate* [Ridgway, PA], August 9, 1877.

Stevenson, Fay. "Using jiu jitsu on time and mashers." *Evening World* [NY], August 17, 1921.

"Street flirtations." *Ouachita Sentinel* [Monroe, LA], April 21, 1883.

"Street loafing." *Daily Press* [Newport News, VA], April 5, 1907.

"Street mashers." *The Washington Times*, September 18, 1905.

"Street mashing." *St. Paul Daily Globe*, March 10, 1889.

"Stuck hatpin into a masher." *Evening World* [NY], May 27, 1903.

"Subway masher gets 10 days." *New York Times*, March 13, 1928.

"Subway masher jailed." *New York Times*, April 16, 1930.

"Subway squeezer squeezed into cell." *New York Tribune*, June 24, 1915.

"Suppressing the masher." *The Daily Journal* [Salem, OR], October 6, 1903.

"Swat the masher." *The St. Joseph Observer* [MO], April 21, 1917.

"Taming the masher." *San Francisco Call*, April 28, 1913.

"Taxi cab masher gets 5 days in workhouse." *New York Times*, August 7, 1921.

"Teaching girls how to deal with mashers." *Washington Times*, February 15, 1918.

"Texas chooses prettiest girl." *San Antonio Light*, April 7, 1929.

"They are blaming low waists, short sleeves, clinging skirts for the bad morals of men even in Des Moines." *Des Moines Daily News*, September 22, 1912.

"They ride wooden horses." *Brooklyn Eagle*, January 26, 1892.

"They'll put an end to mashers." *Evening World* [NY], April 4, 1903.

"This trolley car masher got an awful drubbing." *Evening World* [NY], December 18, 1906.

"Thoughts of a masher." *Aspen Tribune* [CO], October 6, 1898.

"Thrashed by a girl." *Fort Worth Daily Gazette*, January 14, 1886.

"Tight dress cause mashers." *San Francisco Call*, September 17, 1912.

"Tip in headline cost a masher in subway $50." *Evening World* [NY], February 15, 1921.

"To beat up mashers is object of club." *Washington Times*, August 7, 1908.

"To mashers; keep off of 14th Street." *Evening World* [NY], September 30, 1905.

"Too beautiful to remain in city, so judge makes her go home." *Day Book* [Chicago], March 10, 1914.

"Tried to be a masher; it cost him fifteen." *The Minneapolis Journal*, September 28, 1905.

"Tries to flirt but lands in jail." *Weekly Journal-Miner* [Prescott, AZ], February 12, 1913.

"Two mashers erred; jailed." *Chester Times* [PA], November 10, 1930.

"Two mashers punished." *The Sun* [NY], August 1, 1897.

"Two months for Davis." *Evening World* [NY], December 11, 1903.

"Under advisement." *San Francisco Call*, July 17, 1891.

"Used her fist on a masher." *The St. Louis Republic*, April 4, 1902.

"Vermin on the cycle path." *Brooklyn Eagle*, May 13, 1897.

"Victims of the mashers." *Salt Lake Tribune*, September 25, 1904.

"Vigilance committee formed." *Gainesville Daily Sun*, September 19, 1908.

Vincent, Betty. "Betty Vincent's advice to lovers." *Evening World* [NY], June 19, 1914.

"Virginia's anti-flirting bill." *The Anderson Intelligencer* [SC], January 19, 1898.

"War on masher." *The Hartford Republic* [KY], December 25, 1903.

"War on masher in big Chicago stores." *Minneapolis Journal*, October 26, 1904.

"The War on mashers." *The Watchman and Southron* [Sumter, SC], January 1, 1901.

"War on park mashers." *The Minneapolis Journal*, June 19, 1906.

"War on river masher." *Washington Post*, July 14, 1912.

"War on subway mashers begun by lady dicks." *Naugatuck Daily News* [CT], March 15, 1924.

"War upon the mashers." *Salt Lake Herald-Republican*, November 18, 1910.

"Warm weather brings out mashers." *Salt Lake Herald*, May 14, 1904.

"Washington observer." *Berkeley Daily Gazette*, March 12, 1923.

"Watch out for the goo goo man." *Washington Post*, December 23, 1906.

"Weeks news from all over Colorado." *Eagle County Blade* [Red Cliff, CO], March 24, 1910.

"Were almost acquitted." *The Morning Times* [Washington, DC], April 3, 1896.

"What to do with mashers." *The Tacoma Times*, April 8, 1904.

"A Whip for scoundrels' backs." *New York Times*, January 17, 1883.

"Whip the masher." *The Minneapolis Journal*, April 15, 1901.

"Whipped a masher." *San Francisco Call*, October 9, 1897.

"Wife helps free masher." *The Sun* [NY], March 26, 1914.

"Will wage war on the masher." *San Francisco Call*, November 9, 1903.

"Woman and the mashers." *The Sun* [NY], November 9, 1902.

"Woman gives alleged masher big black eye for flirting." *The St. Louis Republic*, April 9, 1903.

"Woman had right to whip the masher." *Evening World* [NY], March 7, 1916.

"Woman has scalps of nine mashers." *New York Times*, August 14, 1921.

"Woman lashes a masher." *New York Times*, January 25, 1904.

"Woman punched on street fails to press charge." *Evening World* [NY], January 13, 1909.

"Woman slugs masher." *The Minneapolis Journal*, July 25, 1906.

"A Woman's essay on mashers." *The Sun* [NY], August 11, 1899.

"Woman's fists land on masher." *Evening World*, [NY], December 3, 1903.

"Woman's modesty saves a masher." *Salt Lake Tribune*, February 2, 1905.

"Women as decoys in masher crusade." *Washington Times*, June 3, 1908.

"Women beat masher into unconsciousness." *The St. Louis Republic*, September 5, 1903.

"Women consider mashing." *The Sun* [NY], November 5, 1905.

"Women in hobble or harem skirts can't blame mashers." *The Tacoma Times*, May 31, 1911.

"Women police grapple with the masher evil." *New York Times*, March 23, 1924.

"Women police to rid Boston of mashers." *Washington Herald*, August 11, 1913.

"Women who fence are terrors to mashers." *Spokane Press*, August 28, 1906.

"Women's blank expression." *New York Times*, December 4, 1909.

"Workhouse sentences to curb Broadway mashers." *New York Tribune*, August 5, 1920.

"Would-be sheiks annoy the ladies." *Carroll Times* [IA], June 25, 1925.

"You won't fear mashers if you learn to skate." *The Tacoma Times*, January 28, 1910.

"You'd better make your eyes behave." *The Ogden Standard*, October 23, 1915, magazine section.

"A Young girl's protest." *New York Times*, December 4, 1909.

"Young woman sends a masher sprawling in a car." *Evening World* [NY], March 31, 1909.

"Young woman uses hatpin on an offensive masher." *The St. Louis Republic*, April 20, 1903.

"Youngstown women look for a masher." *The Marion Daily Mirror* [OH], May 28, 1909.

Index

www.ingramcontent.com/pod-product-compliance
Lightning Source LLC
Chambersburg PA
CBHW031129270326
41929CB00011B/1549